THE LOOKING GLASS WORLD
OF NONFICTION TV

The
Looking Glass World
of
Nonfiction TV

by

Elayne Rapping

South End Press   **Boston MA**

Cover by Nick Thorkelson
Typesetting, design and layout by the South End Press collective

Library of Congress Cataloging-in-Publication Data

Rapping, Elayne, 1938—
    The looking glass world of nonfiction TV.

    Bibliography: p.
    Includes index.
    1. Television broadcasting--Social aspects--
United States. I. Title.
PN1992.6.R37   1986   302.2′345′0973   86-27944

ISBN 0-89608-282-2
ISBN 0-89608-281-4 (pbk.)

South End Press
116 Saint Botolph St.
Boston, MA 02115

for Alison and Jonathan

Table of Contents

I'm looking and I'm dreaming for the first time
I'm inside and I'm outside at the same time
And everything is real
Do I like the way I feel?

> When the world crashes in, into my living room
> Television made me what I am
> People like to put the television down
> But we are just good friends
> I'm a television man.

—David Byrne, "Television Man"

As a teenager, reading both Karl Marx and *Honey* magazine, I couldn't reconcile what I knew with what I felt. This is the root of ideology, I believe. I knew I was being "exploited," but it was a fact that I was attracted. Feelings (ideology) lag behind knowledge (science). We can learn from their clash. We move forward as the revolutionary becomes the obvious.

—Judith Williamson, *Decoding Advertisements*

Foreword

I began writing about television in the early 1970s. I had recently completed a doctorate in American Literature, had published articles in scholarly literary journals and was teaching literature at a local college.

While I was in graduate school, in the 1960s, I had two children and became involved in the political movements of the time, the anti-war and women's movements, and what later came broadly to be thought of as the New Left. The combination of ideas and experiences which these activities presented seemed more and more at war with the ideas, methods and values I had acquired in the academy.

On the one hand, the people I knew and the books and publications I read increasingly forced me to see both literature and personal life in political and social terms. And on the other hand, my daily life as an exhausted mother trying to juggle work, political activism and kids drove me, for the first time, to daytime soap operas. Each afternoon, as the babies napped, I would spend a mindless half hour with my friends on "Days of Our Lives."

Gradually, the parts of my life came together in a unified perspective on art, politics and daily life. I began to analyze the TV shows— which I discussed with other mothers—in terms of my developing views about society as well as in the critical terms I had learned as a student. It seemed so obvious to me that popular culture was a far more important part of daily life than either my academic or political friends considered possible.

When I began writing cultural reviews for various political publications, I found myself increasingly drawn to TV as an important subject. It wasn't easy. Most people—almost everyone really—found the subject embarrassing. "Do you really watch those shows?" I heard from friendly and not-so-friendly acquaintances. It was a kind of joke, I think. To many people it still is. It never seemed funny to me, although it did seem like fun, and I persevered.

1

This book grew out of that time. It is more serious—politically and culturally—than my early writing had been. And it is more insistent on the importance of television as a political force than I then had the confidence to be.

Over the years, many people have helped and taught me a lot. I would particularly like to mention a few of the most important here. I want to thank my students for teaching me as much as they learned; Barbara Miner, John Trinkl, Carol Leven and Jill Benderly of the *Guardian* for encouraging and appreciating my media work before it was fashionable; Anne Steytler and Shelly Chandhok for helping me through the rough times; and Al Petrarca for listening and caring for so many years.

1

An Introduction to the Looking Glass World

July 4, 1986 was more than just Independence Day, a time for picnics, fireworks and waving Old Glory on the front porch. In celebration of the renovation of the Statue of Liberty, an entire weekend— "Liberty Weekend"—was set aside for celebration and festivity. In fact, the weekend swelled into a full week of publicity, anticipation and previews of planned events, as the three major television networks fought to woo viewers to their own particular version of patriotic tribute to Lady Liberty and her still bubbling melting pot.

It was ABC that got the plum, the right to stage the "official" state celebrations in which the President, along with notables from the proverbial "every walk of life," participated. With the expert help of David Wolper, seasoned producer of TV miniseries, the ABC "spectacular" was just that. Part show biz, part national ceremony, the marathon—which drew 100 million viewers over the course of the weekend—presented a picture of American life and American values that must surely have made the Founding Fathers shift in their graves. The fantasy visions of our own towns and regions which all three networks presented periodically throughout the weekend, as a kind of documentary report on the "State of the Union," were nearly as slick and cheerfully hokey as the official ceremonies.

"Is It News or Entertainment?" asked many a headline. It was a valid question, one not easily answered. The program was not unlike a Las Vegas floorshow. In a typical segment, for example, there was Elizabeth Taylor, on a soundstage covered with brightly lit stars, introducing Frank Sinatra, who sang his 1942 classic "The House I Live In." As the Hoboken *cum* Beverly Hills crooner paid tribute to the denizens of a small town America he had never inhabited, and which resembled daytime soap opera's Pine Valley more than any real American town, the camera picked up the beaming faces of "the President and Nancy," old pals to whom the tune was dedicated. Official speeches, dancing girls, beer commercials—all used the same actors and actresses, the same "Yankee Doodle Dandy" show tunes, the same messages about life, liberty and the pursuit of happiness.

3

Somehow, through the wonders of television and the conventions of show business, the leaders of a fragmented, troubled nation had found a way to reassure us that whatever we may have been hearing or feeling about the shaky state of the union wasn't quite so. Unemployment, racial and national tensions, violence and alienation, the explosive demise of the nuclear family—these were not the dominant themes of national experience. On the contrary, what viewers saw on their TV screens—a "looking glass" more marvelous in its promise of wonders, and more deceptive in its apparent "reality," than Alice's—was a nation unified, happy, healthy and having a good old time.

As the weekend progressed, and TV sets clicked on and off, switched from network to network, what emerged was a sweeping picture of every corner of the nation which did indeed resemble the small town, picket fence world of Sinatra's song. From Los Angeles, where no fewer than twenty-three communities of immigrant cultures happily coexist, to New England, where new industries and technologies are replacing old, we saw our problems dissolve in a sweep of glitzy, tune-filled patriotic rhetoric. Not that the networks or government officials denied the existence of problems. There were many moments when one or another of the networks presented excellent segments on troubled areas of national life. At one point, ABC even presented a dramatic reading of Thoreau's essay *On Civil Disobedience*, followed by moving newsreel footage of civil rights and anti-Vietnam War protests of the 1960s. But the dominant theme and tone of the programming—not least because of the ever present jollity of the commercials—was upbeat, pretty and on the move.

There is no question that the long "Liberty Weekend," parts of which must have been seen by nearly every one of us, if only in the teaser clips that dotted the TV day for weeks beforehand, was a veritable national event. Only network TV has the ability to provide that kind of shared political/cultural happening. Only network TV can provide a sense of unity to a nation more culturally and spiritually fragmented than ever in history. And because of the partnership among government, the networks and the sponsoring corporations, the image we see of ourselves when we turn to the TV looking glass usually seems more like a Hollywood movie than anyone's real hometown. The Tulsa of "Liberty Weekend" might have come straight out of *Oklahoma*; the New York City out of Sinatra's own *On the Town*.

To be sure, there is something amazing and delightful about this kind of thing, and about American television in general. To see a picture of American life modeled after a Hollywood musical is not the worst cultural experience one could have. On the contrary, the success of home television in luring us all away from our other choices for holiday celebration is rooted in its positive appeal. Like the best of Hollywood culture generally, TV focuses on what is best in American life, in the democratic rhetoric of life, liberty and the pursuit of happiness. It sees us as we are in our dreams, at our best, at our luckiest and most generous. While quite a few shades rosier than reality, this is hardly a totally false picture.

If we understand popular culture as a form of wish fulfillment fantasy, we can better understand its appeal. To see the worst of human nature, as we in modern capitalist societies know it, exorcised by heroic figures who exhibit only our finest qualities is more than entertaining; it is necessary. Fantasies of worlds in which our deepest dreams come true are the stuff of human and social change. If we cannot envision a better world, a better relationship, a better way to feel, we will never pursue them. And popular culture provides such visions and fantasies. On that level, and in a variety of instances—sports events, moments of comedy and drama, history in the making—television plays a positive role. It can inspire, raise important social questions, suggest solutions to emotional tangles.

Television is also a powerful political and economic institution whose owners and controllers have specific interests. Indeed, television, as we shall see, was developed by the powerful specifically to pursue those interests. And if, in the process, it also became a medium for creating and projecting collective dreams, those dreams take a particular form, in large part because of the political and economic forces which allow them to exist. There is a constant tension, then, between the positive things in mass culture, the impulses to address and change what is bad and wrong, and the overriding need for those in power to manage and limit the range, scope and texture of those impulses, to keep them within certain conservative boundaries which do not threaten to capsize the ship of state. It is this process which I am interested in analyzing because, it seems to me, the role and success of television are so very important to our social and personal destinies.

Television's Power

It seems perhaps too obvious to mention that television has by now profoundly changed the world in which we live, the routines of our daily lives, the patterns of our thought and perception. But the very obviousness of this thought is deceiving. Home television is one of those massive, all-encompassing cultural realities that creates a "forest for the trees" problem in comprehension. We so take it for granted that we may never analyze its role in our lives. For those of us—now the majority—who grew up in post-World War II America, television is a given, a permanent fixture sitting, literally and figuratively, in the middle of our lives, in our very "living rooms." In many homes its flickering images and semi-human drones are almost constant.[1] While we may not be consciously "watching" or concentrating on what is being shown, we do experience it in some sense. TV's images and messages are now an integral part of our home environment. Like the nagging husband we may tune out but can never forget about, or the restless child constantly vying for our attention while our mind is elsewhere, it nags us, it seduces us, it won't let us ignore it entirely. Its images, voices and tunes follow us from room to room, from infancy to old age. Like the intimate family relations whose ebbs and flows it accompanies, its effects and contradictions, its very presence in our consciousness and actions, are difficult to discern, much less get free of.

Complicating the problem even more is our educational system, which subtly instills in us a disdain for "mass culture," for the culture with which we grew up and know most deeply. This is one of the most subtle methods by which our dominant institutions keep most of us—perhaps most significantly those destined to be the future interpreters of culture and society—ignorant of the forces and values governing our lives. The Humanities, according to academic wisdom, encompass only those forms created by dead people to interpret past eras.[2]

And yet common sense tells us there is something phenomenally important about this psychologically addictive, not-quite-realistic cultural junk food. Listen to the conversations at any bus stop, school corridor, supermarket checkout line—chances are you'll pick up facts and feelings about the latest doings of the Colbys and Carringtons, Mr. T. and Captain Furillo, "Love of Life" and "All My Children." These are the human dramas that make up the bulk of our common social gossip. It is TV, its standard structures, personalities, themes and styles, through which our young people learn what it is to be male and female, young and old, Black and white, "good" and "bad." TV provides the dominant system of spiritual, political, moral and social values by which we live.[3]

When we venture into that looking glass world beyond the screen, however, like Alice we inhabit a universe of values, rules and personalities which are a bit fantastic, somewhat contrary to what we know of reality, truth and logic. TV's looking glass world operates according to laws that on the surface seem to make sense, to be familiar, but when we look closer, think harder, we find them to be a bit askew. The justice meted out by the "Hill Street Blues" gang is not really a model for your local ghetto police department's methods. Neither is the family closeness and community coherence seen on "The Guiding Light" the norm for our own crumbling families and hostile neighborhoods. Yet, we live much of our emotional existences in that fanciful, Jabberwocky landscape and we internalize its "reality." The world of network TV influences our dreams, our responses, our values—sometimes for better, sometimes worse.

The political implications of this truth are mind boggling. Culture is the means by which we pass on to new generations our values, beliefs and hard-won wisdom. But, as the term "mass communication" implies, the rise of home TV has taken this crucial socializing function out of our hands and transferred it to commercial network executives. Since these networks are owned by vast multinational conglomerates whose many subsidiaries now use common motifs and images to promote other products—toys, clothing, books, furniture—the characters and values presented on TV shows are omnipresent.[4] There is no escape from their influence, even for parents who forbid TV watching.

Nor is there any sign that TV's influence is on the wane. On the contrary, with the development of cable television, with its links to other technologies such as the telephone, computer and satellite, TV has reached an awesome level of potential sophistication. Its ability to intrude into our daily lives and determine how we live and what we think is, over time, certain to become more entrenched and politically significant.[5]

There is no question then that TV has become a dominant force in our lives. It is no longer a question of owning or not owning, watching or not watching. TV is a fact of our common life. It is there; it molds and shapes; it is the voice and soul of our informing values and social determinants.

Television Experienced

Because television has been perceived primarily as a cultural form, most of the critical attention it receives focuses on its fictional forms—dramas, sitcoms, and so on. When media analysts turn attention to the other kinds of programming—the news, documentaries, coverage of live events like Liberty Weekend or the Olympics—they tend to use different terms and criteria. In fact, as media studies penetrate the academy, it is the literature and film departments that handle fictional forms while these other, "real life" happenings become the province of sociologists (in this country, if not in Great Britain). The distinction between "art" and "reality," "news" and "entertainment," is thus maintained.

Yet, when we are actually watching television, these distinctions become more blurry. The blatancy of Liberty Weekend simply brought into the open something which has characterized network television from the start: its tendency to confuse and blur traditional distinctions between fact and fantasy, and functional distinctions among entertainment, information and marketing, all of which TV is meant to provide. In fact, "real life" events and the "informational" forms which interpret those events for us make use of the same techniques as do fictional forms on TV. More and more, they are as stylized, as dramatically structured, as emotionally engaging as drama. This is even more pronounced in commercials, which are technically supposed to provide another kind of "information," information to consumers about available commodities.

When you watch a typical hour of television, moving, perhaps, from the local news to a TV movie, you find yourself in a more or less ideologically and esthetically unified world. You may see a news segment in which the "news team" beams about a small child who has just received a new liver through the wonders of modern medicine. The movie may well tell the same kind of story. And the ads, in the majority of cases actually, will also be extolling the glories of medical science, the products of which are, even now, waiting for you at your local pharmacy. In most cases, the principals—whether journalists, actors or salespeople—are unusually attractive, well groomed and theatrically expressive. The emotions, typically, are sentimental and melodramatically reassuring. The message, more often than not, is that modern science is out there working its head off so that your kids will not suffer from the variety of illnesses we are prone to. And the dramatic format, most typically, is that of a heart warming human interest story. First the suffering child and worried parents, then the expert, caring doctor, then the cure.

In this way TV, watched as a continuum, or "flow," is—in a broad and, at this point in our discussion, overgeneralized sense—of a cultural and ideological piece. Its messages and their emotional overtones, no less than its artificially framed and glossy views of American life, follow us from dawn to dusk, from bedroom to boardroom. The overriding message it seems to whisper in our ears is that the "American Way of Life" is the best life imaginable; it will provide remedies and solutions to our many, often overlapping, needs.

It is here that the power of the media is most awesome. It creates an entire universe—a looking glass world—which, its many internal contradictions and inconsistencies notwithstanding, is for too many of us more emotionally fulfilling and more intellectually coherent than actual experience. What comes to us as we sit before the little, lighted box seeking escape or remedy for our troubles, trying to fathom the ways of the world and the human heart, is a picture of something which resembles our own world, partakes of it, but seems, somehow, more manageable and reassuring.

Is any of what we see in these forms real? Is any of it unambiguously fact or fiction? Dramatic or informational? Sincere or faked? It is impossible to tell. The questions themselves refer to earlier cultural forms. Television is a new medium designed to perform more roles and play a greater part in our lives than any other. And its way of presenting fact, fiction and product propaganda also differs from other forms.

News and ads are more like dramatic fiction; fiction is more simplisticly didactic and factual than is usual in newspapers, magazines or cinema.

What is Nonfiction?

If the line between fiction and nonfiction is so blurred on television, why write a book about the latter? Doesn't this simply confound the confusion and help it along? It is a good question with a complicated answer. The impetus for writing this book, for trying to single out something admittedly fuzzy and lacking in clearcut boundaries, grew from my sense that this blurriness was an important feature which seemed to go largely unnoticed or undiscussed. What studies exist on the framing and molding of informational television and its institutional context have focused almost exclusively on the nightly news, and often on a single segment of that.[6] While these works are often invaluable in helping to demystify the media, they tend to ignore, for reasons I have mentioned, the specifically esthetic aspects of the form. Even when they are attentive to such matters—the very use of the term "framing" implies a structural device which molds material in the artistic sense—they do not perceive or discuss them in esthetic terms. Yet to see the distortions and manipulations of TV news in a strictly ideological context is to miss the texture, the feeling of these broadcasts, the quality that provides the emotional impact that makes it compelling.

It seemed important, then, that we begin to examine the various aspects that contribute to TV's looking glass world as a whole, that we break through the fragmentation and compartmentalization that keep us from understanding the totality of the TV experience, and so gain power over its effects upon us. Thus, this book is intended as a holistic study which places cultural analysis in a sociological, historical and economic context, as a way of demonstrating the interdependence of these realms.

Since I start from the premise that fiction and nonfiction are so similar, so blurred, I might logically have written about the entirety of TV programming and demonstrated the blend of art and ideology, fact and fiction, that also characterizes soap opera and crime drama. There were several reasons I didn't do that. First, criticism of TV drama and comedy has quite often assumed an ideological component. All literary criticism based on sociological views of art does this. And so there was less need to demonstrate the political implications of, say, "Dallas," than the artistic components of "60 Minutes." I chose not to include a chapter on nightly news itself for a different reason. There are, as I said, voluminous studies of that phenomenon available. That material, along with the direct and indirect references to nightly news in many places throughout the book, seemed to make a full discussion of this more generally understood form superfluous. There is nothing specific to nightly news broadcasts that does not come up, in more sophisticated form, in other program types. Indeed, nightly news has tended to follow the "softer forms" in its development. Nor is nightly news, never high on ratings, nearly as widely experienced as most of the other forms.

The various forms I chose to analyze, on the other hand, from "20/20" to "Let's Make a Deal," have not received the kind of analysis they need in order for their popularity and effect to be understood. What they have in common, loosely put, is that they present themselves to us as partaking in one way or another of "real life." The contestants on "Let's Make a Deal" are not actors but real people who have chosen to participate in a game so that they can win real money. The characters and events in "Roots" have their basis in actual lived history. However much TV has distorted their characters and lives, there is a grain of lived reality at their bases. For this reason, viewers of the series are meant to believe they are getting some version of real history. Viewers of "Dallas" or "Days of our Lives" do not assume this. Even the commercials for Bufferin and Buick are supposedly based on fact. If they were not, we assume, they would be barred from the air as "false advertising."

At times in this study—notably in the chapter on TV movies—I do discuss purely fictional films, films, that is, developed wholly from the imagination with no factual basis. I do this to illustrate how, in this most sophisticated of TV forms, the blurring of fiction and nonfiction is nearly complete. Nonetheless, the main topic of the chapter is TV movies based on real life events. To see the similarities in the two categories is useful critically. But to the viewer, the significance of viewing a film publicized as "based on fact" is different from watching one known to be pure fantasy. The difference may be subtle in some cases, since the ideological message may be as strong in both. But the movie put forth as reality is received with more seriousness, on the very face of it. Teaching guides are prepared for historically based miniseries, no matter how farfetched, and teachers use them in classrooms to teach history. No such guides exist for purely fictional films unless they are based on "great literary works," in which case the guides are sent to literature teachers and the approach is completely different.

Similarly, when one watches "Let's Make a Deal" or "Real People," one may seriously plan to become a contestant or participant and may in fact do so. One cannot, of course, become a member of the Ewing family. Truth and falsehood are, on that material level, distinguishable. Because the game shows, beauty pageants and local news shows have this basis in reality and invite actual participation, they play a more serious role, or at least a very different and more problematic role, in our consciousness than do drama and comedy. That is one of the reasons I have singled out these shows for study. They have an imaginative and emotional power that is bolstered by their apparent truthfulness and the supposedly realizable fantasies they engender.

Beyond their emotional power, the impact of these shows is further embellished by the sheer number of hours per day they are experienced. On a randomly chosen weekday in a typical city, *TV Guide* shows all three networks featuring nonfiction shows—news, morning magazines like "Good Morning, America" and talk shows like "Donahue"—from 5 A.M. until 10A.M. Two of the three then feature game shows until noon, when all broadcast news again.

From 5 A.M. until 12:30 P.M., then, audiences see nothing except nonfiction. From 12:30 until 4 P.M., when soap operas dominate, there is an hour on each of two networks when magazine formats are offered. From 4 until 6 P.M., when local news starts, two of the three feature magazine shows, game shows and real life shows like "People's Court." From 6 to 8 P.M., local news, national news and syndicated magazine and game shows fill all three slots. Primetime begins with fictional series on two networks and a baseball game on the third. At 9 P.M., two networks offer fictional series while the third presents a "based on fact" TV movie.

After the 11 P.M. news, one network features a dramatic series rerun while the others offer more nonfiction—"Nightline" and "The Tonight Show." Even at 3 A.M., two of the three offer game shows, followed by late night news broadcasts, which continue until the morning news at 6 A.M. When one includes the eight minutes per half hour used for commercials, stations breaks, newsbreaks and the like, the proportion of nonfiction, as opposed to strictly defined fiction, programming in a network day looms very large indeed. Except for two of the soap opera hours in the afternoon, there is not a single time slot in which at least one network isn't showing nonfiction fare. Most of the time two or even three are running nonfiction. And so, while the Nielsen ratings tell us that "Murder, She Wrote" and "Dallas" are watched most consistently by the most people, overall, the stray viewer will almost assuredly be faced with an overwhelming number of apparently true to life, factual programs during twenty-two of the twenty-four hours, including primetime.

The sheer quantity of nonfiction in its multiplicity of forms will no doubt surprise the reader. But that is network TV's reality, and as such it seems obvious that a good long look at nonfiction television is overdue. Just what is it that we are being shown in so continuous and incessant a fashion? What version of "real life" does TV concoct for us? And how do styles and techniques of presenting it affect us? How do they jibe with other versions of "reality," whether theoretical or common sense experiential?

Talking About Television: Methods and Approaches

In order to answer these questions, we will need to consider, briefly, what an adequate methodology for analyzing television might be. In the vast and growing body of "communication studies," produced largely by sociologists, there is little serious analysis of what the media has meant to the changing nature of art and information. Gaye Tuchman, one of the most influential and incisive analysts of TV and its ideological implications, bases her work, as do so many others, on what is called the "reflection hypothesis." This, "at its simplest," she writes, "states that a medium's content reflects its society's values, goals, ideals, aspirations and shortcomings."[7] A related theory, the "hypodermic needle" theory, sees the viewer as a passive vessel into which the content of the medium, as described by Tuchman, is simply injected.[8]

This way of thinking reduces TV content to a mirror image of the values of the dominant society and makes of the viewer an inert, spongelike creature who brings nothing of her or his own to the viewing experience. It misses important basic truths about both processes. For one thing, television, by definition, offers a vision of reality which is "mediated," not merely "reflected." And that mediation takes place in specific ways: through the use of such esthetic techniques as plot structure, character development, point of view, camera angle, editing, style, atmosphere and so on. This is as true of nonfiction as fiction. One of the most obvious problems with the reflection approach is that it ignores that TV is a visual form. Like film or painting, it obeys its own laws of graphic organization and movement, what film theorists call *mis en scene* and *montage*. The "meaning" of a TV show is never simply ideological, simply content-produced. Artistic "meaning" must always be understood as a function of esthetic as well as rational, visual as well as verbal, elements. The experience of responding to media is as much emotional as intellectual, and it is often the purely esthetic components that elicit the strongest emotional response.

As for the viewer, here too the reflectionists oversimplify. We are not all identical empty vessels being filled up with TV content. We are active and very diverse human beings, coming to any given TV show with our own histories and experiences, our own ways of understanding and responding to what is shown, our own levels of attention and immediate moods. We do in fact interact with media, participating to some extent in developing the "meaning" we take away from the screen. And that meaning is as much a function of how the images and narratives make us feel as what they seem to tell us in the abstract, informational sense.

We are speaking of a particular medium which is more universally shared and understood than most. That is one of the main points of this book. Television is the place where most of us have learned a great percentage of what we know. It has nursed and shaped our responses to life in ways which are predictable, to a point. But beyond that point we may see and feel things differently. A Black child watching a cop show in which the heroes are white and the criminals Black will get the same message as a white child, on one level. But the emotional response to that message will be more complicated. TV may encourage self-contempt in Black children. But it may also raise feelings of anger at a picture of Black culture that is noticeably distorted in ways the white child cannot know. If the child's family or peers are politically conscious, if the times are rife with racial protest, all this will affect a response. In any case, the Black child will have a personal identification the white child will not have.

To complicate things further, there are certain contradictions and disjunctions even within the scope of network TV's largely coherent world view. What appears to be, and in the large view is, a culturally and ideologically unified universe of images and messages, emerges under closer inspection as more varied and diverse. Even the Liberty Weekend programing discussed earlier contained a variety of segments which contradicted or called into question the tranquil harmony and abundance of American life that was the weekend's dominant theme. Network TV, viewed over time and in quantity, reveals itself to be peppered with such contradictory messages—what Janice Radway calls "ideological seams"[9]—of a variety of kinds, both stylistic and ideological. On a given evening, for example, a police drama full of racist sterotypes may be followed by a magazine program's moving tribute to a Black athlete who has overcome hardship. The news and ads may support one or the other view, or provide different ones. And even among generally racist police shows, there are stylistic differences. Some are more subtle, more intelligent, more visually interesting than others.

Hegemony and Its Complexities

How, then, do we put all of this together and come up with a useful analysis? It will be helpful to begin with a concept developed by Antonio Gramsci at the beginning of this media dominated century: "hegemony." As Gramsci observed, each of us carries within us certain values and beliefs which are handed down from generation to generation and which are inherently conservative because they reflect the interests of those in power, of the status quo. But at the same time, the experiences of our daily lives tend to establish in each of us another level of consciousness which is in conflict with, and implicitly challenges, the established institutions and their "truths." It is possible, even common, for someone to "think one thing and do or feel another"; to act in opposition to her true self-interest because of contradictions within consciousness. Contemporary voting patterns provide an obvious example. Many working people voted for Ronald Reagan because he spoke of traditional values which held emotional appeal, in spite of the fact that his economic policies favored bosses over workers. In the same way, the Black child watching TV may root for the cop-heroes of the racist police drama while, on another level, he understands the falseness and personal injustice of the show he so loves. Clearly, there is a war within many of us between deeply ingrained reactionary concepts and our personal experiences and observations of hardship, misery, injustice and insecurity.

Hegemony describes the system of dominant beliefs and attitudes to which most of us, most of the time, subscribe, and which holds us together as a culture. It is a flexible, dynamic system which manages to accommodate and integrate a great deal of often contradictory experience and thought. It seems to, and at times does, take seriously and respond to our feelings of discontent and disaffection. But it accomplishes this in ways which serve ultimately to maintain the existing power structure. Sometimes it allows for new, divergent attitudes to become legitimate and for limited changes in social practice and belief to occur. More often, it persuades us, disingenuously, that our feelings of dissatisfaction can be assuaged within the limits of existing social practice.

Television, which is owned and controlled by those in power, is the major institution today charged with maintaining hegemony. Because it has become our main source of ideas and culture as a nation, it has the greatest responsibility for projecting a dominant version of reality and belief and eliciting loyalty to that world view. The medium's particular effectiveness in liberal, capitalist societies like ours comes from the institutional separation of media and state. The media is understood to be the "watchdog" of our rights. Its role is to keep an objective eye on those in power to ensure their honesty and accountability. In many dramatic cases it does just that. It was the press, of course, that brought the Watergate scandal to light. It was through the nightly televised coverage of racial unrest in South Africa that the anti-apartheid movement in this country was able to pressure Washington to rethink national policy there. That South Africa saw fit to ban such coverage and deport the media crews responsible attests to its effectiveness.

While such individual cases are obviously important—not only in bringing about politically progressive change, but in creating the environment which makes such change possible—the larger role of the media is not primarily to serve justice or the underdog, but to serve those who own and run it. This, as Douglas Kellner observes, is one of those "contradictions between capitalism and democracy historically typical of the American experience."[10] The media is a business, regulated by the state; but it is also the voice of democratic process. It is meant to uphold the values of truth, justice, "objectivity," and also to present minority experiences and views. This is a tension-filled contradiction. The newscaster is paid by the network. But his or her professional trust is with "the people" and their "right to know." In the media's finer moments—its Watergates—democracy wins out over established power. But these moments of liberation, so to speak, exist within the totality of TV newscasting and must be limited in their expression by the boundaries—legal and formal—of the media.

In other words, what we see on television, throughout a lifetime of watching, is a looking glass reflection of emotional and social life which takes the substance of reality and fits it into a set of molds. The end result is "not like a polished rock face that allows for no scrambling," as one analyst has put it, but "a rough, irregular surface, with fissures that enable one to gain a toehold."[11] Still, its laws and motions, like those of the sea, work to smooth out the fissures over time.

Hegemony is the terrain upon which those of us who work for change must move, but it is not our home turf. We do not have the material resources for the battle that those in charge have. It stands to reason then, that most of what appears on television will—for a variety of subtle reasons—tend to support the status quo. Television will focus on aspects of American life that most please its masters, fit their images of themselves. It is no accident that those who work in decision-making positions for television's owners earn enormous salaries which allow them to live lives filled with luxury and ease, divorced from the landscape of pain and deprivation which so many others inhabit.

But that is not the most important way in which hegemony is secured and maintained. What limits the portrayal and impact of contradictions—what really happens on the TV screen—are the rules that the media follow. And these rules grow out of basic democratic capitalist dogma. We are taught from birth—whether we are destined to own a network, work for one, or watch it—that we have certain options in life and no others. We learn, for example, that "freedom," in its operational sense, is bound by the choices inherent in capitalist life. We are "free" to buy this or this, vote for that or that. We will be "happy" if we have certain things, live certain ways, and so on.

In reality, the system under which we live cannot fulfill the implicit promises of democracy. Inequalities and limitations are everywhere. We hit our heads against them in every aspect of life. But the media, as the greatest socializing agent, insists again and again that we must simply try harder, search harder, think harder and we will realize our dreams. Happiness becomes associated with a Coke-filled picnic basket and a blonde in a bikini; success is a Honda Accord; justice is the Hill Street police force; democracy is a Black athlete making it into the Major Leagues.

To some extent, this set of images and messages has validity. Coke does tastes good. Racial progress does take place. What is left out of the picture, most of the time, is any alternative sense of what might be fun and what might promote collective equality. We get a finite set of choices and they are more slick and shiny than real life's mirror opposites. The Coke doesn't taste that good, nor is racial progress, in the case of one athlete, as emotionally gratifying as in the TV movie. Finally, life itself lacks the closure of these narratives. There is no happily ever after in life. There is the Monday after the picnic; the caffeine, calories and nutritional emptiness of the Coke; the built-in obsolescence and danger of automobiles; and the vast majority of Blacks who don't make the Big Leagues.

"Hegemony," wrote Raymond Williams, is "a dominant system of meanings and values" which "constitute a sense of reality for most people" and which, far from being "static...is continually active and adjusting," able to "accommodate and tolerate alternative opinions and attitudes, even some alternative senses of the world...within a particular effective and dominant culture."[12] It is those "alternative senses of the world" that are TV's highpoints, its glories, at least from the perspective of this book. But they exist within the larger, more complicated universe of ideological hegemony.

When alternative visions and messages do come out—the case of Watergate, of Abscam, even the editing techniques of "60 Minutes" or the sexism of the local news managers—they push at the limits. Sometimes they permanently expand them, as we shall see. And that is what we aim for and try to capitalize on. But it is a tough, ongoing battle in which we are at a huge disadvantage.

The media is not a gray, undifferentiated "they." It enlists workers to produce its product, and they are not by any means in agreement with their bosses, corporate or governmental, in every instance. In fact, it is probably fair to say that artists and thinkers tend—as the Right is fond of accusing—to be more liberal than not. Yet, what they produce is often very different from what they would like to produce, what they may believe in.

For Gramsci, the relationship between media workers and bosses was a cold-blooded sort of thing. "The intellectuals," he said, "are detaching themselves from the dominant class in order to unite themselves more intimately to it, to be a real superstructure and not simply an inorganic element of the economic structure."[13] The taint of blood money and the stench of selling out riddles this statement. The experience of daily life is not so cut and dried. There is no conspiratorial committee of Ronald Reagan or Richard Nixon clones planning the daily schedule of each network. Nor are all those who produce nonfiction television so stupid or disingenuous that they either do not know the grand scheme or deliberately collude with it. The producers of those segments which present critiques, at times even radical critiques, of the status quo generally understand very well the overall thrust of the media. They know how few critical moments they are likely to be allowed. They know how many proposals will be vetoed before they are allowed to do the occasional labor of love that has political teeth in it.

Robert Greenwald, an independent producer of some of the most socially powerful made-for-TV movies, developed his skills and earned the reputation and trust which enabled him to persuade networks to trust him with hard-hitting material, by producing movies like "Story of a Centerfold." "I wanted in," he told me in a recent interview in which he described breaking into the industry. "I wasn't sitting there objectively saying 'This guy's an asshole,' I was trying to analyze the system, to figure out how I could do what I wanted to do."[14]

But we have shifted to another level of analysis from Gramsci's. One of the things Greenwald "wanted to do" turned out to be an above average docudrama about the building of the Statue of Liberty, which aired about a month before Liberty Weekend. But that movie, like the many fine, even radical moments in the hours, weeks and months of patriotic programming, existed in the context of an overall set of images which were mostly jingoistic, plastic, crude. Even the best and most radical of network TV dramas is rarely as texturally or politically rich and challenging as its counterparts in independent media production, or even the mainstream television programming produced in other countries.

But again we are setting up conflicting criteria for judging network TV. From an absolutist perspective, the best of TV drama is obviously and necessarily less sophisticated than the comparable novel, foreign film or independent video production. From the perspective of social impact, however, the effects of even this watered down commodity may well be greater and more progressive. It reaches an audience that is far larger than these other forms, and far more significant in its social makeup, for this is the audience that does not see foreign films, hear about serious books, or read the *New York Times*. The reality within which socially conscious artists work today sets the terms for the choices they must make. Mass audiences can only be reached through mass cultural forms, and this necessitates working within the particular limits imposed by corporate controlled mass culture.

Progressive artists who choose to work in the media which reach this audience—whether TV, film, popular fiction or rock music—must, in Greenwald's words, "analyze the system" and "figure out how to do" what they want to do. "What they want to do" can never move too far away from the artistic and political limits of the form, however. That is of course true for every artist in every medium, but in popular culture, especially network television, the rules reflect particularly blatant economic and political values.

We have been talking about network television in terms of at least three separate levels of reality, from three separate angles of vision. We began with the level of audience experience, in describing, from a critical perspective, the programming for Liberty Weekend. But we have also viewed Liberty Weekend from the highly theoretical level of Gramsci and Williams, as part of a system which produces the dynamic and complicated abstraction called "ideological hegemony." And just now we added a third level of reality, the workaday world of individual producers, writers and network executives, within which Robert Greenwald produced a specific TV movie called "Liberty." This third level includes the various people who run and work for the corporations which sponsor TV programs and the institutions, such as the Federal Communications Commission (FCC), which make and enforce the laws which regulate the industry.

The language used at each of these levels differs dramatically. What to Gramsci and Williams is an "institution" within a "liberal capitalist society," is just "the tube" to the viewer of Liberty Weekend. Whether it was a news report on what is being done to create jobs for the unemployed in New England, or a musical "special" with Frank Sinatra, it was received with pleasure or boredom, belief or skepticism. To the executives at ABC and the sponsoring corporations, it was, during production, an over-budget, controversial headache; while, after the fact, it became a delight—a whopping 35 share on the Nielsen ratings.

One reason the system works so smoothly is that each of these groups uses a language and thought process that is so limited. In fact, the individual members of each group may change identities, angles of vision and terminology. As a viewer, for example, I like to watch soap opera. My daughter and I love to discuss the latest goings on of Brook English, Tad Martin, and the other residents of Pine Valley, a town we often escape to when we're both home. It is one of the ways we have developed for discussing relationships, sometimes as gossip, sometimes as serious mother/daughter talk. But when I talk to her about "my work" on "the media," we use totally different concepts and terms and call upon totally different feelings. We may be contemptuous of plot implausibility or outraged at class bias, where before we were emotionally empathetic.

This ability to hold a variety of contradictory thoughts and feelings is part of every viewer's experience. It enables us, potentially, to challenge the power of hegemony. For that power rests on its ability to make most of us, most of the time, "go along" with the dominant attitudes and beliefs presented.

There are moments in history when significant numbers of us come together around an oppositional set of beliefs. The feminist movement of the 1960s and 1970s both grew out of and created such a moment. As a result, women like Brook English of "All My Children" are now standard characters of daytime soap opera. Brook is herself a TV journalist and a single mother. She is bright, independent and concerned with such social issues as apartheid and the plight of the homeless. It was feminism—women collectively revolting against sexist stereotypes, both as viewers and TV writers and producers—that put characters like these in the place of the "Stella Dallas" types of radio soap opera.

Such examples of political progress take place within the very complicated world of hegemony. In that sense, the struggle for change within the media is a part of the larger struggle for progressive social change in all arenas. And just as groups of viewers may affect progress, so too may they act in reactionary ways. Christian programming and groups like Accuracy in Media are proof of that.

One reason such political struggle seems so invisible is that the people who work within the media, both creatively and administratively, do not use this kind of language very often. They have specific jobs which require, again, specific angles of vision. If one is concerned with profits, ratings and coming in under budget, one's mind will be on the accounts ledger and demographic studies. If one happens to be working as an artist under these conditions, one will need to "push the artistic limits at the same time that you push the financial limits," to quote Greenwald.[15]

In fact, as Todd Gitlin attests in his detailed account of the working world of network production, "the networks generate ideology mostly indirectly and unintentionally."[16] Even the most consciously leftist producers and writers shy away from political concepts because they are not descriptive of the problems and solutions their jobs present. "It wouldn't work dramatically," is the answer to most questions about the elimination of explicit political concepts. Or else, "it wouldn't pass Standards and Practices."[17] This kind of thinking is slippery. It serves, after all, to justify the hedging of political and artistic principle in the interest of expediency, of what can reasonably be done. The danger is that even the best of those who work in television, outrageously overpaid as they usually are, will lapse into an easy accommodation with the rules and stop trying to push the boundaries. But that, as they say, is—quite literally—show biz. It is also an important factor in understanding hegemony.

Television's Political World

Given the general absence of political language, and the many contradictory elements within the broad framework of network programming, it is difficult to determine the exact ideological parameters of the world view presented on television. Obviously, some things are identifiably rightwing and others radical in the leftist sense of the term. At various times in history, and with shifting administrations, there may also be discernible left and right tendencies. When Ronald Reagan took office, network staffs, on the basis of instinct rather than hard information, scurried to adapt to what they assumed was a conservative shift in popular sentiment.[18] And during the Vietnam period, when radical sentiments about the war, minority and women's rights and the broad range of lifestyle issues subsumed under the "counterculture" heading were rising, the networks picked up that cue as well.

Norman Lear's many liberal series—"All in the Family," "Maude"—and the sympathetic portrayal of working women started by the "Mary Tyler Moore" show, certainly were significant and clearly visible in the late 1960s and early 1970s. The shift to police dramas and TV movies based on military heroes and scenarios which characterizes the 1980s, is equally tangible and clear. But beyond a vague sense that Lear is a "liberal," while series lionizing men like Patton and MacArthur are "conservative" in sentiment, we don't have much. "Liberal" and "conservative," as political labels, have extremely fuzzy definitions these days.

According to media analyst George Gerbner, in a study of political attitudes held by heavy TV viewers conducted over a twenty year period, network television itself is responsible for much of the confusion. Heavy viewers of working class origin, for example, were found to feel increasing sympathy for the wealthy and their conservative policies, while conservatives who watched a lot of TV came to feel more open to things like women's rights and alternative lifestyles. Nor could those who called themselves Republicans be clearly distinguished, on the basis of political beliefs, from self-proclaimed Democrats. The terms seem to lose meaning through television viewing. And even on a specific issue, the results of TV watching are contradictory. According to Gerbner, "Viewing tends to moderate some extremely racist views, but it also undermines the support for racial equality, especially among ...liberals."[19] The same holds for views on women.

Gerbner concludes that TV has a "mainstreaming" effect, pulling everyone toward an undifferentiated midpoint which he labels the "New Populism." "Contrary to the charges of some critics," he concludes, "television is no liberal conspiracy. Our data show that if anything its New Populism undermines liberal support for women, minorities, and political and personal freedoms,"[20] even as it may, at the same time, also undermine certain sexist and racist attitudes.

In other words, network television serves to muddy the political waters. It pushes us all toward a center point because it tends to destroy hard, meaningful definitions of policy in favor of mushy, contradictory emotional attitudes toward issues. This is achieved—hardly in any deliberate, planned fashion—as a by-product of the various levels of input it blends, and by the framing and dramatizing patterns created through technical and artistic conventions.

It is probably safe to say that the liberal Left boundary of this "New Populism," in every instance, is a firm anticommunism bolstered by the severe effects of McCarthyism in the 1950s; both are part of the Hollywood atmosphere. On the Right, pure fascism, even on Christian networks, is beyond the pale. What we finally receive is a world view recognizable as corporate capitalist. Sometimes it bears the mark of democratic humanism; sometimes cynical nihilism or Hobbesianism. And, in those moments we work and search for, it may even push beyond liberalism a bit, and, as in the case of feminism and soap opera, hold its ground. On the other hand, it may at times push the rightward boundaries closer toward fascist attitudes.

Within that universe, certain vaguer tendencies emerge. The dramatic conventions of narrative television—fiction and nonfiction—make individualism the norm for understanding all human behavior, even social change. Collective political behavior, except in the negative sense of mob riots, "doesn't work dramatically."[21] TV also tends to isolate incidents in time and social context. The fragmentation produced by commercial breaks, along with the generally segmented way in which all TV is produced, from news to movies, gives the illusion that events happen in distinct isolation from one another, and in very shallow historic and social spaces. Thus, a TV version of history implies that "great men," acting in historic isolation and free of the effects of complex social forces, make things happen.

But these are very general observations. There will, in the course of this book, be numerous other such observations made. They will add up to a world view which is defined more by the nature of human experience as presented on television than by its ideological specifics. That *is* to a great extent the ideology of network television. And it is within this framework that we will be looking at the various nonfiction forms produced by network television. For the most part, the TV world we will be looking at will be characterized by what is most typical. We are interested, primarily, in the largest, and thus most powerful, defining features of the television universe.

In order to create this ideological mosaic, we will be balancing a lot of different balls in the air. Formal and esthetic considerations will be included along with ideological analysis. And the input of the various members of the different institutions which produce shows will be understood to coexist with the complex responses of viewers as a group, their varied and internally contradictory attitudes, beliefs and emotions notwithstanding. Before beginning, however, we will need to examine the history of the networks and their institutional structures.

2
A Look at the Basics: Social Context, Technology and Institutions

The effect of home television on contemporary life—in particular on our understanding and experience of "culture," as both art and knowledge—has been phenomenal. The mass media have changed the meaning of art in the modern world. In fact, much of the confusion and controversy surrounding home TV stems from a misunderstanding of, and resistance to, the way in which social and economic factors always determine the nature of what is called "art." There is a myth that says that art is somehow inspired in the soul of the individual artist; that the artist is a "gifted" seer who produces poetry, sculpture, etc., in a social vacuum, out of visions and impulses that are nonrational, and certainly nonmaterial. In this myth, the work of art is an isolated, pure "object" which bears no necessary relation to or reflection of the material conditions within which it was produced.

This is a myth that is conducive to the maintenance of the current power structure. It tends to obscure the fact that cultural experience in this age is less and less a matter of individual, private creation and more and more an integrated part of the entire social structure. We are taught to view art as that kind of thing—poetry, theater, classical musical—that is in fact, for social reasons, in decline and increasingly marginal to daily life. We are taught to see television, pop music, pulp fiction—the forms that in fact dominate our cultural lives—as something other than art, primarily because they are mass produced and blatantly commercial. But commercialism is almost by definition a condition of modern life. It is hardly peculiar to cultural works. In fact, we are living in an age when most things are mass produced and sold commercially. To deny that mass media products are "art," while still calling a Big Mac or TV dinner "food," is illogical. We may not like it, but, for many Americans, television is the only "art" that has meaning.

It is particularly important to remind ourselves that television is an art form because it is so much more socially powerful than previous forms. It has made dramatic art a universal experience for the first time in human history. This is the first civilization in which people of all classes, ages and educational levels have constant access to dramatic art in the privacy of their homes, and at what seems to be no cost. There are more TV sets than bathrooms in American homes.[1]

Since a huge proportion of the world's population is illiterate, and even in this country, where universal high school education is the norm, functional illiteracy is a massive problem, television, a visual and oral medium, is one of the most significant cultural developments in history.[2] Its universal accessibility makes it the most potentially democratic of cultural forms. Unlike the print media—newspapers, novels, history, poetry—everyone can "get it." Everyone shares in its vision of human values and its version of social truth. It has hopelessly blurred the distinctions between "high" and "low" culture, between "art" and "information," if not made them meaningless. And as we have already seen, it demands a more complex method of analysis than other cultural forms, a method which brings social and artistic categories together.

The Social Role of Television

It is common for people to think of technology as simply emerging from the genius of some brilliant scientist and taking off, automatically becoming a fixture of our lives. But this kind of romantic thinking ignores the real trajectories of scientific development in the modern world. Technologies emerge and become universally implemented in response to real social needs that accompany changes in society. The science needed to develop home TV was understood in the 1920s, but TV did not become universal until the post-World War II era.

What TV—and to a lesser extent radio—offered was a badly needed mechanism for social communication directly into the home in a society increasingly characterized by what Raymond Williams calls "mobile privatization." Where people had previously lived in small, stable, culturally and politically homogeneous communities, 20th century capitalism, with its uprooting of families and "increasing distance between immediate living areas and the directive places of work and government...carried an imperative need for new kinds of social contact," for "news from 'outside,' from otherwise inaccessible sources."[3]

Since the 20th century also saw the influx into the U.S. of huge numbers of immigrant workers from a variety of cultures, the need for standardized social and cultural messages was even greater. As Stuart and Elizabeth Ewen point out, "the growth of capitalism has always depended on the ability to distribute standardized information," and in America this information, in the form of mass culture, has especially been "a bridge between the aspirations of an old world and the priorities of a new one."[4] The role of mass culture and communication has therefore been extremely important in the workings and development of American capitalism since the early part of the century.

The post-World War II era brought even greater changes and put even more demands on the system, making the struggle to shape and control communications production ever fiercer. As the economy came to rely more and more on consumerism—on persuading people to buy things not needed, or replace things already owned—more sophisticated messages and images were needed. The dual role of socializing diverse and/or isolated people and marketing new consumer goods was now more critical than ever. And TV, which was so much more emotionally powerful than radio, became increasingly attractive. In his study of the rise of the advertising industry, Vance Packard showed how the "science" of marketing research was developed in the 1950s to increase the marketing and ideological power offered by mass media. "What makes this country great," he quotes one executive, "is the creation of wants and desires, of dissatisfaction with the old and outmoded."[5] In other words, democracy and freedom had come to mean consumerism—the spectacle of infinite choices among identical, often useless products. And TV was clearly the medium of choice for presenting this vision. Home TV, with its direct line to the most intimate domestic space, and its enormous visual power, was a perfect mechanism for both selling and persuading.

As the size and scope of multinational corporate activity grew, so did the use of television to push more politically explicit values. "The creation and maintenance of demand," says Erik Barnouw, in discussing corporate use of TV advertising, is only one of the needs of modern corporations. "For the multinational corporation a more pressing task is the legitimation of its vast and often mysterious operations which require, for success, an environment of confidence."[6] This "environment" of course was in no small part created by the development of sophisticated "ideological" TV advertisements, touting "progress" and "better living through chemistry." As time passed, the globe-gobbling programs of these corporations required more and more public relations rationalization to keep a shine on their rapidly tarnishing images.

Government/Media/Corporate Complex

The rise of television to its current position of cultural dominance involved far more than mere technological innovation. In ways too subtle, numerous and intertwined to list, TV has become an integral component of our political, economic and personal lives, by virtue of its ability to play a variety of roles and fill a variety of needs. Once it had reached this position of omnipresence, it was inevitable that political forces and figures would also see the need for and advantage of using it. Indeed, by the 1980s, the media has become a central fixture and factor in all major political events and controversies. The cliche that "if it didn't happen on TV, it didn't happen" is too close to the truth to be funny. In fact, every public figure must now shape her or his strategy around media coverage and image. It is unlikely that a wheelchair-bound Franklin Roosevelt could have commanded the same authority in the age of television. The importance of television image is borne out by the careers of such men as Richard Nixon, John F. Kennedy and Ronald Reagan, to name only a few.

But since TV's enormous power to affect political life derives from economic revenues received from corporate sponsors and political and legal sanctions granted by government agencies, relations with these institutions are extremely important. Media power, in effect, depends on its working relationships with those in high places. For that reason, the processes by which media image and coverage build or destroy careers, make or break policies, and determine public attitudes toward issues, is no more random or inherent in technological processes than the development of TV itself. The media work with a set of of priorities, guidelines, values and preferences, which govern what and how they "cover reality."

Consider, for example, the now institutionalized and far from "open" form of the presidential press conference. The network anchorpersons always sit up front and are always called upon. While they seem to be hardhitting and even adversarial, especially in times of social unrest, they do not, except in extraordinary circumstances, go beyond certain standard, understood and rather narrow limits of media/executive protocol.

In return for being "reasonable," the established press, through a now established system of communication, is made privy to "scoops" and "leaks" less mainstream journalists are denied. They attend social functions where they mingle and become chummy with the officials they cover. And while a certain amount of controversy and conflict is expected and required, by and large there is a commonality of values and beliefs that binds all parties to a common vision. The parameters may shift from administration to administration, but the basic structure does not change.[7]

The same relations exist informally between media officials and corporate sponsors. A network will often call a sponsor whose ad is scheduled for a news program in which negative information will be aired—on the dangers of tobacco or over the counter drugs, perhaps—and give them the option to switch their ad to another evening.[8] There are crucial loopholes and contradictions in this system. But in the

larger sense, there is a mutually advantageous and smoothly functioning relationship among the media, the state and the corporations.

Because of the structure of the modern media, and their interlocks
with government and corporate institutions, it is no exaggeration to
say that they have become a major force in the maintenance of the
social structure.

> In a modern capitalist economy...the cultural institutions of
> press and publishing, cinema, radio, television and the record
> industry, are no longer, as in earlier market phases, marginal
> or minor, but, both in themselves and in their frequent inter-
> lock or integration with other productive institutions, are
> parts of the whole social and economic organization at its
> most general and pervasive.[9]

None of this has come about accidentally. The development of
contemporary media technology, the government agencies created to
regulate it, and the role of the corporations in determining its uses,
have all been carefully and deliberately orchestrated by those with the
authority to influence such decisions. We need, therefore, to look
briefly at the history of each of these components, to see how they have
acted, individually and together, to create the amazing world of American TV.

The Technical Framework

There are many interesting questions about the development and
current structure of television which are, oddly, rarely asked. How did
TV rise to its present position of cultural dominance? Why the particular technology of centrally broadcast home TV? Since TV is so politically significant, should it be operated as a commercial business?

We have become so accustomed to the present situation that we
assume—largely unconsciously—that there must have been something inevitable about it all. But no developments of such social magni-
tude are ever "natural" or inevitable. To be sure, the social forces at
work in the 20th century created a "need" for some form of "mass
communication." But

> the key question about technological response to a need, is
> less a question about the need itself than about its place in an
> existing social formation. A need which corresponds with the
> priorities of the real decision-making groups will, obviously,
> more quickly attract the investment of resources and the
> official permission, approval or encouragement on which a
> working technology, as distinct from available technical
> devices, depends.[10]

The particular technology in which our decision-makers invested—properly called broadcasting—is unique in several ways. First, it doesn't presuppose any particular content. From the beginning of radio, in the 1920s, it was a system of distribution, not production, that was developed. Unlike motion picture technology, which developed in response to the demand for the product, radio, and then TV, came about in response to a need for "mass communication" in the abstract.

That the specific content to be broadcast was of three kinds—information, art or entertainment, and commercial advertising—was a result of economic and political decisions about the use of new technologies. Television, for example, is deliberately a one-way rather than two-way system. It is meant to allow messages generated from a central source to be received in the most decentralized of all institutions—the private home.

Unlike the telephone, for example, it is not set up to allow individuals or small groups to produce and broadcast their own materials. Thus it is not, as is commonly supposed, a "free" or "democratic" system.[11] It is a system in which the means of communication, and its products, are owned and controlled by a very few, while the "masses" to whom this product is "communicated" are mere passive receivers of materials over which they have no control. The use of ratings does not give audiences control over programming. It merely tells sponsors and networks, in the most general sense, what sells and what doesn't, always within the limited context of what the system itself has made available. Television, then, is a "commercial, politically regulated, monopolistic form."[12]

Institutional Background

The way in which radio, and then television, came to be regulated was, again, a matter of high level decision-making in a context of dynamic social change. In particular, working out conflicts and contradictions among the economic and political needs of government and industry, and the ideological demands of "democracy," played a major role in determining the often internally contradictory nature of network television. The most politically revealing thing about the history of broadcast regulation is that it was requested by the industry itself.[13] "It was no accident," Erik Barnouw explains, that "in 1922, when ASCAP started to demand royalties for materials used on air, thus eroding the economic base of radio,"[14] the programming and economic structure of radio became a public issue.

While many possible systems were discussed, the final decision, codified in the Radio Act of 1922, was to make radio programming a "tool with which to sell audiences to commercial sponsors."[15] Profit thus was determined to outweigh both public welfare and individual interests as the primary purpose of broadcasting. In 1934, when the Federal Radio Commission of 1927 became the Federal Communications Commission, the rules governing radio broadcasting were more or less transplanted to the newly developing television industry.

That the FCC's "broad-based powers" have always reflected the needs of the industry itself is no surprise. The history of that industry parallels that of all other economic developments in this country. Concentration of power in a few hands tends to bring about the need for some kind of regulation to curb monopolization and lay down the rules of the corporate game. The controversy over "who owns the airwaves" is in many ways similar to the question of who owns any other natural resource. The demands of private greed war against the democratic commitment to the public interest. And as in other such cases, the regulatory agencies which evolve out of this need for order tend to be representatives of the powerful.

As Douglas Kellner notes, "The development of the telecommunications system followed the railroad, oil, steel, and automobile industries in concentrating the means of communication in the hands of giant corporations."[16] In the 1930s, with the invention of television, the struggle for control of telecommunications between AT&T and RCA, primarily, was savage. In the 1940s, government efforts to control the monopolizing tendencies of these giants began. But the regulators of the industry—as is still true today—were primarily members of the industry itself.

By the time the radio industry had settled into a relative calm, the three networks which would dominate television reigned supreme, while the Federal Communications Commission, established in 1934 to regulate the industry, was staunchly committed to "advance industry private interests rather than enforce 'the public interest, convenience and necessity.'"[17] (In 1935, for example, the Wagner-Hatfield Bill to amend the Federal Communications Act by which the FCC was formed was defeated. The amendment would have allotted "one-fourth of all the radio broadcasting facilities" to "educational, religious, agricultural, labor, cooperative, and similar non-profit making associations."[18] And "government and industry frequently suppressed technologies of communication in the interests of their exploitation by hegemonic corporations."[19] The choice of VHF over UHF television systems in the 1940s, for example, hampered the development of cable and pay TV.

The key issue of whether "the people" or private industry own the airwaves has been worked out in a typically contradictory and lopsided way by the FCC. In the Federal Communications Act, the democratic idea that it is "the people" is clearly stated. Yet the industry has operated as a private enterprise. The "public interest" is of course the terrain over which the contradiction between capital and democracy works itself out. It is the legal bone over which the commissioners must contend. And it is the craggy landscape upon which progressive forces must gain their toeholds. But with regulation in the hands of appointed commissioners, the deck is always stacked.

Public Television: The Fourth Network

Certain commissioners—most notably Newton Minow in the 1950s and Nicholas Johnson in the 1960s—have tried to democratize and uplift the industry. Minow's famous "vast wasteland" speech created the push for public television which was established under Lyndon Johnson in the 1960s. But public television has not fulfilled its mandate in terms of democratic access or quality or variety of programming.[20]

For the most part, public television has reproduced the existing order, on a somewhat different political and cultural terrain. If the networks offer "mass culture," PBS has generally offered a certain kind of "high culture," based on the university model of that idea. Chinese art, symphony, ballet and Shakespeare are the norm. Certain dramatic series like "Masterpiece Theater" offer more challenging contemporary drama than the "Movie of the Week," and within limits, PBS has been the only outlet for leftist independent film makers. Indeed, on the face of it, PBS may appear to be the major carrier of nonfiction television, because it has had a reputation for carrying the kind of documentary films which the term nonfiction seems to most classically suggest. Series like "Nonfiction Television," for example, until it fell under the budgetary ax, could from time to time present films sympathetic to the Sandinista government of Nicaragua or critical of major industries. But money, politics and a subtle kind of cultural elitism severely hampers PBS' ability to act as a progressive force. And under Reagan, things have deteriorated to the point where PBS is a pale shadow of its healthier network counterparts.

The limits of PBS were built into its conception and framework. It was subsidized in part by the federal government, and also by corporations and private contributions. Corporate underwriting has served to place the same kinds of cautionary limits on producers as within the commercial networks. (PBS is sometimes called "the Petroleum Broadcasting System.") And indeed, corporations' motivation for funding "quality TV" is the prestige factor. It serves to create the illusion that the oil industry, for instance, really is in the service of progress and culture. But this is also the case on the networks, in series like "Hallmark Hall of Fame." One of the ways in which quality and democracy are served on television, generally, is through the need of corporations and governments to appear nobler and more enlightened than is entirely the case. That too is a given of the primary media contradiction between profits and products. PBS is no different in that sense; its offerings just look a little "classier."

As for government funding, the Reagan administration has drastically slashed that. In the wake of these cuts, made in conservative times by a conservative administration, "high culture," often a euphemism for noncontroversial "classics" from other times and places, won out over socially provocative fare. The biggest chunk of nonfiction funding on PBS today goes to two series which are only marginally different, or better, than the best of the networks. "Frontline" and the "MacNeil-Lehrer Hour" are essentially equivalent to ABC's late night public affairs show, "Nightline." What independent films manage to get aired are few and far between.

Viewer support, without which PBS would fold, is of course a form of charity. It means that only those committed to "highbrow" programming, and with spare cash, will contribute. Thus even when PBS is politically progressive, its audience tends to be largely made up of the more well-to-do and educated among us. A documentary on Black South African leader Nelson Mandela, for example, will not reach many young Blacks in the ghetto. Its appeal, when it does reach them, is usually limited by its stylistic choices. In a nation raised on "The Flintstones," it is not likely that a ten year old in a household with few books or records will choose a talky, visually flat documentary over a flashy police drama.

"Sesame Street" is a rare example of a PBS product which was informed by an understanding of this cultural and political truth. Borrowing from the tradition of literacy programs in the Third World, it used network TV styles and techniques to woo youngsters to its "literacy lessons." Unfortunately, this is not the norm. In fact, there is quite a bit of controversy over this technique. Does it not, say some, pander to the "lower tastes" engendered by TV? [21] While this is an interesting and important debate, it is not likely to change PBS much. It will remain a marginal and not-too-different "fourth network," less varied in its offerings than the major networks and less attractive to young viewers than wholly commercial cable networks like Nickelodeon and MTV. That is why this study is restricted to commercial TV.

The Workings of the FCC

A brief survey of the important tenets and functions of the FCC as it works today will explain a lot about the way the broadcast industry functions and, by implication, about network nonfiction television programming.

The FCC has historically been primarily responsible for granting and renewing licenses. It cannot—because of infringements on First Amendment rights—actually monitor the content of programs. It can only investigate the behavior of a station when a complaint is filed. In fact, it is almost unheard of for a license to be revoked, and the FCC has never revoked a television license (and only once a radio license) for failure to serve the public interest.[22]

It is, then, economic interests tempered—mainly—by the need to fulfill the "public interest" requirements of the FCC that govern programming decisions. FCC regulations, modified to some extent by the political bent of the Reagan administration, require an undefined amount of public interest programming. The effect and intent of the Reagan FCC, chaired by Mark Fowler, has been to eliminate public interest regulation, and to heed the private entreaties of friends in high corporate places to an unprecedented degree. The stipulation that commercial advertising be limited to a certain number of minutes per hour, for instance, has been rescinded by the Reagan administration, as has the rule that networks may only own and operate five affiliate stations outright. Deregulation, in the name of free enterprise, is the blatant and militant policy of the current FCC. Limitations on ownership, as well as curbs on content, are being attacked by Fowler with an almost wild abandon. The few and limited restraints under which broadcasters now operate are at this writing being challenged at every turn.[23]

In the area of content, it is more difficult for the FCC to act than in the more mystified and less visible economic realm. For the rulings protecting individual rights and insuring political balance are of ideological importance in the public mind. There are three tenets, in particular, which network executives adhere to and think about every day. The Fairness Doctrine, which Fowler thinks has become legalistically obsolete in the light of the new technological landscape,[24] is the most publicly disputed. Adopted in 1949, it requires that airtime be given to "opposing views" when a controversial idea of public importance is presented. With the "Equal Time" rule, which requires equal time for political candidates, and the "Personal Attack" rule, which requires that individuals personally attacked be allowed to respond, it makes up the triumvirate of democratic principles upon which broadcasting practice is primarily based. But while the reactionary efforts to drop these rules are dangerous in principle and should be fought, the fact is that all three of these rules fall far short of the kind of political comprehensiveness which would in fact protect individual rights and allow for a broad, all encompassing range of debate on television. For each one assumes a narrow view of controversy which is based on a highly individualistic view of politics and an overly simple understanding of "opposing" political views.

The Fairness Doctrine, which is concerned with "opposing views," states that all controversial political positions presented should be balanced by "opposing views." But it is broadcasters, not any outside forces, that determine what views are heard, who should represent them, and when they should be aired. Nor do the networks have to abide by an Equal Time rule. That applies only to those a network is thought to have slandered.[25]

In an interesting example of how these ideas actually work in practice, Av Westin relates how, while ABC's News Director in the 1970s, he applied the Fairness Doctrine. He became concerned that his staff, briefed each morning by certain publications—the *New York Times, Washington Post* and *Wall Street Journal*—would necessarily have a bias. He was of course correct. What is interesting, however, is his sense of that bias and his corrective. To Westin, these publications represented an "East coast, socially activist view of events" which, according to the Fairness Doctrine, should be balanced. He initiated a process called "reverse perspective" by which the news staff was required to do a certain number of stories which reflected views opposing the "socially activist" assumptions of the east coast press, within seven days of a story based on that bias. For every story detailing the tragedies suffered by women refused legal abortion—an example he gives—he ruled that an opposing story be aired giving the antiabortionist position that "the fetus is a human being," complete with "prolife"-style photos of dead fetuses.[26] In this way, he insured that ABC would not subvert the Fairness Doctrine.

This example, presented in tones of liberal self-congratulation, makes a certain kind of sense. Given that the biases of network news crews will be liberal, an assumption which seems justified, the balance demanded by the FCC becomes traditionally conservative. The problem is that no other choices exist. And yet, while it is difficult for people in this country to see this—because of the very policies followed by Westin—the simple prochoice position is not really "opposite" the "prolife" position. That position, with its ultimate push for a Human Life Amendment outlawing abortion outright, is indeed the extreme Right one. But its actual counterpart is free, safe abortion on demand, not mere legalization. This is the only demand that truly represents "the public interest" in the comprehensive sense. For it alone provides abortion rights to the poor and powerless who do not have the means to obtain even legal abortions.

In areas in which the FCC determines policy on social and political issues, then, it is bound by the common understanding—which exists in the FCC, network offices, the press, the schools and so on—of what the limits of those issues are. In the realm of dramatic programming, the network Standards and Practices office serve the same function. They too decide whether a program will offend "existing social standards." But those standards, like the existing framework for discussing issues which affect us all, such as abortion, are determined in the minds and actions of men—mostly white, wealthy men—for whom the concerns of poor, Black women, for instance, aren't known or relevant.

In the realm of economic power, the FCC has the crucial job of determining rights to use of the airwaves. This is its most important economic function because, when new technologies emerge, major reshufflings must take place in allocation of what is, of course, a scarce resource. Typically, the major players involved are the corporations already invested in media who want to maintain the life of vast monopolistic empires by absorbing and becoming the dominant purveyors of any new technologies that emerge and flourish. Newer businesses, of course, as well as small and politically weak minority groups of various kinds, want to gain a toehold too, whether to pursue financial, political or social ends. The FCC tends—because its members are themselves usually tied to government and corporate interests—to favor existing owners. But it must, in the name of democracy and free enterprise, allow some competition, and some entree for small and poor groups. In the scramble for rights and frequencies on the airwaves created by new technologies, the FCC acts in ways which typically allow a few upstarts to gain ground while essentially preserving the powers of the top corporations and their interests.

An issue currently under discussion by the FCC illustrates more generally how technological decisions are made. Low power television (LPTV) uses weak signals to broadcast over small areas without interference. The technology has been around since the beginning of television, but has not been made available for use. In 1981, the FCC solicited applications for licenses, which was seen as an opportunity for small, populist groups to gain access to the airwaves. In particular, geographically defined ethnic groups, such as Blacks in Harlem, could use LPTV for community broadcasting. The "FCC received applications from black and Hispanic groups, from unions and religious bodies, from radical television-for-the-people types, and from small town folk of all descriptions."[27] Over 6,000 applications were submitted, including many from corporate giants hoping the original guidelines limiting ownership to fifteen stations would be dropped before decisions were made. The FCC, inundated with applications and unsure of direction, put a "freeze" on them, just as it had frozen applications for commercial television licenses in the early 1950s.

In the meantime, deregulation did result in the elimination of the ownership restrictions. Nonetheless, in March, 1982, the FCC, under pressure from Congress, adopted rules giving preference to 50 percent minority owners and those with no other broadcast interests, and giving rural areas a jump on major markets. Since then, applications have swelled to 40,000 but the FCC seems to be stalling; possibly, it is suggested, to avoid acting on its democratic mandate. So far only 109 licenses have been issued. Of those, almost all are doomed to operate at a loss for some time, and possibly fold, because of the cost of establishing and running stations. This expense and bureaucratic stalling have cooled the ardor of the groups that would have benefited most. Large corporate applicants, of course, have no such problems. To them, LPTV is only one more tiny block in a vast and thriving media bulwark. And they can easily afford to wait.[28]

In looking at the workings of the FCC, it becomes clear that the economic functions of the media serve the same political ends as the ideological. In determining economic rights and privileges, as in ruling on concepts like "fairness," the Commission acts to enforce a certain amount of democratic process. Its ultimate function, however, is to ensure that existing power relations and inequalities are preserved. To put it in the most simplistic way, the message of network TV is that the American Dream is working, at least within reasonable limits. It is the FCC's job to make sure that the rhetoric of the Dream is adhered to sufficiently to make that claim believable. But its primary function, which it performs directly and indirectly, is to set stringent limits and boundaries, ideologically as well as economically, on the way in which that message is expressed and enforced.

Networks, Affiliates and Sponsors

The relationship between national networks and local affiliates is also determined by the FCC. As with all other aspects of that body, the basis upon which national vs. local concerns are worked out is a hodge-podge of political and economic contradictions. Nationally, the television industry is dominated by the three major networks, all owned and controlled by multinational conglomerates. Their relations with the local affiliates they own are determined by FCC regulations and by contractual arrangements worked out to suit the economic needs of each.

On the ideal side of this working arrangement—in terms of "public interest programming," such as documentary reports—if, say, the networks can design a suitable non-controversial documentary, the affiliates provide a built-in market. For affiliates are required to present a minimum amount of public affairs programming. And economically, to put it bluntly, "the cost of producing documentaries is lower than...entertainment."[29] While affiliates have other options, however, for financial reasons most choose to run the network programs offered rather than produce their own. They may reject as much network product as they dare without risking such blatant disregard of FCC public service requirements that they might—and again, this has yet to happen—lose their licenses.

In 1970, in response to arguments about the loss of "local auton- omy," the FCC passed the Prime Time Access Rule, freeing the 7:30-8:00 P.M. time slot for local programming.[30] But it has not been local public service material with which this slot has generally been filled. It has again been programming which local affiliates found more profitable than what the networks offered. In other words, affiliates had to sell this time to local sponsors by running either non-network syndicated or locally originated programming rather than network shows. In fact, the vast majority of local affiliates run syndicated programs in this slot. Whatever expansion of locally originated pro- grams has occurred has been in the interest of financial gain, not public service. The best way to gain audiences for national network news, for example, is to have a popular local news "lead-in." Local news, it turns out, is not only the most popular form of nonfiction television (with the exception of certain made-for-TV movies), it has become the most popular form of local programming.

The complicated history and development of nonfiction pro- gramming—both local and national—can best be viewed as a process determined in great part by the financial concerns of national net- works, local affiliates and commercial sponsors. To understand this harmony we need to look briefly at the way the industry works as a financial enterprise. Virtually every analyst of the television industry has pointed out the primacy of financial over artistic values, and the ultimate concern with selling audiences to sponsors, rather than pro- grams to viewers. "Network TV," said Edward Epstein in 1973, "is in the business of attracting and holding large audiences."[31] TV historian Les Brown said the same thing in his influential *TV: The Business Behind the Box.* "Nielsen ratings are not about TV shows but the people who watch them and it is they who are the real products of the wonderful electronic picture machine."[32] And most recently Todd Gitlin, in *Inside Prime Time*, wrote that "the networks as a whole aim to create not purposeful or coherent or true or beautiful shows, but audiences."[33]

If the networks' mad scramble for audiences is orchestrated through the ratings system—an inexact but hallowed process whereby more or less representative audience samples are presumed to tell how great or small a "share" of the total viewing public watched each network at a given time—the recent addition of demographic studies, whereby the mass audience for a given show is broken down by age, income, lifestyle, etc., has refined the process. But whether sponsors are looking for total audience size, or a more select, upscale group likely to buy a specific expensive product, the process is the same. Ratings determine the price networks may charge for a spot on a given show.

In the early days, sponsors actually produced and sold shows to the networks themselves. In those days, they could and did directly monitor and control program content. Today the system is more rationalized. Sponsors either buy "spots" in specific shows scheduled for specific viewing times, or a series of scattered spots to run periodically over a longer span. This sponsor "control," while less direct, is still of primary importance. In the broadest sense, corporate producers of consumer goods will not, with significant and regular exceptions, risk selling their wares during shows which contradict or seriously attack the values upon which their livelihoods depend: consumerism specifically, and advanced corporate capitalism generally.

Erik Barnouw, in his study of the role of the sponsor, chronicles the rise and fall of the "Golden Age" of television drama, when serious, often downbeat dramas of common—nonwealthy, nonglamorous—people were regularly aired. Working class settings were another source of exasperation

> to sponsors. The enormous success of Paddy Chayevsky's "Marty," about the love problems of a butcher in the Bronx, inspired a flood of plays about..."the marvelous world of the ordinary." Sponsors...were meanwhile trying to "upgrade" the consumer and persuade him...to "move up to Chrysler," and "live better electrically" in a...suburban home, with help from "a friend at Chase Manhattan." The...sponsors preferred beautiful people in mouth-watering decor, to convey what it meant to climb the socio-economic ladder. The ...commercials looked out of place in Bronx settings. The drama...undermined the message.[34]

This economic and ideological control by the sponsor is felt no less deeply by those who produce the news and other nonfiction "public service" programs. The history of decision-making by networks and affiliates about running such shows, and the whens, how muches, and whats of it all, show a clear determination by financial realities, tempered by a marginal concern with FCC requirements for public affairs programming.

It is impossible to determine the actual workings of network decision-making, or the role of sponsors and government officials in actually censoring programs, or seeing that they are dropped, for political reasons. When controversial shows are in fact dropped, or when—as is more likely—they are not produced at all, there are a myriad of sound, or not so sound, artistic or economic reasons to be freely handed out by network executives. The "Lou Grant Show," a progressive program which stayed on the air long past the beginnings of the Reagan years, was dropped after its star, Ed Asner, came under public scrutiny for his political activities. Asner was president of the Screen Actors Guild and an open supporter of such controversial projects as Medical Aid to El Salvador. It is widely known that one of the sponsors of the show, Kimberly-Clark, had economic interests in that region. Still, when the show was finally dropped, there was no possible way to prove that sponsor pressure had been applied. Had this been the case, according to NBC head Grant Tinker, the word would never have gotten past the mahogany doors of the network executives. It would be, in his words "an inner sanctum matter."[35]

The reason released to network offices and the press was that ratings were slipping. But because the rating system is so imprecise, and decisions based on them are subject to all sorts of whims—"Hill Street Blues" and "All in the Family" both had poor ratings for a long time, but were kept on the air—ratings are an all-purpose excuse. What is easier to chart, although still filled with the kind of ambiguity which makes "censorship" a useless word in TV circles, is the role of sponsor influence in ongoing decision-making about what shows to carry in the first place, and what they should contain.

In a broad sense—born out by a long term analysis of isolated events which seem superficially ambiguous—the network heads tend, consciously or not, to keep the limits of most programs within the ideological and stylistic range of a world view in keeping with consumer capitalism. While sponsors have no direct input into production, as a group they are all-important and never forgotten. According to Grant Tinker, TV "is an advertiser-supported medium and to the extent that support falls out, programming will change."[36]

Since the early 1960s, when advertisers lost the right to read scripts in advance and veto them, their power has been indirect and weakened by being given such rights only after the fact. But they are still allowed to opt out of shows detrimental, in the narrow sense, to their interests. A CBS vice-president explained,

> Maybe it's a show on toxic [shock] syndrome, and Procter and Gamble [manufacturers of Rely Tampon, which is identified with the illness] says, "Hey I really don't want to be on that show tonight." The network says, "Okay we'll flip you to next week."[37]

In a more unusual and problematic set of circumstances, there are certain programs which the networks choose to run despite being so controversial they cannot get sponsor support even by making trade-offs among different companies. Some things so worry the corporate world that no sponsor will touch them. It is to the credit of the networks and their staffs that such shows may ultimately run. "Quality" is, in fact, a value creative staffs never wholly give up. It is justified in the name of "fairness" and "public interest," and it is often fought for by those in the business who care. Movies like "The Women's Room" and "The Day After," about the controversial issues of feminism and nuclear war, were both produced by ABC in spite of sponsor boycott. Sponsors actually cancelled ten of fourteen minutes of spots from "The Women's Room." But when it garnered a whopping 28.8 share, its producers were proved right in taking the chance. The sky high ratings for "The Day After" were an even bigger surprise to sponsors who wouldn't touch the show, and a more significant tribute to the network.

On the other hand, a close look at the process of producing these movies reveals that even the most daring social issue movie gets a certain amount of declawing in the name of "dramatic necessity" or "Standards and Practices." NBC for example aired a "based on fact" TV movie called "Bitter Harvest" about a Michigan farmer whose cows died because of a mispackaged chemical. In the process of filming, a variety of changes were made, many of which served to take the political bite out of the story, and to preserve a world view less challenging to the image of American big business than the events suggested. The most revealing was the deletion of a single line: "Don't think it's an isolated case. There are 35,000 other chemicals out there." To the director, this line smacked of "didacticism," and was therefore not artistically effective. In cutting it, the only hint that chemical poisoning was a general corporate practice, rather than an isolated "mistake" or "crime," was erased.

The Balance Between Local and National Interests

One of the most intriguing FCC tasks is to mediate between the demands of local and national welfare. It is here that issues of democracy come up most clearly. There is some—in my view, false—controversy among media analysts about the position of the FCC on this matter. The real language of FCC documents insists on the primacy of the "Local Service Objective."

According to economists at the Brookings Institution,

> the primacy of local service reflects a deep-seated view of how television ought to be organized... It foresaw a local television station in as many communities as possible. Stations would be owned and managed by local residents, and would devote

considerable broadcast time to information and commentary on important local issues. The stations would be instruments for community enlightenment and cohesion, much like the hometown newspaper of an earlier era.[38]

The FCC has viewed local ownership as a social ideal and the local owner as a "kind of latter day Mark Twain who understands the needs and concerns of his community in an imaginative and sensitive way."[39] In the late 1960s and early 1970s, Nicholas Johnson, the most progressive and independent commissioner ever appointed to the FCC, was a strong supporter of localism. In the FCC document known as the "Oklahoma Report," authored by Johnson and Kenneth Cox, he says

The greatest challenge before the American people today is the challenge of restoring and reinvigorating local democracy. That challenge cannot be met without a working system of local broadcast media actively serving the needs of each community for information about its affairs, serving the interests of all members of the community, and allowing all to confront the listening public with their problems and their proposals.[40]

Despite all the juggling up and back of primetime allocations between national and local programming, 82 percent of all programs broadcast by affiliates remains national in scope and origin.[41] The thrust of FCC rulings generally has been to maintain—ideologically and materially—a strong local presence, while in fact maintaining a primary national (read: corporate) favoritism. This is not really contradictory.

The relationship between localism and nationalism in media is essentially parallel to, as 1960s feminists were fond of pointing out, "the personal is political." What they meant was that our experience of personal life, while seemingly wholly private and disconnected from larger political matters, was in fact determined by the workings of the larger institutions in the public sphere. In much the same way, local and national television are generally distinct in subject matter and style, but ultimately connected and complementary. "They are in perfect harmony"[42] in presenting a total picture of American life. They are mutually dependent.

Local television, which is dominated by local newscasts, tends to deal with those issues that affect us personally: our communities, schools, personal disasters and achievements, and so on. Its style, which is so distinctive and popular that it has had major influences on national shows, is personal, informal, chatty and light. National programming, on the other hand, is more educational in the sense of explaining and highlighting major national and global happenings and issues. It is the voice of our national leadership telling us what's going on, what it means and where it is leading.

* * *

The organization and approach of this book is based on the framework developed in these first two chapters. On the one hand, I have stressed the role of visual and dramatic art in creating meaning. On the other hand, I have assumed an economic, social and political context for the creation of culture. Through the interactions of the FCC, the networks and the corporate sponsors, as well as the technical and esthetic bases of the medium, television creates and presents a view of reality which, in all its variety and contradiction, expresses the ideological hegemony upon which corporate democracy rests.

In particular, I chose to begin with local programming and then move on to various national forms because of the view expressed above: that they are two sides of a coin, two aspects of a system that is ultimately integrated and harmonious. I put local news first because I believe, contrary to most approaches, that it is the qualities of local news, and the economic, social and "social scientific" principles that created it, that most fully typify what TV has come to mean to this nation and its people.

3

Local News:
Reality as Soap Opera

Local news was not always the jazzy package we have come to think of as "Happy News," "Eyewitless News" and "Newzak." In fact, local news, until recently, wasn't much of anything. Even national news was, until the early 1960s, a mere fifteen minute segment which affiliates were reluctant to carry because it was not a moneymaker. National news has always been a difficult thing to sell. An FCC ruling requires that it be a regular programming feature, but it doesn't draw viewers well and has never warranted primetime scheduling. Even the special events and reports, which networks carry largely for prestige and to fulfill the "public interest" requirements of the FCC, lose money.[1] Apparently, most people, most of the time, don't like to be educated or informed; after a hard day's work they prefer lighter fare, escapism, something that either numbs or stimulates intense emotions.

The expansion of national news to thirty minutes came about because of technical innovations at a time when public life was particularly dramatic. The 1960s were heady days for American news-watchers. The Vietnam War, violent police reactions to massive protests, ghetto riots, public figure assassinations, "all converged to attract nightly viewers in unprecedented numbers."[2] The sophistication of the new TV technologies, especially the portable minicam which allowed live, on-the-spot coverage of breaking news, added to the appeal. So did the highly televisible space flights with their accompanying development of global satellite communications technology. Now major news stories from distant places, as well as the most mundane local fire or car accident, could be brought to audiences as they happened, in full, bold color.

Local news was the primary beneficiary of this technology because it enabled stations to turn trivial local events into sensational, colorful dramas. But there was another reason for local news' rise to prominence. By the 1960s, local news had become almost the only original programming produced by affiliates. The networks had become so powerful that they had been able to produce and sell their own shows to affiliates very successfully. They offered an arrangement the locals could not refuse. In exchange for running nationally produced programs, rather than their own, affiliates received "compensation" from the networks. Since the local affiliates could sell their own spots in the network shows, the arrangement was both profitable and efficient. Affiliates no longer had to hire large production staffs and produce elaborate programs. They merely used nationally relayed material, which was slick and popular. Thus, local happenings became the only area which required local production.[3]

Another factor in the rise of local news was its growing role in the evening's primetime schedule. Local news is, by default, the program which establishes the personality and tone, the "signature," for each local affiliate. Whatever the quality of the news team and its coverage, that is what viewers come to identify as the quality of the entire station. And whatever local news show develops the biggest audience is also the show which is most likely to carry its viewers with it through the rest of the evening's shows. Network news as well as the entire schedule of primetime programming for each network thus depend on the ratings of their affiliates' local newscasts. So do the affiliates own revenues for local commercials.

As a result of this importance, as early as the 1960s audience research specialists were hired to help in attracting audiences. Paul Klein, a brilliant analyst hired by NBC, came up with the concept of "Least Objectionable Programming." It was based on the insightful idea that audiences did not really "watch a program" so much as they "watched television." The handwriting was on the wall. The move from information to broadly appealing entertainment was a foregone conclusion.[4]

The affiliates, sensing the rising appeal of news in general, as well as its pivotal importance in primetime ratings, began to think about the news more carefully. With their eyes fixed on greater profits, commercialization of local news was inevitable. As Ron Powers has said, "the TV newscast was a victim of its own success."[5] Advertisers were quick to zero in on the growing audiences and were willing to pay higher rates for even bigger ones. How to deliver them? The answer came through the services of market research consultants. And when their services paid off more handsomely than anyone had anticipated, the future of TV news was a *fait accompli*. It was to be—in ways more profound and disturbing than anyone imagined—a commodity, a combination of various show business staples packaged and promoted like perfume or pet food.

In 1974, local use of media consultants hit the jackpot. NBC's New York affiliate was running a poor third in ratings. Compared to its

333,000 adult viewers, ABC had 697,000 and CBS a whopping 937,000.[6] NBC hired some experts who, using standard marketing techniques, found they could gauge audiences' tastes and their attitudes toward various news features and styles more effectively than the networks had dreamed possible. Seventeen months later, NBC's "News Center 4" was number one with 708,000 viewers to CBS' 696,000 and ABC's 610,000.

At that point "television news had become too important to be left to the newspeople." Marketing whiz kids and TV production experts began determining the content, look and delivery of what was supposed to be important political information and analysis. No expense was spared in what was quickly recognized as a near foolproof investment. Suddenly budgets went sky high. NBC built a $300,000 set, raised anchor Tom Snyder's salary to $500,000 a year and put a staff of 200—"the largest group anywhere putting out a news program, local or national"[7]—to work. Local news had become big business, big show business to be exact.

Marketing research is a system developed to determine "what people want," but always within the limits of what the market is prepared to offer. Viewers participating in the research had their past experience to use as a guideline—not some ideal informational universe in which relevant, significant events were offered in a meaningful context. The choices presented by researchers necessarily reflected some variation of selections from within that range. Similarly, once the results of the research are put into practice, and ratings rise accordingly, viewers are not necessarily confirming that their needs have been met. They are merely confirming that as network news goes, they prefer the new arrangement to the old.

The researchers discovered that what viewers "chose" to see on local news—and increasingly, over time, on all news— wasn't more in depth reporting on politics or social issues. Far from it. They were dying for something which was not technically news or information at all. They wanted more human interest stories, more personable anchors who would communicate a sense of intimacy and warmth, more sports, more weather, more jazzy graphics and more on-the-spot coverage of community events—no matter what they were. In a word, audiences wanted local newscasters to create for them a sense of "community."

If the results of these findings, in terms of news production, have at times seemed appalling, that is by no means because of "what people wanted," at least not in some absolute sense. The direction of local news reflects two facts about contemporary life and network TV. In the first place, it reconfirms the thesis of this book: the social role of television, in its broadest sense, is to provide that lost sense of community integrity in a fragmented world. That is a legitimate need and, to the extent that local news alone provides it, its popularity is justified. That this society needs to manufacture a synthetic version of community in this way is a reflection of its structural values, not its citizens. It is the economic drive of capitalism, after all, that subverted the homogeneous communities of the past. And it is capitalist economics, more than any human "want," that led to the particularly plastic version of "community" local news came to offer.

To provide "what people wanted," local news producers began to revamp their entire newscasts. Everyone needed a "media consultant"—it was not enough to have a general sense of what was wanted. Competition demanded specialists in creating sets, weather maps and other graphic aids. National trends began to emerge, as each station adopted a tried and true format established elsewhere. "Eyewitness News," "News Center 4," and so on, came to represent standardized sets and program formats seen all over the nation. Even some packaged, generic-style news items began to appear. Human interest and other light features are highly transportable in a society which has increasingly given up local color for the modern uniformity of mass-produced shopping malls, fast food chains and eight-screen movie complexes showing the same eight movies from Anchorage to Atlanta.

All of this is considered nonfiction. It pretends to present "reality" in the raw. But in truth it could hardly be further from reality. The superficially unique but essentially clonelike communities portrayed on local newscasts everywhere are utopian fantasies. They are Emerald Cities conjured up by the hidden Wizards of marketing research. They construct a false version of reality, a false sense of community and intimacy which, in many lives, must substitute for the real thing. That these Tinker Toy towns are taken at face value by most viewers, are embraced and smiled upon as their own, is a sadder commentary on American life than the much scapegoated media "sex and violence." For the "have schmaltz will travel" anchors that smile out at us from news desks and other cozy local spots are not journalists, strictly speaking, but rather paid performers, impersonating the friends and neighbors we all wish we had.

It is all too easy to condemn the audiences whose apparent attitudes and desires brought all this about. That, in fact, is the standard line we get from most educated people and indeed many media workers themselves. It is worth looking at the implications of this position. On the one hand, there is no question that the networks are in the business of manipulation and profiteering. They need to attract and hold audiences and they have found that the best way to do this is with this pseudonews. But if people enjoy and look forward to watching this stuff, it is not because they are stupid; it is because their immediate human needs are not being met elsewhere. What people in this country crave, and increasingly feel the absence of, is human intimacy and a sense of meaning in their lives. They are lonely, confused and increasingly terrified of what the world "out there" might have in store for them.

The lack of interest in hard news and analysis is in part attributable to this greater felt need for security and well being. But it is also a function of the educational institutions—of which the media is by now perhaps the most influential—through which we develop our ideas about the world. Functional illiteracy in America is a well known scandal. Even those who are "educated" are not taught to see events in an historic context or to question the information they receive. When you put together the commercial, show biz style of TV generally, the lack of critical skills in the population at large, and the very real—almost heartbreaking—need for emotional and social gratification, you have a world readymade for the gift of Newzak.

A Day in the Life of Hometown, USA

Local news is now quite standardized. It is made up of a series of formulaic features organized in a way which prioritizes things for us. To scan the agenda and time allotments of the items featured on a typical local newscast is to see at a glance what a typical American day is supposed to have been like in Anytown, USA. I have selected, at random, an 11 P.M. Action Newscast from the ABC affiliate in Pittsburgh, on the night of September 26, 1984. First there was a report of a fatal car crash. Then a three year old "was found beaten to death." Then came the death of an eleven month old baby, possibly a result of neglect. A man, we heard next, was sentenced to twenty-five years for arson, followed by a report about a local county's budget problems. All this took four minutes. It was followed by a "teaser" for upcoming stories and a commercial break.

At 11:06:50 the national and international news began—with a noticeable local slant. First, and supposedly most important, a local speech by Anwar Sadat's widow was cancelled because of a bomb scare. Then came a quick report on the activities of the President, Secretary of State and Vice President—all of whom had spent their important days delivering speeches. After a quick report on a study of the dangers of tobacco, and another commercial, we were ready, at 11:13, for the sports segment which ran over six minutes—as compared to the seconds-long reports on political and social matters.

After the sports came a report on the beginning of the Jewish New Year, a report on the lottery winners, and a commercial break preceded by a teaser for the weather report. The weather itself, second in time-measured importance only to sports, ran for over five minutes. It included footage of the weather reporter's visit to a local grade school that day, complete with pictures of the signs made by the kids—"The Weatherman Cares"—and the refreshment table, jello molds and all. Finally the anchor told a cute story about tourists stealing sherry glasses from an English Earl and said good night.

With a variety of other similarly earthshaking options, this is what local news does. It sends us off to bed with certain images, ideas and attitudes dancing in our heads. First there is local catastrophe, the more heartrending the better. Kids in need of organ transplants are often featured in the early minutes, along with pleas for money and/or donors. Lately, reports on missing children have also become big news. Any story in which warm feelings combine with dramatic visuals is a shoe-in. Pets stuck in trees, or kids falling into wells are always hot. They allow for sympathy and for a chance to show our local fire fighters and law enforcers on the job, being heroic, making our neighborhoods safe and happy. Whatever national news is shown is usually locally oriented and, if possible, sensational too. Big names are featured doing ceremonial things. If there is a bomb scare, all the better. The local heroes are on the job again.

This series of disasters and tragedies may not seem particularly cheering at first glance, but given the realities of modern life, it presents a picture that is in many ways reassuring. In fact, the world it presents to us is remarkably like the fictional world of daytime soap opera. There is a preponderance of trouble and disaster, to be sure; but the trouble and disaster take timebound, physical forms. The tragedy is always personal, not political, even in the major national news items. It takes the form of illness, natural catastrophe and human failure of a very personal, immediate kind. The father who beats his child is, by the very fact of his deeds having been reported, already taken into custody. And if the missing child, the child in need of an organ transplant, the victim of fire, are in very bad—even terminally bad—shape, it is not the fault of society or the political system. On the contrary, to the extent that local or national officials enter the picture, they are seen as heroes, good guys—not by dint of any political virtues, but because of their official status. The implication is that given disaster and tragedy in our community, more often than not, there are good professional father figures around inventing new surgical procedures, putting criminals and child abusers where they belong, saving family homes from fire.

The very ways in which social leaders are portrayed is reassuringly apolitical and noncontroversial. Speeches, acts of derring do and so on, have no political, social or historic context or implication. Local news, again like soap opera, makes no judgments about issues, except an occasional emotional endorsement of "Democracy" and repudiation of "Communism." It omits any historic or social background information to tie personal events—and even national speeches by individual leaders are personalized—together or make them part of a larger social world. It moves from visually sensational or heart stirring image to image quickly, with each report separated from the other by breaks. Overall, it provides a sense that the average citizen, as victim, patient, frightened worker or homeowner, is important, is cared about and cared for.[8]

Local news stations do deal with larger, more ongoing social issues in their own way. But it is not a way which leads to deeper understanding or raises any kind of question about differing policies or strategies for solving such problems. Rather, the ways of solving social problems on local news are wholly in keeping with the ways of solving private problems. From time to time, special reports are run on recurring problems. If there has been a rash of rapes, teen suicides or the like, locals will often run a series of brief reports on the topic. Incest, teen sexuality and other sexually titillating topics are particularly popular. Mostly, they are nothing but interviews with victims and local experts in the field. A director of a shelter for battered women may say a few sentences about the number of cases and the gory details of the typical situations. Footage of crying children, bandaged women and—if all else fails—the exteriors of family homes is *de rigeur*.

These special reports are usually run during the sweeps seasons to boost ratings at the time when advertising rates are set. When media consultants are brought in, the topics covered can be pretty flimsy. "Bikini fashions" was a hit in one city. A series on "Super Rats" sighted around town actually boosted a Chicago station's audience by 30,000 homes. "We thought it was a joke," said one of the reporters involved. While media experts tend to believe that the popularity of this kind of thing "brings out the worst in human nature," there is more to it than that. This, after all, is just the kind of thing people in a small, close knit community would talk about quite naturally. It is only because of the atomization and impersonality of most cities that we do not normally have these discussions, even when the situation at hand is one that affects an entire community. People often do not know their neighbors anymore, and may even be hostile or fearful of them. Local TV, by acting as neighbor substitute and telling us this kind of story, may not be giving us the news, but it is giving us something we don't get anywhere else and would naturally find interesting or at least useful for small talk.

Another feature of local news which is both disheartening and understandable is the increasing use of prepackaged items distributed by independent producers or the networks. While the independent items are generally used as fillers on slow nights, the network packages are different. They are produced and distributed so the affiliates can publicize, through popular local newscasts, the network's other programming. As competition from cable and video cassettes impinges on network entertainment audiences, it has become common for the networks to send affiliates whole series of pseudo-promotional clips to be run as news. Most typically, a "report" on a sitcom or soap opera will air, accompanied by guest appearances by stars, or even appearances by newscasters in the shows themselves.

This serves two purposes. First it helps boost the shows. But more interestingly, it adds to the personalization of the newscasters, to their transformation from journalists to show business personalities. There they are, acting out a fantasy viewers can only dream of—mingling with popular stars and appearing as actors on television. Never mind that they are already more actors than information gatherers. This ploy intensifies and glamorizes a process which is not consciously understood by most viewers, but which is perhaps the most important ingredient in the success of local news.

On another level, of course, there is a great deal of public awareness of much of what I have just described, although not in any coherent, systematic context. And the media itself, in its other forms, often satirizes and criticizes the excesses of news trivialization. Recently, one of the networks aired a very good TV movie about the dangers of sensationalizing the news, and the moral and social issues the practice raises. This is where television acts in its most healthy capacity. The tendency of TV movies to individualize and limit issues is always present, but the process of consciousness raising is nonetheless begun.

Late night TV comedy has always been the domain in which social satire flourishes best, and TV news has often been its target. As early as the 1960s, "That Was the Week That Was" began mocking TV news as a genre. HBO's current "Not Necessarily the News" updates the effort. In fact, the best TV comedy today—"Second City TV" and "David Letterman" for instance—takes its humor from its knowing "defrocking" of the hallowed traditions of its own medium. The demise of "Saturday Night Live" was probably in part attributable to its failure to focus on a salient aspect of the social world and mock it. Its best features, in its early days, were its parodies of classic TV genres. That it is now the media itself that most demands satiric comment is a reflection of the "looking glass" hypothesis: that social reality, as we experience it, comes largely through the mediated glass of network convention.

Howdy, Neighbors!

If satiric take-offs on TV news have focused mostly on newscasters themselves, it is because the personalities of these people, "the news teams," as they are euphemistically called, are the dominant elements of the genre and the biggest factors in the ratings wars. Most local newscasters have had no experience in print journalism. They were trained and hired to do what local news does: create a sense of "family." So important is this role that local newspeople have become marketable commodities. No longer do they hail from the cities they report on, and pretend to be a part of. They move from town to town in search of the bigger buck, the bigger market, the bigger chance to hit the TV bigtime. "They circulate through the ranks of the farm-league stations on their way to the majors with maximum fanfare."[9] You only need to check the trade paper, *Variety*, to see what has happened. Each week, space is devoted to the moves and salaries of local newscasters. Anyone with appeal will move from Omaha to Denver to Washington so fast they will have no time to learn the local landscape, slang or dialect. Newscasters even have agents to negotiate their salaries and career moves.

In order to capitalize on, and increase, the sense of family closeness and community solidarity which the news team is supposed to reflect, stations now regularly hire ad agencies to create very elaborate, almost sitcom-like ads for their crews. They are seen doing their shopping, visiting their grandmothers, tending their babies and so on. They are tracked to the bank, the local diner and the Little League in order to promote their local roots and "just folks" personalities. An anchor who has just barely unpacked will say "I love my neighborhood" to attract viewers. And during the sweeps season, when the ratings are monitored, the stations go all out to do more and more of what works best—colorful, emotion-charged stories full of sensational visuals and community spirit.

There are anchors who cannot pronounce the English language, much less names and cities of other cultures. There are anchors who cannot read a sentence and make it seem as though they understand their own words. And these people may be the most popular. Grooming, dress and the all-important ability to interact in a chummy way with the other reporters and exude cheeriness and charm are what producers look for. After all, with a script full of half-minute hard news stories stuck between mountains of shocks and tearjerkers, the only reactions really needed are horror, pity and sentimentality.

The advancement of women into anchor spots has been heralded as a victory for feminists. Certainly there is truth in this. The change in newscaster image, from the fatherly authority of Walter Cronkite to the informal sister-brother camaraderie of today's local and national teams is one of the many salutory effects of feminism on the mass media. It is also one of the most dramatic illustrations of the often kinky workings of hegemony. On the one hand, even that bastion of male privilege, "60 Minutes," has introduced a woman, Jessica Savitch, to the team. And Barbara Walters' position of prominence in the news world would have been unthinkable a decade ago. On the other hand, the image projected by these women is not exactly a model of feminist dignity. And the worst of the negative features foisted upon women newscasters is seen in local news.

It is difficult to sort out the convoluted minglings of the demands of feminism and the marketplace in discussing women on the news. For if, on the one hand, women newscasters—like women in every field— must be faster, brighter and more aggressive than their male counter- parts, they must also conform to an image of femininity which is saturated with negative stereotypes. Women anchors are invariably young, pretty and ever-smiling. Since they are meant to perform as good neighbors and family members, they mimic the most traditional female versions of those roles. They coo at babies, cluck at naughti- ness, sigh emotionally at stories of human tragedy.

The case of Christine Craft, the thirty-eight year old local anchor who brought suit against her ex-employer on grounds of sex discrimi- nation, explains it all. Craft was let go because, among other things, she did not take enough care of her appearance and failed to show "deference" to males. The attractive, personable woman won her case, although it was appealed and is still unresolved. But the contradictions in local news shows brought out in the case were enlightening. For it is not only women, but men too, who have been "feminized" by Newszak. Good journalism is in fact a matter of aggressiveness and integrity, not deference or grooming. But since ratings and human interest, not truth, are most valued in local news, show business standards over- take those of journalism. And show business is built on charm and affability. For women, this translates into an image too close to "sweet young thing" for comfort. For men, it comes across as "good old boy." In both cases, it reflects a move from the "watchdog" role of profes- sional, independent journalists to a more entertainment-oriented image of the untroubled Yuppie enjoying his or her lifestyle.

In the process of creating the "team," local news has followed another trend set by dramatic series—presenting an image of the family in which authority figures are downplayed, while youth and equality are stressed. Sitcoms have long projected this view of family life. Father has not known best in TV families for a long time now. More often, as in "Family Ties" and "All in the Family," it is the youngsters, more in tune with social reality and often more sophisti- cated and intelligent, who shine. Bumbling old Dad, with his outdated ideas about life, is the butt of many jokes on TV. (The popularity of

"The Bill Cosby Show" may reflect popular discomfort with this trend and a return to patriarchal dignity.)

As a trend, the elimination of the strong father figure, and his replacement with a group of palsy-walsy kids who get along fine without him, is at the heart of the news team concept. Expertise and authority are less and less centered in the home, after all. And a family living the good life presented on TV is in fact caught up equally in the concern with youthfulness, fun and being "with it." And so, while Dan Rather and Ted Koppel still affect a patriarchal kind of authoritativeness, the local teams, reflecting personal life and private values, share in the playful, egalitarian image of family life projected by commercials. Sometimes—often, actually—a team will burst into theatrical giggles when a line is flubbed. This collective cracking up emphasizes the childishness of what's going on, the playfulness and the element of leisure activity. Needless to say, such behavior would be unseemly in a serious analysis of the arms race. But such material is not found on local news.

In place of old fashioned journalism, local news inserts interpersonal relations, jokes and teasing. "Where did you get that jacket?" says a woman anchor to the weatherman—who has developed a reputation for slightly out of the ordinary attire. Or perhaps we hear about someone's failure to change her snow tires or stick to his diet. Just like you and me, we think, as we smile warmly to ourselves.

The actual coverage of events, and choice of stories, reflects these human, neighborly criteria for news. In fact, the media—especially local news—have become a kind of substitute for all the things a good society is supposed to provide, but which our society dramatically lacks. We live in a world in which social service agencies are underfunded, inefficient and often cruel and insensitive. The police and the courts are filled with corruption and bias in their enforcement of "justice." The sense of community has been replaced by a plastic, nationally uniform series of commercial enterprises. Do you need child care? You won't find much in the way of public assistance and what is available is expensive and corporately owned and managed. Do you worry about the dangers of drugs and violence for your kids? The streets and schools are full of both and there is little being done about it. Government agencies are often as not in on the take or responsible for the violence.

But when you turn on the local news, it's a different world entirely. There you see any number of encouraging and reassuring things. The pretty reporter who jokes with the weatherman every day is right there in front of City Hall, or the local prison, keeping us informed of the latest developments in a scary situation. The robber is just now being apprehended, she'll assure us. The city council is carefully considering bills to stop drug traffic, to tighten up regulations for child care licenses, to bring more jobs to our city. We ourselves might be frightened to go out and observe these things—especially with the media so eager to scare us to death about street violence—but we know if "our Mary" is on-the-spot, it cannot be too bad for too long.

News Teams as Public Servants

Serious city council debates on troublesome issues do not in fact bring results very often. So, besides reassuring us that things are being "considered," local newscasters have another, even more important job. As the world and its problems worsen, and the proposed plans to make things better fall by the wayside and are forgotten, the media has become the primary source of its own "good news." It is no exaggeration to say that most of what passes for good news—as opposed to reports that our officials are on the job, working on solutions to social problems—is manufactured by local news stations themselves. More and more, local news stations have been taking their responsibilities as agents of the public interest seriously. News stations and crews are responsible for any number of campaigns and programs to solve community problems.

The sign in the grade school lunchroom announcing "The Weatherman Cares" is a symbol of the main role of local TV. It presents an image of an institution—the media itself—that is wholly concerned with us and our needs. Newspeople now traditionally visit schools, lead parades, head charity drives and open malls—all in the name of public interest. In any city you visit you will find that each network affiliate has its own little do-gooder bailiwick. One may focus on collecting food for the unemployed and homeless. One may provide information for returning veterans. One may provide health information.

This trend began with the now standard "Action Line" segments in cities everywhere. People, desperate for help in solving everyday problems, took to calling their local TV stations for advice and information. From there it was a quick move to the institutionalization of a special feature in which anyone with a problem calls a certain number and talks to the person in charge of that beat. Say the garbage on your street has been sitting there for weeks, attracting rats and looking generally grotesque. Call "Action Line" and the newscaster will put in a special call on your behalf to the appropriate agency. In a flash your problem is solved. Then you will find yourself on the evening news telling your story to other sufferers of governmental neglect.

This is a technique which President Reagan has used with great success. Single out one person, solve her or his problem, and then announce to the world that the system works. Never mind that it took clout to do the job for which every citizen pays taxes. Never mind that one case means nothing in the scheme of things. The point is that help is available, caring and effective. No need to organize, protest or—perish the thought—change any institutional structures or power relations. In fact, one result of this technique is to individualize the whole concept of social problem solving. While giving us a sense of belonging to a cohesive, caring community, it also reinforces the sense that each problem is unique and personal and must be solved on a case by case basis.

When this technique took off, stations recognized a real gold mine of viewer loyalty and commercial revenues. And since the world is getting harder and harder to deal with anyway, it was inevitable that bigger problems and bigger media extravaganzas would soon arrive. Following in the tradition of the TV marathon for charity, the stations began running lengthy broadcasts devoted to one particularly serious community issue. Typical issues treated in several-hour long, or even whole day, marathons are those which first speak to local concerns and crises, and second, have great emotional appeal. The plight of Vietnam vets, for example, might be treated as a day long "workshop" in which local news teams and public officials participate.

This "group effort" image is one of the most important aspects of this kind of program. It adds to the image of the station as a caring, effective community institution. The hitch is that the TV crews can do nothing beyond publicizing, and exaggerating, the existing programs and agencies and their effectiveness in "solving problems." In fact, these problems have deep social, historic and political causes. They arise because we live in a society which does not provide needed services and benefits for those on the bottom, those who have the least opportunity and are therefore most often exploited—a perfect description of the Vietnam vets. But the day long attention to their "problems" gives the false impression that this society is functioning in a healthy, just way.

One of the most common issues to be treated in this way recently is unemployment. No fewer than sixty cities have in the last few years run lengthy primetime extravaganzas called "Job-a-thons."[10] These shows, sponsored by local stations in areas hard hit by unemployment, are paradigms—almost parodies, really—of what local news is all about. Following the charity marathon format, they pretend to be offering a vital service: a "job exchange." The entire news team is on hand to facilitate the event. Publicity begins early and is relentless, leading anyone with a problem finding work to anticipate the day with great hope. First, every possible employer in need of workers lists openings, complete with job description, requirements and pay. Then everyone seeking work is invited to come on the show and give her or his story and work qualifications. Viewers—both employers and jobseekers—can also call in to offer jobs and request interviews for those listed.

This format—part "Queen for a Day," part cattle auction—is both dishonest and exploitative. First of all, the jobs listed are almost invariably minimum wage dead ends that no one else wants. Some are downright Dickensian in their demands. A position as the sole live-in "counselor" at a halfway house for delinquent and addicted teenagers is typical. Most of the opportunities are of the custodial nature, and many are very short term. The "applicants" for these positions are often positively tragic. Most are highly qualified for much more meaningful work. They are people laid off from good jobs, with families to support, and are forced, through sheer desperation, to parade themselves before the TV audience, dressed in their best and nervously trying to make a good impression as they tell their stories. What should elicit outrage brings pity. The always smiling newscasters look dutifully sympathetic and concerned—as they do about everything else they report on. The experience is humiliating and, worse yet, largely useless. In Pittsburgh, one of the hardest hit cities economically, 4,600 people, many with advanced degrees and special skills, applied for about 1,500 jobs. Only 300 fulltime jobs were filled. Almost all were far beneath the talents of their applicants. In Milwaukee, 860 jobs were offered. Of 2,800 applicants, 460 found jobs. Most were with food chains.[11]

The sheer number of offerings and ringing phones, seen and heard on the TV screen, give the impression that there is a lot happening, that people are being helped out of seemingly hopeless situations, that a huge social problem is being solved. This impression comes almost entirely from the visual and dramatic format of the programs. The hosts seem to be sweating away, aching hearts in throats, in the interest of the poor souls they exploit as they comfort. Soup kitchens are shown feeding smiling children. Volunteer health care workers describe free health care. Never mind that in reality these institutions are few, understaffed and very limited in the services they are able to provide. It looks impressive on TV. Periodically, local politicians come on or call in to applaud the effort and pledge their support (whatever that means). President Reagan himself called in to the "Virginia Job Day" program. And why not? That is just the sort of "safety net" he loves—one which gets lots of media coverage and almost no meaningful results.

The society at large is clearly not dealing with the problem of unemployment, or health care, or illiteracy, or any other widescale social crisis affecting the poor, the disabled, the minorities of the country. Nothing vaguely related to the real causes of structural unemployment, or any other social crisis, ever comes up in these shows. There is no analysis of historic causes, no economic analysis, no attempt to look for broad solutions to endemic problems of capitalism.

Instead, out of a few bad jokes, crocodile tears and completely misleading images of activity and progress, the viewer is led to believe that no matter what might befall you in these United States, help is just around the corner.

So successful have these features become that many stations take on long term commitments to their pet social crises. The station that ran the Job-a-thon in Pittsburgh has continued to collect food for the unemployed on weekends. Each week you see your local favorites—out of their tailored suits and dressed in jeans and parkas—going out to various town centers to personally collect canned goods from viewers and load them onto trucks. Such is the job of a TV reporter. Not only do these people fail to report news, they often collude in increasingly important ways with the corporations and government agencies responsible for the policies that create these problems. This is because they tend to create a false sense that society is in fact working more effectively than is the case to solve problems. Where collective agitation to demand government action might be a more useful response to a crisis, those who might protest are led to believe the issue is being resolved, that no further action is necessary. In this sense, the media have become an indispensable part of the established power structure, ameliorating anxiety and defusing mass anger.

The Real News: Game Cancelled Because of Rain

As dramatic as these special marathons are, they are obviously not what keeps people watching local news every day. What makes up the bulk of the nightly newscasts are sports and weather—issues of no social import at all. Each of these segments runs far longer than any hard news story, no matter how earth shaking. The allocation of time for these segments is based on the findings of market analysts. It was sports and weather, in particular, that viewers were interested in having expanded. Over the years, this has been happening almost on a daily basis. Anyone returning from a trip of any length at all will notice at least minor embellishments to the weather and sports reports. Maps of various aspects of the weather proliferate endlessly. And sports reports are continuously being changed, and changed again, in efforts to make even more attractive what is already the highlight of the broadcast.

Sports and weather may be the most vacuous things on the air. They provide very little in the way of real information, and what is presented is nearly drowned in glitz. Sports news is the most repetitious and non-analytical thing on TV. There is no sense that economic or social factors come into play in the sports world. On the contrary, the typical sportscast is predictable to the point of self-parody. Athletes are interviewed about a game coming up or just played. The questions and answers are always the same. "How do you think you'll do this season, Bud?" "Well, gee, we're just gonna get out there and give it our best and all," is recognizably typical. (Actually, it is the prototype of most TV interviewing. "How do you feel about your daughter's murder?" "Well, it's hard to put into words. We're just broken up about it." Pointless questions and obvious answers are the stuff of TV "reporting.")

The appeal of these reports cannot be understood in terms of news criteria. It is the very desire to escape from "news," from the pressures of social reality and personal woes, that draws viewers to sports and weather. In that sense, the blurring of entertainment and information creates a situation in which critics, puzzling over entertainment presented as news, may be missing the point. It is because sports is so universal a form of "fun" and relaxation for Americans that it is so talked about and watched. It provides needed "play" after a busy day.

That sports seems to be news is related to the role of sports teams in community identity. If football is fun to watch, rooting for a home team is a more significant pastime. It provides one of the strongest forms of community "glue" left to us. There are few activities—none in collective daily life—that provide that sense of belonging and sharing that sports do. In workplaces, where competition and tension rule, the time spent talking about local teams is a welcome respite from the anxiety and hostility of other activities.

The weather report plays a similar role. Even those who don't like sports must discuss and concern themselves with the weather. It too binds us together as a community; it too is a common element of our collective daily life. When personal problems—money fears, sexual anxieties—plague us, we often hide them from others. With the weather, we really do share them. That is an important social fact. An interview with Phil McHugh, of the media consultant firm McHugh and Hoffman, explained some of the reasons for emphasizing weather on local news. The interview took place in 1974, at a time when weather was only, on average, about three and one-half minutes of the newscasts. In ten years it has just about doubled. According to McHugh, "People are very much interested in weather. They plan their life around it...the mass audience, the people who have to go to work for a living...all the mothers want to know how to dress their kids for school."[12]

The elaborate, sometimes downright gorgeous graphics used to show us everything we could conceivably want to know about the weather are interesting examples of the way in which television's visual sophistication has improved its ability to provide this kind of shared intimacy and personal advice. Because there are so many different maps and radarscopes available, the weatherperson can stay on screen, saying nothing much, for a very long time. Weather people are usually the homiest, wittiest (actually silliest in most cases) and most informal members of the news team. They are often loved by community members, who will choose a particular news station as much for the weatherperson as anything else. If there is no one at home to commiserate with about the eight days of rain we've just had; no one to complain to about having to cut the grass, miss the softball game; or whatever may happen, we still have good old Bill What's-His-Name to share it with. He understands just how we feel. He too forgot his umbrella, or had to shovel his walk four times in one week.

That these weather reporters are in some sense informing us of a phenomenon which has all the trappings of science produces interesting side effects. For one thing, the sexy blondes who reported weather in the 1950s have gone the way of all such blatantly sexist stereotyping on local news. Men do most weather reports, and the women who do it are all business. In that sense, weather and women have made progress toward respectability. But on another level, the pseudoscientific mystification produced by the sets and charts is excessive. It reflects another trend in media toward taking authority away from us and putting our fates in the hands of scientific experts who are knowledgeable about things beyond our comprehension. Science and pseudoscience are the delights of television, for they justify so much that is done to us and for us. The folklore and finger knowledge that Grandma used often worked after all. She didn't need TV to tell her what nature was up to. While there are positive elements to this trend, it also creates one more area of daily life over which we have lost control and forgotten how to use our common sense.

In essence, all these aspects of local news combine to create a feeling of family for those who have none, and for those who have little in common with the one they do have. In so doing they reinforce the corporate definition of family relations too. As one TV station promo promised: "It's not like watching news, it's like watching family!" And it is a family more to your liking than the one you may be stuck with at that. There is a phrase that has gained currency among TV folk lately: "Reality Programming." It is the industry term for the phenomenon signalled by the success of local news—the fact that more and more people seem to prefer nonfiction to fiction on TV. They watch local news in the same spirit that they watch soap operas—in an effort to feel some intense, ongoing human drama in which no matter how bad things may get or seem, there is always a silver lining, an upbeat ending, a hero to solve the problem or at least explain it. They get that from local news. But it is in many ways a more dangerous addiction than the soaps. Soaps after all are—for all but the borderline psychotic—clearly unreal. Local news, on the other hand, is presented and accepted as all too real. What it tells, what it leaves out, how it explains and solves problems, have a lot to do with the way people have come to understand and respond to their daily experience. And yet local news is every bit as much a creation, a fiction, a story as a soap opera. Its characters are playing roles, its stories are distorted and falsified versions of life, and its values are those of the people who make the decisions governing our lives, not our own.

4

Local-Style
National Programming:
One Big Small Town

The enormous success of Happy News, as perfected during the the 1970s, represents the consummation of "reality programming." It has been around, in one form or another, from the start of network broadcasting. As long as there has been home TV, there have been game and quiz shows, and shows like "Candid Camera" and "Divorce Court," all of which derive their appeal from the illusion that they are showing us "real people," like you and me, doing, saying and feeling things that seem typical of real life and its embarrassments, joys and sorrows.

While local news has received a certain amount of critical attention because it is news, these other genres are consistently ignored by those for whom TV is a medium to be analyzed. Shows like "Real People," "People's Court" and "Let's Make a Deal"—and their loyal audiences—represent, to most educated people, the dregs of American culture and American life itself. With the possible exception of the *National Enquirer*, there is nothing in our culture which seems quite so embarrassing as these public displays of greed, misery, emotional excess and freakishness.

But there is another perspective on all this. "Reality programming" is based on the same conventions and principles that have made local news so important in peoples' lives. In fact, its appeal is identical. The people who, in voyeuristic fascination, watch the acting out of personal life in public on these shows are the same people who sit charmed before the spectacle of local newscasters joking around, caring, sharing community trivia and commiserating with local victims. And they do it for the same reasons: they crave a sense of community, of human intimacy and sharing, that modern life has largely eliminated.

What distinguishes these game shows, and the "show and tell" shows like "Real People," from the news itself is their element of exhibitionism, especially of emotional excess. While local news is criticised for "exploiting" its subjects in moments of emotional vulnerability, these programs rely on peoples' apparent willingness to "exploit" themselves. They come before camera crews and act out their most

intimate and intense feelings—elation, despair, pettiness, exhibitionism itself.

The embarrassment felt at the sight of such displays, when examined, reveals itself to be rooted in certain class-bound assumptions
about public behavior. It is after all the more powerful and "cultivated"
among us who are most emphatically taught to repress emotions in
public, and to a great extent privately as well. The ruling classes,
especially males, are trained early in life to keep a stiff upper lip, and so
on. Words like "tacky" are themselves expressions of a kind of class
judgment. To be garish, loud, even flamboyantly sexy in our world is to
mark oneself as "lower class." And the dominance of the mental over
the emotional marks our cultural value system in matters of sex and
race as well as class. Women, Blacks, and oppressed classes in general
have historically been labelled more "emotional" than their superior
master class. That is one of the ways in which oppression has always
been justified. It is obvious then why emotion on television makes us
uncomfortable, and why people raised without these class constraints
are more likely to watch and participate.

Once we get beyond these reflex responses, we can more easily see
the role these shows play. In a world in which emotion is repressed and
privatized, there is something almost liberating about sharing in such
displays of understandable feeling. And they *are* understandable. Who
doesn't long to strike it rich in a single blow? Who doesn't crave justice
after a difficult, draining hassle with a neighbor or merchant? Who
doesn't desire, just once, to be publicly lauded and rewarded for some
special trait or ability that has no dollar value? Participants on these
shows act out these very feelings and let us share in them. These shows
follow the tradition of church revival meetings—also scorned for class-
bound reasons—in encouraging and making space for collective,
shared demonstrations of ecstasy, or at least a secular version of it.

There are various forms of this kind of thing. There are the many
shows which present "real people" doing various things that inspire
and move us. That the vast majority of such shows feature these people
competing avariciously for cash and commodities is not surprising.
That is exactly what most people in this society spend most of their
energy doing or at least fantasizing about. Winning, making money,
the thrill of the gamble when the stakes are high—it's as American as
McDonald's apple turnovers.

Along with games and quizzes, there are shows like "Star Search,"
which feature "regular folks" again competing for big stakes—this
time in show business—and shows like "Real People" and "That's
Incredible" in which, again, regular working class folks appear and are
celebrated for doing extraordinary feats. The psychodrama that makes
up "Divorce Court" and "People's Court" is a little different in focus

and appeal. These two shows are similar to game shows in an important way. There is still a sense of public ritual being presented, but this time the issue is not making money. Instead, we are actually allowed to see the workings of the state legal system as it examines the daily life problems and conflicts of real people and solves them.

Finally, there is a very important variation on these shows that turns the system upside down, making stars—the people we envy and emulate because they have made it financially and have glamorous personalities—into just folks. All the shows with words like "bloopers," "bleeps," "foul-ups" and so on in their titles fit this formula.

Games of Chance

When you consider that there are, in 1986, no fewer than thirteen game shows taking up a full four and one-half hours of network time—mostly in the morning, late afternoon and early evening—and that does not include the near constant airing of reruns of shows sold into syndication—it is impossible to deny their appeal. These shows speak to real needs, fantasies and desires shared mostly by the less privileged people in American society.

The appeal of the game show goes back to the beginnings of television. Shows like "What's My Line?" in which a panel of celebrities tried to guess a guest's odd occupation, with cash given to the guest for stumping the panel, were among the earliest TV hits. In the early 1960s, "The $64,000 Question" combined big prizes, rewards for knowledge (largely a false impression), a suspenseful atmosphere in which the viewer could identify with the contestant's nervousness, and greed. It set the stage for a barrage of such high stakes, personally involving game shows. "The $64,000 Question" was later proved to be a dishonest and rigged show in a "payola" scandal. But the form itself evolved in ways which avoided that danger.

In fact, what was discarded in the aftermath of this scandal was the pretense of being highbrow and rewarding people with unusual knowledge of obscure subjects. Game shows today don't need to "fix" the questions because they no longer focus on esoteric knowledge. On the contrary, the entire spectrum of questions asked on game shows falls into the category of trivial pursuits. The knowledge required is invariably superficial knowledge of facts about mass culture itself, or history as presented by the mass media—isolated facts and names memorized in the process of growing up American. Game shows are the TV version of a continuous national pop quiz on American culture and society—all the facts and events disconnected from their historical significance.

These programs take a variety of forms, some more flamboyant than others. But they share certain features. First, they select contestants on the basis of how personable they will be, how much emotion and excitement they will be able to communicate. Second, they choose questions and topics that fit the criteria just described. Third, they offer huge sums of money and consumer goods as the ultimate reward for "performing"—whether intellectually or emotionally—in the game. Most shows are thirty minute advertising marathons for the products offered. Usually the products are luxury leisure items that exude glamour, fun and privilege. They also reinforce the desire for more commodified leisure time activities, a big part of the contemporary consumerist message of network TV. They use sets that are excessively glamourous (or tacky, depending on your taste), but which primarily promote love of flash and up-to-date ornate decor as American values. Finally, they all present an extremely chummy and affectionate dynamic between contestants and hosts. In this way they are most like the local news shows. They give us real people interacting in an emotionally intimate and caring way with TV stars, who also appear as "just folks."

The most bizarre of these shows—and among the most popular—are the ones that eschew all semblance of "educational value" and base everything on knowledge of, and boundless lust for, current consumer goods. Shows like "Let's Make a Deal," where guests must estimate the prices of various items rather than recite historical trivia, are state of the art game shows in this sense: they integrate entertainment, sales and information into a totally consumerist display of American life as exciting and fun. In these shows, people willingly dress up in silly costumes in order to be chosen to participate. They also indulge in the most uninhibited displays of emotional excess on TV. For the love of a three-piece living room set or a cruise to Hawaii, these people will shriek, dance, cry, hug and kiss anyone on the set, and generally make what the polite world would call "spectacles of themselves."

There are two important features of these displays. The first is the dramatic communication—by our peers, rather than hired commercial actors—of the key feature of consumer ideology: the idea that consumer goods and services are in fact capable of fulfilling our deepest needs, filling us with near orgasmic excitement. Commodities are presented as symbols of a kind of "success" and "winning" that few things in daily life can approximate. The people who come on these shows, like those who buy lottery tickets and fill out the endless forms required to compete in the Publishers' Sweepstakes, are driven by frustration and financial difficulty. They want—just once—to "make it big." This desire is entirely understandable; it's promoted by every mass medium we encounter.

Here is where the limits of hegemony, of what we really can expect in this life, glare at us in all their cruelty. Those who openly reveal the sad truth of so many American lives—that indeed a refrigerator-freezer *is* a moment of ecstasy in a gray and troubled world—will be scorned or pitied only by those privileged enough to think otherwise, those who have learned to expect more and to get it. There is more than a bit of hypocrisy in the scorn. To be in a position in which a major appliance is beyond reach is a reality of life many people cannot imagine, not because they are morally superior, but because they are richer. Contempt for "consumerism" often reveals a limited experience of American life. "Things" are indeed what we are offered for our troubles, and what, for the most part, we take. They are quite literally "better than nothing." They make life easier, more pleasant, more beautiful.

Those who go before the TV cameras and uninhibitedly display the very appropriate emotions connected with the possibility of getting more and costlier "things" than they have had reason to dream was possible, are more in touch with their feelings, and more at ease with them, than most. We are, as Madonna sings, "living in a material world." Cyndi Lauper, another realistic young woman, sings, "Money changes everything." That is the sad truth behind the lure of game shows.

The idea that only one person wins (or at most a select few) is one of the most cruel ideological tricks the media play on us. They promote the idea—inherently competitive and individualistic—that if a single person overcomes difficulty, gets a lot of money for nothing, or even an organ transplant or a special medal of recognition from the President, the system is working, offering real hope of reward to everyone.

Predictably, the "questions" asked on "Let's Make a Deal" are about prices of commodities. And the negotiations for winning involve various aspects of guessing and gambling. On more conventional shows—those that feature quizzes about general topics—the content of the questions is different. But contestants must summon up endless facts out of context, most of which reflect the love of consumerism and the commodification of life in general in this country. "Sale of the Century," for example, features luxurious commodities, displayed with the help of sexy models, as prizes. But the contestants are expected to answer questions, on topics they select, to get them. Typical categories range from "The Movies" and "Literature" ("Who wrote a famous novel about the Spanish Civil War?" "Ernest Hemingway!" "You're right for twenty points, dollars or commodities!"), to such trivia as "Games Kids Play" and "Things to Hang over the Fireplace."

The worst thing about all this is not the trite and meaningless subject matter. It is the way the process itself reinforces the basic fallacy of the public school system: that learning is essentially memorizing rather than thinking, applying or relating knowledge; and that the reason for doing this is to make money, or to achieve success in some other crass way. The style and format of these shows reinforce this implicit value. There is nothing thoughtful about the quizzing and answering. It's a fast paced, cut-throat race to be first to the buzzer, or to see where your "bet" will take you on the giant roulette wheel. Glamour, color and speed are what happens to items of information in these shows. They are transformed—more dramatically than in any other form—into entertainment and power to consume.

The hosts of these shows are cloying. They are show biz hacks who gush and manhandle their "real people" guests day after day. Kissing and hugging, and a manufactured instant intimacy are their stock in trade. On "Family Feud," for example, we have two groups of family members competing for prizes. Family closeness is played for all it's worth—although the joint family project, of course, is to aggressively pursue the chance to get more material goods than the other family. The way this show presents and "promotes" family life and ordinary people is very much in keeping with the principles of local news shows. The difference is that on these shows the advertising—the selling of consumer values and ideas about success—is built in. Commercials are not required to carry the entire ideological burden, since the shows are themselves commercials in which personal joy and happiness, emotional intimacy and well being are seen to derive from consumerism.

Real People as Stars

The popularity of shows like "Real People" and "That's Incredible," tends to fluctuate according to the number of spin-offs and imitations the networks schedule. Nonetheless, the genre has become a primetime staple, and as such is a tribute to the success of the Happy News concept. These shows, more than any others, derive directly from the principles learned in the marketing research done for local news shows. Where local news shows tend to feature a lot of personal interviews with victims and spokespeople of community crises or projects, these pure entertainment shows expand that practice to longer segments. Whether it is acts of dangerous derring do, or simply unusual hobbies or projects that make ordinary people in some sense special, these shows work to spotlight people who are—by sociological standards—losers. Nonetheless, as we learn through television, they have a special trait or talent, and have managed to get in on the big time for at least a brief moment.

On the local news you may see a weepy flood victim survey her devastated house, recount the personal momentos now lost forever, and commend the support and help of the larger community in helping her and the other victims to clean up and survive the interim. On "Real People" you will see an entire segment devoted to a community pulling together to rebuild after a natural disaster. Often a single person, the prime mover and organizer, will be featured and honored.

These shows often present truly constructive and meaningful activity. But, like the "Action Line" features on local news, they glamourize and glorify individual effort and self-help in a way which implicitly lets the government and society at large off the hook. "Look what these folks do to stop drunk driving, to round up, house and counsel alcoholics, to raise money to save a small rural school," they exhort. Heartwarming, inspiring and constructive, these examples act as models for others, proof that we ordinary folks can be pretty effective and heroic, that—as you can see—a little personal and community effort can actually solve problems.

These shows also feature lots of silliness, joking around by hosts, and segments showing people being more freakish and amazing than simply "special." When we come to shows like "That's Incredible" and "Ripley's Believe It or Not," the drift into the superhuman and magical is carried to an extreme. These shows feature truly amazing—and mostly pointless—acts and bizarre facts of natural history. People who have devoted their lives to developing some bizarre or even self-destructive skill are the shows' heroes and heroines. ("That's Incredible" was faced with a series of law suits because so many would-be performers were seriously injured while trying out. Needless to say, these now disabled daredevils were not selected. That the producers were willing to allow such people on the air marks an all time low for the triumph of the material over the human in network TV.)

When the segments portray bizarre or abnormal natural phenomena, which defy common sense, the point made is a bit different. We are shown a picture of the natural world as irrational and beyond comprehension. The chaotic and freakish are presented in an aura of religious wonder. Ordinary life, ordinary people, are revealed as truly extraordinary—even mind boggling. Like the *National Enquirer*, and much of Christian evangelist TV, these shows appeal to the need for magic in common life. They seem to endorse the idea that miracles and irrational, atypical phenomena really do exist, maybe right in your own back yard. In this sense, they are extreme expressions of the nonanalytical, ahistorical and largely information-free content of local news itself. They don't ask us to think or worry about world affairs. They tell us that the world is essentially marvelous and surprising; that if we wish on a star, we too may become special, unique, worthy of "getting on TV"—the current equivalent of having some social and historic existence. Once more, it is important to see that it is the perpetrators of the hoax, not those drawn to its offers of wonder, who are flawed.

The spectacle of someone scaling a building or leaping over a string of cars on a motorcycle may not seem terribly compelling. Neither would the fact that a snake and a kitten, or whatever, had become fast friends. But these items, like those in *National Enquirer*, are of enormous fascination to many bored, lonely souls for whom life has lost any semblance of magic or excitement, and any glimmer of hope. Their obsession with the bizarre events of many shows is based on a longing for personal specialness and excitement. But it also serves to focus the attention of the most unhappy and unsuccessful members of "this great country of ours" on magic and trivia, rather than anything that could actually help them to understand their plight and do something to change their lives. You can get on TV, and so be a momentary star, in so many ridiculous ways today. These shows play up that idea, and the false democracy of its appeal, to the hilt.

From the Ridiculous to the Truly Depressing

"People's Court" and "Divorce Court" are two shows in which people appear not as winners, but losers. They are often hilarious because the producers—as in game shows—consciously choose participants and cases which contain elements of absurdity or nuttiness. It is easy to laugh at the people who are willing to parade their private sexual and financial problems for all the world to see. Horrors! Such lack of middle class posing and privacy! Yet these shows are the closest many of us come to seeing our legal institutions at work. To put a live dramatization of a small claims case on television, so that the audience can see it resolved by a wise, but humorous judge, and then hear what the opponents feel about the verdict, is on one level an appeal to pure voyeurism. But on another level, it serves to give the impression—so important to local news shows—that there is someone out there who cares and will help.

Typical cases involve the meting out of responsibility and ownership rights between a separated couple, or the monetary compensation of a consumer ripped off by a small businessman. A woman once came on to demand a refund for an unsatisfactory permanent she had gotten from a hairdresser. Someone else once wanted an ex-boyfriend to pay the huge phone bill he had run up during the time they lived together. And who watching the proceedings at home could fail to sympathize?

People come on these shows for the same reasons they enter game shows. They want the money. And they also want to appear on television, to be recognized and acknowledged, to have their problem taken seriously. There is something very sad about this need and the routes that people see as open to them in getting it met. But that is what TV is about.

"Divorce Court" is different in that the actual marriage partners do not appear. But for similar reasons they allow their cases to be dramatized. The show is popular because, again, it presents an arena for resolving commonly experienced, painful, but generally private problems. Many people have few helpful, sincere friends to talk to about these things who won't exploit the anguish of their lives. Many people have no intimate friends at all. For those living out their married lives in quiet desperation, keeping up appearances, putting up with pain and humiliation, "Divorce Court" is a vicariously cathartic show.

On a recent segment a woman, planning to marry a Black co-worker, wanted custody of her child. Her husband, an obvious racist and—it became clear—an obsessively jealous, sexually troubled man, was contesting the divorce. The judge ruled for the woman and her fiancee; the husband was beaten. How many women watching daytime TV could relate to that public humiliation of a husband who appeared, in public, to be a paragon but was in fact a tyrant? That this show also scored a point for the right of a mother to break a social taboo—in this case interracial marriage—is not necessarily typical. But it is not atypical either. The cases heard are filled with genuine contemporary sources of suffering with which many people can empathize.

Stars as Ordinary Folks

The final nonfiction form that takes its cue from local news is the Blooper-type show, the show in which behind the scenes tidbits and outtakes of stars being klutzes and jerks are collected and aired, with the help of jokey, chatty hosts. These shows, too, are silly and lowbrow in their exploitation of pratfalls and practical jokes. Sometimes stars are brought on as guests to be made the butt of practical jokes *a la* "Candid Camera."

What could possibly be the appeal of these conglomerations of useless videotape and badly done slapstick? On the one hand, everyone wants to make it, to be Hollywood-style, glamour-perfect. And on the other hand, since most of us have no chance at the brass ring, we also like to see that those who have reached this privileged pinnacle, whose personalities feature so significantly in our daily lives, are human, vulnerable and just like us. Thus, the appeal of the many celebrity athletic contests in which favorites are seen, out of costume and character, failing and making fools of themselves in the everyday world of sports or the behind the scenes world of rehearsal and production for shows that—when seen—seem so seamlessly slick.

The networks, using standard public relations thinking, have recently been working more and more ingeniously to solidify the bonds that keep people watching certain shows. One standard method of doing this, common in the print media, is to create public images of the stars themselves as real people, people we imagine we somehow know, care about and so share something of human importance with. These shows reveal private aspects of celebrities' lives, so that viewers feel they "know" them, even though half the nation knows the same (invented) things and none of us has ever seen any of the media stars in the flesh. This is also the role of publications like *People* and *US*, and the tradition dates back to the days of movie fan magazines. The difference is that TV, unlike a magazine, is more widely experienced and more emotionally vivid.

The flipside of this tendency is a show like "Star Search" in which an ordinary person aspires to, and sometimes achieves, real stardom and the image of perfection that goes with it. The host will encourage contestants—in categories like acting, singing and fashion modelling—to begin by telling their personal stories. This is similar to the "Real People" shows. But the point this time is that someone just like you and me can, on rare occasions, jump the track, move from the minor momentary celebrity of "Real People" to the major leagues, the permanent show business big time. Like the 1930's and 1940's movies—of which current films like *Flashdance* are updates—which showed working class kids being "discovered" and going on to stardom, these shows celebrate the shot-in-the-dark chance every kid dreams of. That this movie genre, and this TV variation, are again surfacing is a predictable sign of economic hard times.

Finally, there are the many shows, from the "Battle of the Stars"—in which teams of network stars compete in sports events against other network teams—to the endless award show presentations, in which we glimpse our heroes being "themselves." Like the Blooper shows, these shows allow for less than perfect behavior. Some stars are nervous and inarticulate. Some are more competitive than sportsmanlike. Some ramble on and on like idiots when receiving awards, and so on.

All these shows present down home, just folks people as celebrities, and vice versa, so that the viewer gets an even stronger sense of intimacy with and involvement in the social world projected as real on nonfiction television. Again, the often heard comment that journalism has replaced fiction as the most popular art form of our day seems to be true. The examination of local news and its nationally broadcast offshoots, or relatives, is the best way to understand why this has happened.

5

National Rituals:
History as it Happens

To move from the homey world of local news and its national offshoots to the more dignified and serious world of national nonfiction television is quite a jump. There are many similarities and overlaps between the two realms, in fact national nonfiction has increasingly incorporated the laid back, informal touches first seen locally. There are still important differences though. Local TV served to create a sense of community, intimacy and emotional depth to fill the gaps left when modern society became excessively atomized, mobile, and lacking in cultural and emotional cohesion. National TV was developed with other needs in mind.

The flip side of the casualty of emotional community wreaked by modern capitalism is a parallel kind of ideological loss. In order to keep a sense of national unity and shared assumptions on the intellectual and political front, widely accessible, uniform, public debate on social and political issues was needed. With the decline of the schools and other socializing institutions, TV provided an arena for projecting common national assumptions and goals, for building loyalty to our national policies. This is the mandate of national nonfiction television: explaining controversial issues and laying out an acceptable range of opinion and belief.

This realm is actually quite varied. "Controversial issues" include things as serious as presidential elections and global military crises, and as apparently frivolous as late night talk shows and quiz programs. Each of these forms has an important ideological function which differs from that of local programming. Collectively, they set forth our values and beliefs as a nation.

The best place to start is with "history" itself, as TV has come to define it. TV is nowhere more influential in molding political opinion than in its presentations of "real history" and national ritual in the making. Every other national form tends to comment upon, analyze or embellish the material seen on TV as raw political experience. From there, the move to shows which analyze and interpret history is a logical one. Once these have been covered, the ideological components of the lighter national forms, those thought of as pure escape and entertainment, will be easier to uncover.

You Are There: History as Experienced Through the Small Screen

"History is made in prime time," wrote Tom Shales in the *Washington Post* in July, 1985. Nothing new there, you say. We've been hearing about TV's influence on our collective political life—its power to shape and distort reality and history—for years. Like so many other aspects of popular culture, the way TV presents "historical reality" seems to most of us so obvious, so much a cliche that we don't even think about it.

Yet, there is quite a bit that still needs to be analyzed about the way TV "creates" our political and cultural lives. For one thing, real public happenings—not only presidential nominating conventions and election night returns, but also sports events, beauty pageants, space flights, and cultural award ceremonies—are among the highest rated TV shows of all. Something like half the population of this country can be counted on to watch events iike the Super Bowl, the Academy Awards and the Miss America Pageant. Often the viewing is itself collective and social. Parties organized for the express purpose of watching these rituals are a common American institution. As often as not, the socializing takes precedence over the viewing. Making fun of award shows, beauty pageants and political conventions is as much a part of our casual social lives as viewing them.

No one ever seems to "like" these shows; yet few of us would think of missing them. They are the major rituals of our culture and as such they both reflect and help mold the values we share as a nation. Whether it is political oratory, scientific or athletic prowess, female virtue and beauty or cultural excellence, it is these televised rituals of competition and reward—winning and losing—that define our collective identity. They tell us what we mean by success and failure, masculinity and femininity, political leadership and scientific progress.

The fact that 70 percent of Americans get all their information about the world from TV is obviously important.[1] But it takes on an even greater significance when we consider that before the rise of TV, most of these people were not getting any information at all. The death of four-term President Franklin Delano Roosevelt, for example, was a national event of enormous import. But because the news came to us through newspapers and radio, its impact was limited. Only those who read newspapers—beyond the headlines—knew the details. And radio reports, while more widely heard, lacked the emotional impact and visual detail that TV provides.

The death of John F. Kennedy, by contrast, was a far more widely experienced and deeply felt public event. The constant TV replays of the dramatic events—from the traumatic shooting to the funeral, where we shared the grief of the immediate family, to the shooting of Lee Harvey Oswald at the hand of Jack Ruby, to the swearing in of Lyndon Johnson—created a powerful national experience in which an entire nation sat rapt before their TV screens for several days, sharing in a national tragedy which was both personal and political, emotionally and historically significant.

This is not an entirely bad thing. In many ways it is a miraculous and wonderful thing. In a truly democratic society such universal access to, and experience of, important public events—in a way which integrates information with emotional and visual richness—would be a great advance over the more limited and socially selective coverage of the press. But, given the nature of our TV system, the power of TV to provide such universal experiences is fraught with peril. The collusion among state, media and corporate officials in selecting and presenting such events has been unfortunate in many ways. It has trivialized, distorted and limited the nature of public discourse on political issues. It has reinforced some of the most undemocratic and distasteful values of capitalist life. And it has created a kind of pseudo-world of shared values which obscures the appalling absence of truly meaningful cultural, political and spiritual values in American life.

Writing at a time when the presidency of Ronald Reagan has brought the integration of government and media to a garish and frightening extreme puts a particular slant on this subject. Reagan, a movie star whose greatest assets are glamour and charm, has brought the art of Hollywood to Washington in a more blatant and politically significant way than any previous executive. Reagan's media strategy, and its enormous success, did not emerge full blown out of the brains of his advisers. Actually there is little about it, except its smoothness, that has not been around from the beginnings of broadcasting.

What characterizes Reagan's political image and strategy is a combination of qualities reflecting the ways various institutions have cooperated to create the reality put forth on the TV screen. Politics for us today is a combination of rhetorical oratory, show business, sports and salesmanship. It is from these arenas, and their respective institutions, that we get the values and images we have come to accept as the stuff of American democracy.

That those who have created this marvel are unaware of its effects and powers, except in part and in distorted ways, is perhaps its major achievement. What John Berger has said of advertising could be said of network TV as well. "Publicity has an important social function... The fact that this function has not been planned as a purpose by those who make and use [it] in no way lessens its significance. Publicity turns consumption into a substitute for democracy."[2] In just this way, network TV turns its spectacle of variety and choice among ideas, programs and candidates into a substitute for real political debate, discussion and freedom of choice among alternative visions, values and structures.

When television hit the scene, there was an automatic and understandable move to make the most of it by those in the White House and Congress, by those trying to sell things and by those with something to say—artistically or as informatively—to the American community. Once the FCC had set the guidelines for use of the new technology, it was a ready made outlet for messages from the Capitol, Madison Avenue and Hollywood. Public interest requirements made coverage of nationally significant happenings an obvious TV function. What better way to serve the public than to allow us, for the first time, to share in historic moments?

Since such moments, whether state funerals, moments of scientific breakthrough or national political processes themselves, logically belonged on TV, were meant to be shared by all simultaneously, as they occurred, this aspect of home TV cannot be overestimated in importance. It is an aspect of national life we would suffer greatly for losing. While, superficially, the process of transmitting such occasions seems simple, it is anything but. Reflectionist theorists notwithstanding, there are a multitude of transformations in the meaning and nature of events, as they are translated—by way of federal regulation, network artistry and commercial and executive demands—into "media events." As each set of experts and actors participates, the shape of "history" emerges. It is different from a textbook version, and it is different from life as lived. Most importantly, it is different from history before TV.

From Ike to Ronnie

It is fascinating to trace the day to day decisions and workings of those powerful (mostly) white men as they set about to determine the conventions and techniques which were to characterize TV's way of presenting history. So much that had profound political implications was assumed or taken for granted. The use of makeup, only a small example, was ultimately dictated by television technology and the esthetic standards of show business producers. One could choose either to appear looking worse, or at least noticeably different from, the announcers and commercial actors, or to appear looking better than one did in reality. As the lesser of two evils, makeup became standard equipment for political leaders in public appearances. From there, the drift toward an over-emphasis on cosmetics and appearance—on youth, fitness, grooming and clothing—was automatic. Only later did it become apparent that serious political issues had mysteriously been decided upon, decisions more serious than they then appeared. The very qualifications for becoming a national leader were being rewritten. One cannot imagine Abraham Lincoln passing muster at a network rehearsal for a presidential debate.

The use of media professionals was not universally and swiftly absorbed into political life, of course. Many balked at the indignities of being dressed, painted, positioned and cued by the same people who produced dog food commercials and "Your Show of Shows." But over time, when the costs of sticking to the old ways became too high, show business, with its unrefusable offer of national audiences, won out.

The first political leader to wholeheartedly adopt TV's order was Eisenhower. Surprisingly, his methods were as slick as his image was not. Running against Adlai Stevenson, the liberal intellectual's darling, he chose tactics which his opponent would not have dreamed of adopting. While Stevenson continued to write and polish scholarly speeches, refusing to use a teleprompter and continually running overtime, Ike had already hired a staff of campaign experts from the world of advertising. Using the firm of Batten, Barton, Durstine and Osborn, he devised a media strategy to be admired. For a thirty minute TV segment, he had speeches written to be no more than twenty minutes long. The telecasts were carefully orchestrated in three stages. First came the entrance, complete with pageantry and hero's welcome. Next came the speech, with carefully arranged camera cuts to Mamie, adoring crowds, and so on. And then the hero's departure. Camera angles, visuals, short speeches, emotional phrases—these were the concerns of his advisers, not issues or ideas.[3]

His short spots, written and directed by adman Rosser Reeves, were equally professional. Slogans were quick and catchy; locations and questioning "citizens" carefully chosen; effects planned and tested. When the results came in, Ike is said to have quipped to his campaign manager, "Well, you certainly got your $75,000 worth." The rates have gone up of course, but the methods remain pretty much the same.

The real TV event of the 1952 campaign was the Nixon "Checkers" speech. The vice presidential candidate had come under fire for financial hanky panky and had chosen to go on national TV to respond. The event drew nine million viewers and seven million radio listeners. The speech was set up more carefully than most people ever knew. First, the admen from B,B,D&O contacted AutoLite, sponsor of the popular "Suspense" series scheduled opposite the speech, who amicably cancelled their broadcast. Then they solicited the help of a whole crew of professionals from NBC to stage the Nixon broadcast, using what they called "preventive television" to ensure the professionalism and effectiveness of the show before Nixon ever arrived. Nixon himself thought up the idea of the "Checkers" speech, using melodrama to take attention away from questions about his campaign fund. The age of TV-produced history had arrived.

The ease with which all this was accomplished came more from naivete than conspiracy. The medium was new and the rules governing media/presidential relations were as yet unwritten. There were no precedents. To TV executives, the plum of broadcasting such momentous events was irresistible. The more seriously TV was taken and used by the powerful, the better. As an art form, TV was low man on the totem pole, and indeed still is. That is the fate of every new popular medium. But when it took on the dignified and nationally momentous role of "producing" history, its status changed.

As for the sponsor's easy ceding of airtime, the same reasoning applied. There was no reason not to, really. Surely cancelling a single episode—for which they would be given public credit for acting in the "public interest"—was preferable to being in the awkward position of refusing a presidential request.

Today, after decades of such arrangements, things are a bit different. The arm of the media that acts as effective watchdog is leary of open collusion. President Reagan has requested airtime and been denied it several times because his request was deemed partisan. It is nevertheless still standard for sponsors and networks to yield to the interests of state in matters of national urgency. Presidential press conferences, debates and live coverage of crises are almost always given airtime at the expense of regular programming. No network or corporation would dare balk at this exercise of television's most important function, although viewers often complain about missing their favorite series.

From the examples of Eisenhower, Nixon and Reagan, it might seem that TV has favored Republicans over Democrats. This is untrue. While there may be ideological and practical reasons for Republicans to have had more smooth dealings with advertising and network executives, the media itself favors the two-party system and works to preserve the image of competition inherent in it. The TV system is structured to transcend party loyalty, to work with corporate heads and government agency officials of whichever party is in power. If it inadvertently favors anyone, it is the candidate who makes the best media.

John F. Kennedy managed to challenge and destroy Nixon's carefully groomed image in 1960. Kennedy was not only better at the game, he had a better sense of what the coming age was going to be like. He chose young filmmakers, like the documentarist Don Pennebaker, the master of *cinema verite* who made the Bob Dylan film *Don't Look Back*, to produce his campaign publicity. He carefully cultivated the role of hip, young liberal leader whose family loyalties and cultural and moral standards were extremely appealing to the new generation of young idealists. As we now know, the truth about JFK, politically and personally, was in no way reflected in his image. His imperialist aggressiveness toward Cuba and the Soviets, evidenced in the Bay of Pigs and the Missile Crisis, revealed a hardline cold warrior. And his sexual escapades, only later made public, were not the stuff of *Good Housekeeping* fiction, to say the least.

The media innovations of the Kennedy years went far beyond manipulation of personal image. The stage set by the 1960 presidential debates had deeper ramifications for our collective political life. Nixon, no media slouch himself, was outclassed by Kennedy. Kennedy's charisma, his tan, the careful coaching about responses for reaction shots, and so on, are well known. So are the details of Nixon's abysmal showing. He was ill, refused makeup, and so on. (The career of Richard Nixon actually presents a fascinating document of one man's ups, downs and coming to terms with television.)

There were two other factors at work though. For one thing, there were no real issues involved in the campaign. Since no one cared too much about content, media appeal had a chance to rise to the highest prominence. But there was another factor. In 1960, the FCC had set a precedent by suspending Section 315 of the Communication Act which required that if a station gave free time to one legally qualified candidate, all candidates must get free time.[4] Such suspension meant only those candidates considered "important" or "real" needed to be included in televised campaign events such as conventions and debates. This allowed the major parties and networks to work together to plan political broadcasts in which only they could participate. The two major parties were now immune from any challenge to the dominant ideologies both shared. Today such action is evaded by giving sponsorship to a private organization, the League of Women Voters. Freed of the need to answer questions that challenged mainstream hegemony, party spokespeople focused their energies on beating one another. The ball game was on. Scoring points took precedence over developing ideas. Personal skill and style were the topics of newscasters' comments, not political differences.

This is the way in which debates work to this day. There is little real debate in presidential campaigns. There are polite questions and answers which may or may not be to the point. Candidates do not face each other and challenge positions. The media, as it is meant to, mediates, making sure that things run smoothly, that no candidate is embarrassed or shown up too badly. These, after all, are the two people deemed most worthy to lead the nation. And the media, more than most observers, has a stake in maintaining the illusion, even—especially—when its illusoriness is most transparent.

History as Spectacle and Special Event

There is much more to national life than presidential candidate debates, of course. The rituals of power, as presented on television, owe much to the general idea of the TV "spectacle." Pat Weaver, who in 1949 left the presidency of Young and Rubicam Advertising to become head of NBC, introduced the concept of the "spectacle" to TV audiences. Among his innovations were the shifting of programming control from sponsors to networks, and the idea of breaking the tedium of regular series by promoting a variety of major special events to add spice to a season and draw new viewers. It worked. Since the spectacle could be fiction, variety, sports or historic event, the rules for staging all these things were much the same. As we shall see, the road from Pat Weaver to the David Wolper of "Liberty Weekend" runs straight and smooth.

The first political extravaganza to fill this bill was the Eisenhower Inaugural of 1956. By then the Republicans were adept at using the medium. They understood that it was entertainment value more than political substance that made for successful spectacles. The Inaugural they planned was as much show business as pomp and circumstance. Just as business and government began to overlap under Eisenhower, so did government and entertainment, although as Erik Barnouw reminds us, "Accepted doctrine had it otherwise."[5] The media had no interest in being recognized for its artfulness.

From Cowboys to Astronauts:
The New American Heroism

The TV spectacle that most captures the spirit of what TV has come to mean to this nation is the space flight. Astronauts, spaceships, communications satellites, rockets around the moon—these are the images that represent our national sense of heroism, adventure, progress and global political power to the generations growing up in the age of television. In fact, space travel, taken at face value, has always been a media event in essence. It has little scientific value, and if it weren't for its power to unify the nation—through the universal home TV set—around a patriotic and romantic spectacle, it is unlikely that manned space flights would be undertaken.

The real purpose of space exploration has always been military, but the practical military aspects of the work are hidden, "classified." What we see of this military activity is a mere symbol, a poetic metaphor. In fact, the race between the United States and the Soviet Union for mastery of space is as much a product of popular culture as the *Star Wars* movies. (The lackluster reception of the movie about the astronauts, *The Right Stuff*, may be due to the fact that it had already been done so much better by George Lucas.) It is a glamorized fantasy in which certain Cold War values—"beating the Russians," being tough, adventurous, competitive, daring, macho—are put forth in a mythic form which sugar coats the realities of imperialism. It is fitting that John F. Kennedy was the author of this myth because he was so adept at using the media to cover over political truth.

In 1962, Kennedy's promise, made months earlier, to have "a man on the moon" was kept. John Glenn (whose political TV career continues) became the first man to orbit in space. The TV cameras were there at lift off and landing as a nation watched with rapt attention and pride. A few months later, the first Telstar Communications satellite was launched from Cape Canaveral. Telstar I made possible the transmission of American television programs all over the globe and prompted the networks to expand nightly news from fifteen to thirty minutes. It "was comparable to the laying of the first [transatlantic] cable"[6] in import. The space program, and Telstar, were NASA projects with clear military implications. But the American public was told that AT&T, not taxpayers, had paid for the satellite.[7] To this day the powerful links among the military, the White House, the corporate world and the media have continued to be obscure.

The space program itself has been put forth as an image so powerful and appealing that the realities upon which it is built are rarely mentioned. But the development of space technology and communications satellites have profound political implications. They make possible new extensions of American imperialism, both cultural and military. The invention of a new American hero, the astronaut, is the cultural expression of these changes. Heroism is now connected not with physical strength but with technological prowess. It is less individualistic and more collective—although hardly in a healthy way. It is still essentially male, militaristic and conquest-oriented.

The most recent and dramatic instance of TV's handling of the space program was the explosion of the Challenger space shuttle. President Reagan began his announcement that he would cancel his State of the Union address to allow for collective mourning, saying, "By now we have all seen the pictures..." We certainly had. Of the many significant aspects of the media coverage, the most telling was its self-consciousness. The excessive concern over a media issue, the exploitation of family suffering, took precedence over any political issue. Questioning of the NASA decision process came much later. For days we read and heard only media self-congratulation for "tasteful coverage." This seemed to become the major political issue. It was as though we had collectively admitted that media presentation had come to outweigh all other considerations—military, political or humanist— in evaluating the historic import of events.

From its conception, the shuttle flight was designed to use a television spectacle to obscure a serious social problem. The very idea of sending a teacher and mother—Christa McAuliffe—into space, thus amending the all-male rule, was a typical Reaganesque subterfuge. Teachers were then demanding much deserved pay increases. Reagan responded by singling out one media-ripe teacher and shooting her into space as a national heroine. Meanwhile, teachers everywhere moonlighted as cab drivers.

So great was the aura of this event that no criticism of any kind was uttered for weeks. To suggest that these victims were not "tragic heroes" was almost treason. No wonder a stream of truly "sick jokes" about the dead astronauts cropped up everywhere. There was no other outlet, save this subterranean one, for expressing discomfort with the thick smog of sentiment that fell in the wake of the crash. As in soap opera, when television writes, produces and directs our national life for us, it omits the complex social and political context and melodramatically exaggerates the emotional.

We Interrupt Our Regularly Scheduled Programs

Much of the collective excitement of American life comes from the various "special events"—like the space flights—with which our "regularly scheduled programs" are regularly interrupted. In fact, the apparatus set up by Pat Weaver has come to be used again and again for on-the-spot media emergencies. Whether it is a global crisis or an assassination attempt, the camera crews and reporters can be gathered in moments to organize and create history for us on-the-spot. The political fallout from this development is often hidden. The Kennedy assassination set the precedent. All security and civil liberties concerns were ignored in the face of the national need to be involved in the procedure from beginning to end. The networks carried no commercials from Friday to Monday. The American Civil Liberties Union was appalled that police procedures had taken on the "quality of a theatrical production for the benefit of the television cameras."[8]

While many critical voices—religious, legal, political—were heard at the time, the primary feeling about the television coverage was that it was masterful. Television had created a national arena for public feeling and sharing in a time of crisis which had not existed for many decades.

> In one decade—the Eisenhower and Kennedy years—American television had reached fabulous proportions. It had developed its technology and skills to a degree that earned astonishment. It had become not only a national but an international institution, helping to consolidate—along with other forces, such as the military—the world reach of American business.[9]

The interruption of the day's broadcasting for national and global occurrences is one of the most important ways in which presidents and their administrations, as well as other officials, maintain support and solidarity in the face of disaster, failure, or gross miscarriages of justice or judgment. It is by now a truism that the nation rallies around its leaders whenever such crises occur. The invasion of Grenada in 1983, for example, was met with general disapprobation when first announced. It was a tiny country and the given reason for the act—to protect medical students—was patently flimsy. Within twenty-four hours, however, after everyone had come home from work to watch the newscasts on TV, the mood of the nation had changed. There was little doubt that the invasion was necessary to "preserve democracy," "fight Communism," save lives, etc. Even the gross manipulation of the press, the refusal on the part of Reagan to allow reporters or cameras to see what was going on, was ultimately, after much "debate," acknowledged to be a reasonable, if not universally condoned, decision.

Grenada is one of the most dramatic examples in recent years of the power of television over American minds, and the ultimate loyalty of the media to the president, no matter his party, no matter his actions. Most frightening is the quickness with which such things are forgotten, and the ways in which they become precedents, part of what we continue to call "American democracy" and "freedom of the press." What Eisenhower and Kennedy, a Republican and Democrat, began, Ronald Reagan, more profoundly than anyone since Kennedy, has consolidated and institutionalized in ominous ways. The handling of the space shuttle explosion is a prime example. From the start, the mission was a planned media event. Win or lose, as it turned out, Reagan was able to use media coverage to his advantage. Intense, shared emotion—whether pride or sorrow—was built in.

Regularly Scheduled Spectacles: The Rituals of American Life

In the years between the Eisenhower and Reagan inaugurals, a series of national rituals of competition have been institutionalized in the areas which most firmly define American values. Beauty pageants, cultural awards ceremonies and major sports events are national, even historical events which are anticipated and shared as though they were holidays. Indeed, it is easy to argue that while actual holidays—Christmas, Easter, and so on—have become wholly commercial rather than spiritual, these TV events have replaced them as celebrations of national spiritual and cultural values. Because the success of the Reagan media strategy depends so heavily on the incorporation of motifs and forms from these other rituals of national life, it will be useful to stop here and survey those ceremonies—their forms and meanings—before looking at the state of the mediated nation in the 1980s.

All these rituals share a common format. They are competitive; they allow us to vicariously experience a process whereby the values we share seem to be reinforced through a competition among those most highly endowed with those qualities. In each case there is a series of stages, well known by all, through which we move, like sleep-walkers, until the final moment when the "Champions" are crowned amid tears, hugs and general joy. And last but not least, there are commercials. The commercials which periodically interrupt the proceedings are as much a part of the spectacle as the events themselves. They reflect the material and personal values which each event is about. The prizes given winners of American competitions are always, at least implicitly, the ones offered in the ads, whether material goods and glamour, or happiness, love and friendship.

Fighting for America on Land: Athletic Rituals

The recent TV event which most flamboyantly captured the power of television to create a culturally and politically rich and moving spectacle of American values was the 1984 Olympics. Like the space flights, the Olympic games combine athletic prowess with the values of Cold War militarism in ways which cleverly obscure the realities of war—the bloodshed, pain, trauma and, in recent years, national humiliation and shame. From start to finish, the televised Olympics merged and blended the political, the emotional and the patriotic in ways which made even the commercials—especially the commercials—a major part of the meaning of the event. In reality, the event was preceded by a series of political disasters, most notably the Soviet boycott. Without the chief competitor, the event was robbed of its grandeur and the American victory diminished politically and athletically. There were also a myriad of demonstrations outside the stadium and a variety of logistical mishaps. None of this, however, was allowed to intrude upon the reality that was presented on our television screens.

The elimination of unpleasant externals was no big trick. That is a standard aspect of the framing that network TV uses on a daily basis. What *was* truly remarkable was the way television created a magic mirror which in most ways distorted and transformed the political and even actual facts. The ability of the medium to create a largely false picture through the selective placing of cameras and the decisions of commentators about what to emphasize and how to present it was masterful.

Almost every detail chosen for expansion by background facts and autobiographical materials was of a highly emotional, not to say schmaltzy, nature. Every athlete with a heartrending personal story was dragged onscreen shamelessly to be sobbed and smiled over. An athlete who once had cancer, but had since recovered and become a champ, was exploited endlessly. Any homey or sentimental tidbit was highlighted. Hurdler Tonie Campbell was a gold mine of soppiness. First he went on and on about his grandmother's cooking. Then he knelt and crossed himself before hurdling. Gold medalist Edwin Moses introduced his wife. Greg Foster announced to the nation that he attends bible class. Carl Lewis found God in the Coliseum and introduced him all around, saying "It's great to know you have God on your side." One poor guy, criticized by commentators for not showing sufficient enthusiasm after winning a round, actually apologized "to everyone" as though we were one big happy family that he had let down.

The commercials continued these same family and religious motifs. McDonald's, "the family restaurant," told us to remember that "When the U.S. wins, you win." United Airlines saluted "The best friends an athlete ever had—Mom and Dad." Budweiser showed a group of hardhats cheering a friend's daughter. The daughter? None other than the little girl who went on to TV stardom first as a regular Wheaties hawker, then as a model for her own clothing line, and then as commentator and talk show host in her own right—gymnast Mary Lou Retton. Immediately after the Bud ad—far from the only commercial to enlist the services of actual athletes as "actors" in commercials—the cameras actually shifted to the stadium in which Retton was then competing, to flash on a sign from the stands cheering Mary Lou on, held by someone from her own hometown. If viewers weren't totally confused by then about what was real and what was fictional, they just weren't paying attention.

The strongest note sounded at the Olympics was red, white and blue patriotism of the most sentimental, rightwing sort. Even filmmaker

Steven Speilberg, an expert at creating American pop culture, was impressed. It was, he said, "the most patriotic event [he] had ever seen." The *New York Times* media critic noted "more flags" than were present "on the floor of the Democratic National Convention on closing night." The cameras had not failed to pick up a single one. His closing thought was appropriate: "Media consultants will kill to attach their political candidates to images like that."[10] By week's end, no one remembered that the Russians weren't there.

Not surprisingly, the Super Bowl, which is watched by a full half of the population every year and brings in more advertising revenues for networks than any other single, regularly broadcast show, is sponsored by the same corporations that sponsor the Olympics: United Airlines, McDonald's, Bud, IBM and a few others. In 1984, the going rate was $525,000 per half minute, a cool million for the whole sixty seconds. Jerry Della Famina, an advertising king, explained it easily. "You're talking about a Super Bowl that's a happening," he told Ted Koppel's "Nightline" viewers. Other experts, many from the world of high finance and academia, came on to expound on the political significance of the event. The Super Bowl, we were told, was "an event experienced by Americans as deeply meaningful in ways that go beyond the surface. It is a ritual of American life."

What are the values manifested in this spectacle of male competition? Well, maleness and competition are quite obviously two of them. Where the Miss America pageant blatantly, if contradictorily, sells female sexuality, the Super Bowl embodies an image of masculinity that is physical but not sexual. In that sense, it is similar to the image of masculinity put forth by the astronauts. Women have no part in male activities of this kind. In the realms of power, whether symbolic or real, women and sex are dispensable. Team spirit, male bonding, the will to win, the need for mass adulation and reward for destroying an enemy and achieving dominance and glory are all part of football. So, increasingly, is violence. That football has replaced baseball as the national pastime is surely—as so many have observed—related to its glorification of violence. As a metaphor for American military values, football reveals an increasing brutality in the national soul.

Of course there are positive values connected with sports. There is a sense of community identity and shared values and goals—in an abstract sense. When one quarter of America roots together for a team, there is a shared sense of community that nothing else in American life affords. Sport—in its original sense—means play. It is a necessary element of every life, both physically and emotionally. We need not belabor the obvious point.

Since organized team sports are the primary form of physical, collective play in this society, they play an important and in many ways healthy role. The extent to which politics and economics have come to dominate them, however, is dangerous and sad. Even on the level of individual participation, the pressures of competition and the lure of big money transform play into very difficult, stressful work. When nationalism takes over the realm of sports and uses it to further military values, more is lost. The sense of spontaneity, sensuality and camaraderie which play provides naturally for young children is wholly lost in the spectacle of televised sports today. The use of numbers and statistics to measure every movement and its value is at cross purposes with the desire for physical pleasure and social relaxation.

As in every other form of mass culture, what is essential and positive in the realm of spectator sports is still present. The excitement we feel in a close, well played game, the wonder and admiration at the sight of exceptional physical skill and grace, are quite real. The social aspect of spectator sports is also real and important. Shared rituals are indispensable to life. In the social context created by television, though, raw beauty and power is harnessed and channeled in troubling directions.

Beauty Pageants:
American Womanhood on Primetime

When we come to beauty pageants, we hit the other side of the American value structure, the "female" side. The existence of beauty pageants is proof positive that no matter how much woman's condition has changed, no matter how far she has moved professionally, athletically, politically and in lifestyle and relationship choices, sexism still affects her. Sexism is the value system which beauty pageants reinforce. The values of the Miss America pageant in particular (and by extension the Junior Miss America and Mrs. America pageants) are those of middle class, white, sexist society. Physical endowments, youth, prettiness, charm, elegance, sweetness and malleability are what these events are about. There is an attempt to promote the importance of intelligence, talent and personality. But these are well known frauds. What passes for intelligence is really the ability to perform verbal exercises in charm and malleability on cue. What passes for talent is, with few exceptions, mediocrity.

Miss America, in reality, must be able to exude sexual purity, eternal youth, wholesomeness and passivity. She must be able to mouth Americanisms and charm old and young middle Americans of both sexes. She must shock or threaten no one. She must be sexually bland and plastic. What she promises in that area is as predictable as everything else about her. Nothing kinky will be done to or by Miss America. She is the official version of what good American males are allowed to dream of. She is the embodiment of the qualities that make a proper First Lady.

There is a contradiction here. Miss America, after all, does parade around in a swimsuit, chaste and demure as it may be. She competes for glamour and gifts. Every smile she beams out at us is paid for in dollars and diamonds. She symbolically offers her sexuality to those who can give her these things throughout life. Yet she is pure, Christian and decent. The difference between "good" and "bad" female sexuality is based on class and race distinctions. "Good girls" can be relied upon to follow the rules of white, middle class respectability. They will reserve their sexuality for the one man who has legally purchased it for life. "Bad girls," on the other hand, exchange their sexual favors in a variety of ways that are less manageable and passive.

Vanessa Williams, the only Black Miss America so far, learned quickly the cost of crossing that often hard to recognize line. She was forced to relinquish her crown in 1984 because she had posed nude with another (white) woman for *Penthouse* magazine. She allowed the dark side of the material and sexual contradiction of American womanhood to surface. Swimsuits and *Good Housekeeping* covers are one thing; nudity, lesbianism and *Penthouse* are another. The distinction is blurry, and it is appropriate that it was a Black woman who got caught. Black women, poor women, lesbians, prostitutes and other rejects from the haven of white, middle class respectability know that the road to and from the Miss America title is generally paved with sexual and spiritual compromise and humiliation. But like the political realities TV hides, these sexual realities are also largely hidden. To the media— at least on primetime—femininity is embodied in the image of Nancy Reagan: passive, charming, loyal and devoid of independent activities or desires.

The Age of Celebrity

The Miss America pageant is part of show business. For all the protestations of altruistic ambition, of desire to "do good," to make a contribution to humanity, to cure sick kittens, what most pageant entrants want and have trained for is a career in show business. The relation between the pageants and the Academy Awards is the same as the relation between raw sexism and the more complex and contradictory world of show business itself. Sexism is a major part of American show business—surely there is no need to list the ways. But show business involves talent, art, women of all ages and physical types and of course men, very masculine men, as well.

Athletes are exploited by American institutions and money in the same way. On the rare occasions when issues of unionism or team ownership come up in professional sports, everyone becomes very uncomfortable. No one, least of all fans, wants to be reminded of the cash nexus propping up our favorite national fantasy. But just as sports teams tend to recruit from the ranks of the poor and minorities, from the immigrant groups not yet fit—if they will ever be—for more responsible work, so does show business. Acting, dancing, playing ball, these are all careers that demand physical rather than intellectual skills, the ability to perform rather than manage or buy or sell.

What is confusing about the exploitative aspect of show business and sports is that the rewards—far from approximating the meager salaries and oppressive working conditions that characterize the world of most exploited groups—are in fact enormous and ultraglamourous. There is perhaps no work in this society more appealing and sought after than that of movie stars, models, athletes and rock stars. Every small child dreams, at least on occasion, of walking in the shoes of these cultural heroes. In fact, every job that puts its workers into the media limelight, makes them a part of show business, is tinged with glamour, adoration and respect beyond all sense of what the actual work entails. The great majority of professional actors, models, and musicians who struggle with unemployment and low wages are rarely allowed to intrude into this picture and sully the grandeur of our dreams.

The rise to the position of heroism of the manned space flight astronauts is a perfect example of how this weird system works. As military men, the astronauts (as the movie *The Right Stuff* almost comically revealed) are almost wholly passive and idle. The need for the media to beef up their images by adding elements of physical danger and courage, competition and leadership skills, is understandable. The actual job of an astronaut is to be strapped into a capsule and shot into space like some carnival performer being shot from a cannon. It is clearly not what they do that makes them national heroes and celebrities, somehow deemed fit, through this "work experience," to run for Congress and even the Presidency. It is rather the media image painted over them that gives them this aura of heroism and specialness.

Once a person has, through deliberate "image making" or by chance, risen to national prominence as a celebrity, he or she is incredibly important to those with real power, those who do the real work of running our institutions and making our national decisions. The economic and social rewards these people receive is in keeping not with what they do but with what they are willing to be. Nothing reveals the importance and illusory quality of the media more poignantly than the existence of this strange new category of "worker" who does little and is treated, economically and socially, as though he or she kept the world spinning. But there is a sense in which these people do keep the world running—the world of television and publicity, which has come to be, for so many, more real than daily experience. If we can understand the appeal of the local news and its neighborly news teams, and the validity and importance they have for viewers, we can also understand the emotional and political significance of celebrities to people's lives. Whether they really are the way they appear to be doesn't matter. For the media itself is real, and media personalities are, in that socially significant sense, real too.

In the age of television, the role of public official has come to include many of the qualifications of show business success. Politicians are increasingly youthful, telegenic, personable, charming. That is the legacy of JFK, but its germ is with Eisenhower. It is no accident, and should not be dismissed as lightly as it usually is, that Ronald Reagan, while the oldest and probably among the least intelligent and informed of all presidents, should also be among the most popular, and certainly the most accomplished at using the media to create his own image. His skills are in the realm of show business more than traditional statesmanship. His term in office marks the highpoint of the integration of show business and public life.

Cultural Awards Shows: The Politics of Show Business

The Academy Awards, and the many other award shows like the Grammies and Emmies, are the rituals in which our media heroes are rewarded for doing their jobs well. They are deemed champions of public communication. While acting and musical talent are in many—not all—cases evident, that is not what is really at stake. Personalities and the qualities celebrities seem to reflect in their acting or singing roles are what usually are judged.

Just as in the Olympics, where the camera sought human interest touches and moments of "real life" behavior, the Academy Awards try to show us the real people (as they are supposed to be) behind the movie screen roles. We ooh and aah at dresses, hairdos, shots of wives, husbands, lovers, dates. Who is she sitting with? Who will he thank? Real political speeches, of a kind that attack hegemonic belief in any area, are met with almost overwhelming hostility. TV wants us to see the "real people" being what they seem to be on screen. Illusion upon illusion.

The Academy Awards are less about movies than movie stars. It is the individual stars who receive awards that generate the greatest emotional response. Viewers identify with a has-been who "comes back," a rock singer who becomes a "serious actress" or any of a number of other American myths about going from bottom to top, rags to riches, as it were, overnight. In this way, award shows honor—and reinforce—values deemed acceptable while ignoring those that reveal actual economic or political truths about our institutions, especially show business itself.

This holds true for the award-winning movies too. There are two kinds of films that are rarely nominated or chosen for Academy Awards. These are the really innovative, socially insightful films that look with jaundiced eye on the official social image, and the frivolous blockbusters that really bring in the box office bucks. The 1984 Oscars were typical. The movies that won were all mainstream, unimaginative, liberal social issue films. *Places in the Heart, Passage to India, A Soldier's Story*, and so on, were all very safe, very serious, very worthy. Films like *Repo Man* and *Stranger than Paradise*, two offbeat, small budget, independent films that satirized official social myths, were ignored. So were truly popular films, like *Beverly Hills Cop*, which represent what Hollywood does best: make lots of money by being silly. Hollywood rewards only those films that maintain official myths about dominant values.

Mixed in with the many elements of falsehood and hypocrisy in all these rituals is a healthy element of things unambiguously meaningful, beautiful and true. The myths, dreams and fantasies presented in American popular culture are precious to us for valid reasons. They embody, at their roots, our yearnings for heroic deeds, objects of beauty, relationships based on pure passion and selflessness—things the media alone can give us as a national community. There are wonders to be dreamed about in the romance of space, the tragedy of Rick and Ilse in *Casablanca*, the triumph of the winning touchdown, and even the image of Miss America. Whatever is authentic in our national culture we find in these realms, even if we must sometimes dig very deep to retrieve it.

When cultural fantasy becomes hopelessly entangled with political reality, however, dangers emerge. The fascist films of Leni Riefenstahl and Abel Gance stand as historic evidence. The kernel of beauty or truth in a cultural work can be separated from its contradictory elements and understood for what it is. But cultural analysis is one thing; political reality another. Lou Grant is not Ed Asner and Ronald Reagan in *King's Row* is not Ronald Reagan in the White House. It is important to distinguish fantasy from fact. We can dip into fantasies and nourish ourselves on various aspects of them only as long as we know where we are and when and how to get back. Alice's journey to the looking glass world is again a perfect analogy.

I have spent a lot of time on Hollywood and show business in particular because this aspect of our national political world, as seen on TV, is the easiest to misinterpret and underestimate. It is an informing element in every one of the national rituals discussed—sports, space, beauty and art. It is responsible for the coating of mythic grandeur which so moves us when we view these spectacles—and so clouds our vision. Show business is every bit as important to national hegemony as the salaries of stars suggest. There is no way to understand what has really happened to our public political arena without taking show business more seriously than we are encouraged to do by the media itself. There is no way to understand Ronald Reagan's success, and the precedent he has set for the future, without understanding the Hollywood connection.

Presidential Politics in the Age of Reagan

Having looked at the rituals that define American values, we can return to the national political life which revolves around the extravaganza of the presidential election every four years. Almost immediately after the inauguration in January, speculation about the next election begins. It is a kind of year round media spectacle which is constructed out of the forms and values of the various rituals we have just reviewed. The worlds of sports and show business, in particular, are used to create a set of myths and pseudo-events which represent but are not, political reality.

Once begun, the actual process of choosing and installing a president is drawn out and politically insubstantial; it is a ritual in which things that have no importance are taken seriously, even made to seem momentous. In this way, the process not only deceives; it also keeps more important issues off the news and out of public consciousness. In the primary period, TV shows us quick, visually and emotionally striking shots of candidates making dramatic or clever remarks. "Where's the beef?" for example, unexpectedly became Walter Mondale's only memorable media line in 1984. If a candidate captures a bit of attention through a veneer of "newness" in some area, as did Gary Hart that year, he will make the networks very happy by giving them a new topic and image. Most candidates are soon gone from the arena. Still, for the time being, they are talked about—on the news and in private—as though their positions in the "race" were of earth-shaking import.

Two things are very noticeable in the TV coverage of primaries: polls and stars—sports and show business. "Hart wouldn't even be in the race if not for Warren Beatty," said a *TV Guide* article in May 1984. Since election laws were changed in 1974, eliminating large financial backers and allowing only $1,000 in contributions per person, "the money must be raised in smaller chunks."[11] What better way than with celebrity fundraisers? Hart had lots of them. He was their type—youngish, attractive, apparently liberal. What difference the endorsement of Donna Mills could make may puzzle you. The answer, connected with celebrity and show business values, is that it is not what one knows, does or believes that counts, but how popular one's image is, and to what segment of voters.

The polls are among the most misleading of media gimmicks. They waste time by their circularity. A poll is taken, the results of which give newscasters "scientific" bases for announcing "who's ahead." From there the poll results themselves become self-fulfilling prophesies, since the media uses them to justify coverage of the winners. And coverage on television, no less than paid commercials, serves as propaganda for a candidate. People often vote for the most familiar name, especially if they know little about anyone else. In this sense, newscasters invent and create news.

The networks' job is to promote the electoral process, the sign of a functioning democracy in countries everywhere—at least according to our leaders. If voter turnout is high, democracy is said to be healthy. As ABC chair Leonard Goldenson explains, the networks pay close attention to the "needs" of government. When voter apathy was discussed at a symposium on voter participation cosponsored by ABC and Harvard, "all three broadcast networks took up the call to action in an unprecedented nationwide public service effort that blanketed the nation with information for viewers on the importance of voter participation." [12]

In other words, the networks see themselves not as reporting objectively on the state of things, but rather as key participants in the political process itself. They, no less than government, need to project an image of democracy at work. The way to keep people interested and involved is to translate political matters into terms that are entertaining. Since sports and celebrities are among the most entertaining media staples, elections are presented as star-studded "horse races" or "ball games."

Blacks and the Media's Democracy

We have already looked at the debate process as initiated in 1960. 1984 was particularly interesting, however, because the Democrats had a "horse race," to use the media's favorite sports vocabulary. Eight men, including astronaut John Glenn, were in the running, but the star of the proceedings was the Rev. Jesse Jackson, the first Black candidate to be a finalist in the run for a major party nomination.

While much attention is being paid to television's treatment of women and women's issues in this study, less space is devoted to the equally important issue of television's treatment of Blacks. This is because so much of television—especially daytime and commercials, but also domestic, family-oriented drama—is implicitly about and for women. Women buy most consumer goods, and women are expected to do most of the socializing and domestic work which television so often treats. White, middle class women, that is. Black women who make it into series and commercials most often are overhauled to fit white, middle class standards. Rarely are poor women of any race featured. When they are, they are either degraded because of their obvious failure to fit the feminine norms or, more often, simply remodeled to resemble their wealthier sisters. The lure of consumer society is felt by all of us, and Black and poor women to some extent share in the idealized lifestyles and values promoted by corporate America.

The appearance of Black women on TV is minimal, though, because Blacks of either sex are so rarely visible. This is particularly true of nonfiction television, since Blacks so rarely figure in the official political events that comprise much of what is featured on primetime TV. When we look at the world of sports, entertainment, and beauty, we see more Blacks than elsewhere for obvious reasons. Women, the poor, Blacks and other minorities make up the class of people most likely to turn to these fields because they are excluded from positions of power and expertise. Outside of sports, Blacks are probably most prominent on TV as newscasters. Like women, they are given these positions for two reasons. They serve as tokens, symbols of the media's good faith in our commitment to equal opportunity. And, as news becomes more entertainment than analysis, appearance more than ability is the criteria for newspeople. There is a kind of feminization of TV news which is inherently sexist, and to the extent that Blacks are swept along in the same tide, it is also racist. Bryant Gumbel, an athlete, is allowed to host a morning news show, because charm, not a veneer of authoritative knowledge or intelligence, is required. But he would not be given Dan Rather's job.

When Blacks are featured on television, in dramatic or comedy shows, they are generally forced to fit a white, middle class mold, as indeed they do as newspeople. "Miami Vice'''s Tubbs, and Bill Cosby of "The Cosby Show," are only vaguely tinged with racial characteristics. They are culturally identical to the whites with whom they co-star or compete in other series. While there are periods of social unrest when more realistic Black figures are presented positively, for the most part the media works to create the illusion that Blacks are fully accepted in American life, without calling attention to the white, middle class models they must learn to imitate in order to get the rare position offered members of their race.

It is in this context that the candidacy of Jesse Jackson must be understood. In ways which go beyond the limits of American political discourse, Jackson challenged the cultural and class biases of television. He forced the small screen to expand its boundaries in a variety of areas. And he did it by understanding the rules by which the media operates and sometimes beating it at its own game. While much attention was paid to Jackson's surprisingly successful candidacy, commentary was largely confined to matters of policy position, constituencies and such, not his interesting and politically significant media presence. Jackson made one of the most successful attempts by a leader of a social constituency identified by its powerlessness and media invisibility to deliberately exert effort to push hegemonic boundaries in the interest of those for whom he spoke.

Primary coverage, as just described, is meant to limit the scope and depth of political discussion about presidential candidates. In the place of economic and social issues, we get scores and singers. Jesse Jackson set out to change that media pattern. He had an agenda which was broad and coherent in perspective. It was focused on economic and social justice for those—whether women, the poor, gays or minorities—who are left out of the two party social pie. Where the media and the major candidates consistently worked together to obscure these issues by the use of sports terms and formats, sensational or comic ploys, and the elevation of politically trivial issues to major concerns, Jackson insisted on raising them. In particular, he was successful in expanding the limits not only of electoral debate, but of media subject matter as a whole, to include the Third World as an issue affecting Americans. Again and again he managed to make links between the suffering of Blacks and Latinos in this country and in Africa and Latin America by calling attention to the real workings of transnational corporations in this country and the Third World. This is just the sort of thing the media does not do. Since it is owned and sponsored by these corporations, it is particularly careful not to spell out very clearly, or very often, the uglier aspects of corporate behavior. It is so much safer to focus on details, drama and competition for competition's sake.

Jackson's media strategy is worth examining because it is an example from which all who share progressive concerns can learn. For one thing, Jackson understood the importance of visual images on television. In his brief term as a candidate, he managed to bring legitimating images of Third World leaders and countries onto the screen. He used his position as a candidate to do some dramatic things. He went to the Middle East and negotiated a hostage release. He visited Cuba and was seen embracing Fidel Castro.

What the media shows us of Third World life is almost exclusively of a frightening nature, mostly images of violence. This is easily justified by the dramatic nature of war situations, but it serves to create an image of the Third World as barbaric and warlike. Of socialist countries like Cuba, we see almost nothing beyond an occasional May Day parade in which military forces march through the streets of Havana. Again the threat of war and violence is the message. However, when Jackson visited these places—and forced the media to accompany him—it was in the context of civilized diplomatic relations between statesmen. Jackson himself appeared as a significant political figure, achieving real gains without military conflict. The leaders of Third World nations—Castro, Arafat—also appeared in this unusual, even unique, light for American television.

To have broadened the range of what TV shows us in so important a way is remarkable. Jackson forced us to look, if only briefly, at something different from the media cultivated image of "enemy" nations and peoples as "terrorists." He forced us to see the links between the treatment of Blacks and Latinos in this country and their counterparts abroad. It is surely in part because of his candidacy and its media effects that the media gave such extensive coverage to the situation in South Africa in the next year, thus aiding antiapartheid organizers in their efforts to raise consciousness. Here is a rare example of a political leader seizing an opportunity to push against the limits of hegemony, in the case of South African coverage, with a significant and perhaps lasting impact.

The other amazing aspect of Jackson's candidacy was cultural. Where Blacks on TV programs are forced to imitate whites, Jackson insisted upon using street language, experiences and ideas to make his points as a presidential candidate. In this way he broadened the range of acceptable television language and experience to include the disenfranchised. Where American culture generally stereotypes or lies about Blacks, Jackson brought the truth of Black culture to the screen. And he did it in a way which called attention to its vitality, humor and attractiveness, as compared to the often distasteful, phony and anemic culture of mainstream American life.

We have already looked at the media image created around the space flights and astronauts and the values they were made to reflect. The importance of this set of cultural images to American life was not lost on Jackson. In the year that *The Right Stuff*, in which John Glenn figured as a heroic character, was released, Jackson found himself debating the real Glenn. Not surprisingly, Glenn was a washout at TV debating once the rules changed. But Jackson did not attack him personally. He attacked the very media image which was being used to sell him as something he clearly was not—a hero. At one point Jackson spoke of his success in the primaries. He spoke proudly—and why not?—of having defeated Ernest Hollings who, when governor of the state in which Jackson grew up, lived in a public building whose lawn Jackson was not allowed to sit on. "We done passed him," he said proudly, and the racial idiom was important to Blacks watching. When he came to Glenn, he spoke graphically of the capsule in which the astronauts were strapped, called him "Mr. Right Stuff," and said that while he might have orbited in space, "we done shot on past him, too."

The use of street language was important, for it called attention to the cultural biases which keep poor and minority voices from being heard. Also important was the derision of the very white, very milita-ristic, and very phony image created of the astronauts, for it pointed out how silly the linkage of astronauts with leadership and heroism really was. Finally, he told Blacks in the national audience that they could beat these people at their own game, something rarely said or done by a Black man on TV. As one Black political analyst said, he was "the first candidate for the presidency to talk in a language and form alien to the image-makers, who are conditioned by bureaucratic doublespeak."[13]

As proud a moment of television history as the Jackson campaign was, it was necessarily limited and marred by the standard network practices in dealing with minority characters, idioms and viewpoints. The commentators never stopped reminding us, even when Jackson was one of three left in the race of the original eight, that he could not be considered a "real" candidate. Nor was he ever given the quantity or quality of coverage men like Gary Hart—a noncandidate if ever there was one—received. Any white party regular, even a woman, would have been, and was, treated with more respect than Jackson received. He was personally responsible for forcing himself into the limelight when he managed to be there at all. As in the case of feminism, the boundaries of hegemony were expanded because political activity in the outside world reached into the TV studios and forced it to bend its images a bit to the left.

Even when a progressive movement or individual manages to get into the network limelight and force its agenda upon the news makers, as Jackson did, the coverage will be contradictory and limited. Todd Gitlin, in his study of media coverage of the 1960's Students for a Democratic Society, documents the many standard techniques by which progressive movements—once honored by ongoing media cover-age in the first place—are redefined and undermined. He lists the "customary mixture of undercoverage, trivialization, respect and disparagement."[14]

Among the many ways in which the New Left was hurt by the media even as it seemed to be lionized, was the tendency to separate and glamourize leaders and to select the most militant, sensational footage. Much the same thing happened to feminism. Gloria Steinem became the media spokeswoman of choice, even when she did not represent a political organization. "Bra burning" was widely believed to be the major activity of feminists. Footage of antiapartheid protests indicate that even in the 1980s this policy holds. Moments of violence are sought by camera crews, rare as they actually are.

Both tactics are readily explained by news people in the same technical terms used to explain the elimination of political movements and statements from TV movies. Drama and sensation are what TV crews are after; they look good and hold viewers. As for individual leaders, TV in all its forms tends to individualize social and political matters for the sake of "dramatic effect." Viewers get to know and recognize particular people who are particularly effective on TV. Jackson cashed in on that in the primaries and debates, rituals developed by TV professionals to fit TV methods.

Despite its attendant risks, media coverage is crucial to political movements today. We do not have the luxury of opting out because we don't like the rules. We must learn to play by them as best we can, winning some and losing many. The ultimate defeat for a movement is to be ignored by the cameras and thus rendered historically nonexistent in the minds of most Americans. As in everything else about television, it is a tough game but it's the only one in town. To Jackson's credit he understood this and acted effectively upon it. He pushed his way into the major media event of American political life—the race for the presidency.

The Presidential Awards Shows

After the primaries come the conventions. From the start, back in 1952, the networks placed great importance on these high stakes national rituals. NBC spent $3.5 million on coverage, and Westinghouse made Betty Furness into a celebrity with their refrigerator commercials. However, the institutionalization of these rituals on TV has had antidemocratic effects. "There is greater effort by political leaders to keep their battles in the hotel rooms and caucuses, away from the eyes of the public."[15] There is also an increasing tendency to organize the entire event as a TV show, saving hot speeches for primetime and skipping much important business completely. What we see on the convention floor in fact is very much like what we see in Olympics coverage: human interest, patriotic hoopla, celebration.

According to the *New York Times*, the local news stations are taking over floor coverage, giving the folks back home even more of what local news thrives on—quotes from local folk out in the big city, oohing and aahing about their political sight-seeing adventures. "Only television has the immediacy and impact of the electronic images that convey a convention to millions instantly, and it was mostly on that strength that the medium first developed its news reputation."[16] The very qualities that have made local news so popular are already turning national politics into a similarly apolitical TV event. President Reagan, not surprisingly, understands and appreciates this. "Television," he told Americans during the 1984 campaign, "is becoming the American neighbor" and providing "continuity and reassurance in place of the traditional extended family."[17]

The election night return reports are where the influence of sports becomes most dramatic. "Some measure of the importance attached to the coverage is indicated by the fact that all three networks now have permanent year-round election night units at a cost of $3 million each and cover the 'off-year' election results with almost as much fanfare as the Presidential year election."[18]

Few aspects of national politics are as devoid of meaning as the scoreboard keeping that goes on for hours during an election night. Percentages, computer projections, and other numerical rigmarole are intercut with bits of background on past campaigns and personalities. The computer, introduced in 1960, is a prime example of technology affecting media content. Computers can fill primetime with the most trivial details. All the better if they make the anchors look smart and charming—by human standards. Actually, the anchors these days do not do much beyond what commentators at sports events do. They root, they groan, they get visibly excited. "What a ball game!" they try to convince us. This is really exciting.

The Reagan Touch

Perhaps the most interesting, and least commented upon, event of the 1984 presidential race was the truly amazing inaugural ball planned for President Reagan. Having gained confidence in his first term that his show biz anecdotes and wealthy cronies were not liabilities to his leadership image but great boons, Reagan chose to pull out all the stops for his second sendoff. There was little discussion of this primetime TV spectacular. It was perhaps too embarrassing to be taken seriously by journalists. It would, after all, have gone too far toward ruining the authoritative image of the office to have called attention to what was surely the most tasteless and politically offensive national political ritual of all time. The media, once again, chose not to present as a national news event the one ritual in which show business values were embarrassingly dominant.

The Inaugural was sponsored by such products as Budweiser Beer. It was planned by Frank Sinatra and was in every way identical to a TV special honoring Bob Hope's birthday. It was a "roast" of the federal government, complete with reaction shots of a deliriously amused President and First Lady. There were jokes about Dean Martin's drinking and obliviousness. Apparently ignorant of the election's outcome, "It was our guy!" Sinatra informed him.

The evening consisted of one celebrity after another singing and speaking patriotic drivel. Mac Davis crooned "Cause the Flag Still Stands for Freedom," Donna Summer sang "You Can Do It/Your Time Will Come/You're Living in America," and another Black performer,

Lou Rawls, sang "Did You Ever Know that You Are My Hero?" to the President.

The ads, again, were appropriate. A bank moralized about how "the pioneer spirit made our country grow." Patricia Neal spoke about Anacin being a fighter and the similarities between the ad and the Reagan philosophy were hard to miss. All in all it was an eerie event, not least because it was largely unnoticed by the media. It was a full integration of Hollywood culture at its flashiest into national life. The head of state of the most powerful nation on earth was being brought into office with a nightclub show. It was as though the White House had moved to Caesar's Palace.

The national presidential election process has become a spectacle in which show business and sports themes and forms determine national consciousness about the meaning of the democratic process. Nor is this the extent of the chief executive's use of media tricks. Once in office, Reagan instituted a system of relating to the media which is at least as deceptive and distasteful. Every day in the White House is a TV mini-spectacle. To be sure, much of the structure has been in place for a long time, but Reagan's media staff has found ways to use and expand it that set precedents.

In a recent study of the media's portrayal of the president, Michael Grossman and Martha Kumar conclude that "in contrast to the view that they are adversaries...the argument here is that the White House and the news media are involved in a continuing relationship rooted in permanent factors that affect both sides no matter who is president or who is doing the reporting."[19] The minicam made it possible to place a network news person at the White House all day every day. ABC White House correspondent Sam Donaldson has been known to complain that he often is forced to appear on the nightly news when in fact he has no story.[20]

Grossman and Kumar describe several institutionalized communication systems by which the president determines what is said about him. There is the deliberate leak, the creation of staged media events, the staff's deliberate creation of an image that will be popular with the public, and so on. We have already discussed the presidential press conference and the complicity and cooperation between network reporters and the administration. The authors bear this out: "The fact that the president decides which reporters to recognize helps the staff guess what the questions will be," they explain. They also comment on the use of "ceremonies" to "demonstrate presidential policy commitments" because these events "are easy to stage...and invariably receive coverage."[21]

Reagan and his crew needed only to apply a bit of professionalism to this situation to make it work even better for them. Before he left the team, David Gergen was Reagan's chief media strategist. Responsible for communications under Reagan, he had learned his trade during Nixon's Watergate years, and knew about media manipulation first-hand. Gergen's rules were simple: "plan ahead; focus on specific goals; stay on the offensive; control the flow of information; limit reporters' access to the president; talk about the issues you want to talk about; speak in one voice; and repeat the same message many times." [22]

It was Michael Deaver who invented the "line of the day" to simplify this process even more for the aging Reagan. Deaver believes, with reason, that "television elects presidents," and he is known to be a master at exploiting visuals. Deaver and Gergen both know that "the eye always predominates over the ear when there is a fundamental clash between the two." They have been heard to boast of turning "bad news into good" simply by flashing "your friend and mine, Ron Reagan, onscreen." They know that "he's an actor" after all and "he's used to being directed and produced. He stands where he is told and delivers his lines, he reads beautifully, he knows how to wait for the applause line."[23] Sam Donaldson has commented on the staff's handling of the president. "They use him like a puppet. When you want coverage, you put him out there."[24]

Again, there is something truly eerie about all of this. "There are a lot of people going to school on this administration," fears Jimmy Carter's former press secretary, Jody Powell. "Future administrations will copy the Reagan approach to news management and the American people will be poorer for it."[25] In particular, he worries that the press has surrendered its adversarial role too easily. The variance between pronouncement and reality in the invasion of Grenada, for example, is a source of anxiety for many journalists. Says Jack Nelson of the *Los Angeles Times*, "There are still people who think the place was crawling with armed Cubans. It doesn't matter how often you say that in fact there were only five hundred or six hundred Cubans, that you got the truth from Havana and lies from Washington."[26] People believe images more than words.

There is nothing new about what Reagan has done. The potential to exploit was there for anyone to figure out. The fact that it was a Hollywood movie star, who learned how to be a hero and leader from Samuel Goldwyn, is almost predictable. Had we seen it in a movie we would have called it simplistic, melodramatic, silly—adjectives that apply to Reagan himself. They are also major features of show business and sports, of beauty pageants and even space flights. Considering the grip these rituals have on the American consciousness, it was inevitable that our most popular and media proficient president should be a movie star.

6

TV Documentaries
and Special Reports:
What it Really Means

The rise and fall of the TV documentary reveals more clearly than in most genres the ways in which hegemony's limits were staked out early in the game. During the highly charged period when McCarthy brought his Red Scare to the public, two charismatic men, Edward R. Murrow and Senator Joseph McCarthy, locked horns in battle. McCarthy represented a political position far to the Right of the spectrum of opinion; a position ultimately judged to be beyond the pale of democratic thought, at least at that time. That it was network television, in its role as national arbiter of such ideological conflicts, that saw McCarthyism out attests to the power of the medium, even in the early 1950s. Murrow, the foremost television newsman of his time, took McCarthy on—in a one-on-one battle that set the individualistic tone for ideological contest on television. In the name of true liberalism, Murrow banished McCarthy from the network kingdom. While Murrow was an avatar of the best of American journalistic values, his ultimate political role, in the McCarthy case and later, revealed those values to be more politically limited than they might have seemed at the time.

The importance of Murrow's work as a documentarist may seem puzzling today, since documentary reports have become a rare and marginal nonfiction form, taking a back seat to the nightly newscasts and morning and evening magazine shows that dominate the weekly schedules. But this was not always the case. In television's early days, nightly newscasting was quite primitive because it was technically difficult for the networks to produce material. Early newscasts were almost wholly made up of newsfilm items threaded together by an anchorman. There were a few news crews and stringers in other cities, but they were inadequate. As a result, the news depended on staging its own events, press conferences and so on, for the bulk of its material. Anything happening in Africa, for example, was considered "covered" in Rome. Editing and transmission were also new and unsophisticated processes, and as a whole, TV news could not compete with radio or print journalism, especially when important stories broke quickly.[1]

As a result, there was an information gap on TV which was filled by special documentary reports which could be produced over time, using footage from various sources selected to fit the sense and structure of the report as a whole. Rather than reporting "what just happened," these shows, many weekly anthologies, were meant to give in depth coverage and analysis to a variety of topics. It was what they could, technically speaking, do well.[2]

While there were many serious nonfiction anthologies—"Project Twenty," "Omnibus," "CBS Views the News"—Murrow's "See It Now" was the most important and controversial. Murrow, always quick to sense television's potential, jumped into the documentary field at the historic moment when movie theaters were giving up their role as news distributors. Until 1951, Americans got the only visual newscasts available through the newsreel series *Time Marches On*, shown as trailers to feature films. As this series was dying, CBS launched the first Murrow series, co-produced by Fred W. Friendly, "See It Now."

Critics today still wax eloquent on the subject of this series' merits. Where most TV is commonly dismissed as a "wasteland,"[3] "See It Now" is consistently "numbered among television's hours of greatness," and "a prototype of the in depth quality television documentary." Praised for its intuitive sense of television's ability to communicate "intimacy and immediacy," and its "probing, controversial treatment of...events and conditions of our existence" in a way which commented on "the best of pictures with powerful prose," it stands today as a model of what series television is capable of achieving within the limits of hegemonic thought. Individual efforts in response to specific events and trends may at times stretch the political boundaries further, but "See It Now" consistently presented a strong, serious liberal perspective on important issues.[4]

Strange as it seems, much of the quality of the series was directly related to the technical limitations then imposed on TV production. What one critic describes as a "sense of intimacy and immediacy" resulted in large part from the tension and stress involved in getting the show on the air in "a pressure cooker atmosphere." There was no "live on tape," minicam, or computer-assisted editing in those days, of course. The ninety-six hours before broadcast were hectic. Things wouldn't have worked without the long hours willingly put in by the staff, "a band of brothers under Ed" who usually worked through the night. In what was called "three track production," the picture was printed on one track, the sound recorded on another utilizing radio techniques, and Murrow's final remarks were delivered live, and therefore subject to no editorial controls.[5]

The show, rough as it was in spots, always reflected the immediacy and tension of its production process. TV documentaries of today, produced with great technological sophistication and at the ease of producers, necessarily lack this excitement. They also lack the real personal control which Murrow had then. Technology and politics are intermingled here in a particularly clear way.

Murrow and Friendly were technically innovative. Their first show made use of the newly developed capacity for coast to coast broadcasting (using coaxial cable and microwave relay) to present simultaneous views of both the Atlantic and Pacific Oceans. But their innovations were substantive too. While they were intrigued—and rightly so—with the enormous technical wizardry available through the new medium, they never saw this as "gimmickry." Technique, in their hands, was in the service of another kind of innovation: controversy. Their commitment to this was not in the interest of drama, but principle. They planned to report "not only what was happening but what was wrong with what was happening." They believed that "television was an entirely new weapon in journalism," one which made possible the exposure of "injustice," and the possibility, by way of this exposure, "of redressing or eliminating" such injustice.[6] "Justice" and "injustice," to these staunch liberal journalists, were presumably clear, easily recognized and readily achieved or corrected within the confines of mainstream American thought.

On October 20, 1953, Murrow and Friendly aired the first of their challenges to McCarthyism, "The Case of Lt. Milo Radulovich." Radulovich was an Air Force officer who lost his commission and was removed from the service as a security risk because his father and sister allegedly read "subversive literature." At the time, the chill of Cold War sentiment had long been in the air. J. Edgar Hoover had begun, years earlier, to send memos to FCC personnel questioning the "Communist leanings" of people associated with stations applying for licenses. The House Unamerican Activities Committee (HUAC) hearings had had their effect on the entertainment industry as a whole. And a publication called *Red Channels: The Report of Communist Influence on Radio and Television* had been distributed, with effect, in 1950.

To Murrow, McCarthy's beliefs and tactics were an affront to liberal democracy, and he set out to demonstrate that. The Radulovich show, much admired even today as "a first-rate example of advocacy reporting,"[7] began with a mild introductory statement in which Radulovich was described as "no special hero." Family members, co-workers and neighbors testified to his character. A filmed interview with the accused himself followed, and the program ended with Murrow's live concluding remarks. He called for the Army "to communicate more fully than they have so far done, the procedures and regulations to be followed in attempting to protect the national security and the rights of the individual at the same time." Finally he made a personal proposal: "It seems to us, Fred Friendly and myself," he said carefully, "that this is a subject that should be argued about end-lessly." He also invited the Army to respond.[8] These remarks, and the political context they assume, fairly reflect Murrow's own political position. The redress of grievances, within existing structures, was all that was required. Nor did he attempt to establish a richer historic or social context within which to evaluate the case. In these senses, Murrow operated in the tradition TV has kept.

The response was immediate and positive. Critics and viewers were full of praise. CBS said nothing at all. "See It Now" continued. After several other shows along the same lines, Murrow, on March 9, 1954, "decided to lunge for the heart of the beast," McCarthy himself. The staff had been collecting film for the show since early 1953. The show was exemplary in its careful editing. It managed to indict the Senator by telling his story wholly "in his own words and pictures."[9]

Murrow then aired an ineffectual reply from the Senator, which sharply polarized national opinion. He did several followups based on bizarre charges made by McCarthy himself in his public response to Murrow. The Senator had hinted, for instance, that the hydrogen bomb was delayed eighteen months in production because of "traitors" working on the project. These Murrow-McCarthy shows "helped to make television an indispensable medium" and also "set the stage for the televised broadcasts of the Army-McCarthy hearings, in which McCarthy—scrutinized continually by the harsh light of the TV cameras—put the final nail in his own coffin."[10]

McCarthy was gone and Murrow, having garnered endless critical praise as well as huge ratings, emerged triumphant. But when the dust settled, network response was not what one might have expected. For one thing, Murrow, who had been so instrumental in making TV the major medium of our day, was tactfully eased out of the picture. The fear of controversy had not been quelled. On the contrary, the spirit of McCarthy was what sponsors and networks most feared. Apparently reasoning that money could be made and audiences drawn in safer ways, they preferred to avoid the chaos and disruption to business as usual caused by such political controversy. It is fair to say that a kind of preventative caution, which persists in network television today and is its characteristic method of "censorship," is the most significant legacy of Mccarthyism.

While Murrow's documentaries on McCarthy aired, CBS had been hedging its bets. There was never a question of direct censorship, which was considered too violent an attack on the accepted political rhetoric of democracy and free speech. But there were other ways to eliminate controversy. CBS began shuffling "See It Now" around on the program schedule, making it harder to find. The network refused to place ads for the series, and acted in other ways to limit its audience. The sponsor, Alcoa, while not openly censoring the prestigious show, felt increasingly uncomfortable about the possible contradiction between the content of certain broadcasts and their own advertising copy. Murrow had once been proud of his relations with his sponsor. "They make aluminum and I make films," he said. But as Alcoa branched into the consumer market, they became more cautious. They questioned a program on the Salk vaccine, for example, which in their view espoused "socialized medicine." They applied no direct editorial pressure, but in 1954, they severed relations with the show. And on June 7, 1955, "See It Now" was replaced by a newer, lighter program, "The $64,000 Question."[11]

Ironically, "The $64,000 Question" caused a greater scandal—over issues of money and truthfulness—than any political issue Murrow raised. When the payola scandal surfaced, CBS rushed to get Murrow and his documentary series back on the air. "CBS Reports," which Murrow and Friendly produced, was a regularly scheduled weekly series during the 1961-2 season, and again during the 1970-1 season. It was during that second run that Murrow's "Harvest of Shame," an expose of the conditions of migrant workers, was produced. At that time NBC and ABC also began the documentary series "White Paper" and "Close-Up" which, while never regular weekly shows, still crop up, usually when a national crisis of belief occurs.[12] Regular documentary series no longer exist.

While Murrow condemned McCarthyism in the name of democracy, he was no martyr to democratic principle. The end of Murrow's career points emphatically to the contradictions within and limits of his political perspective. Information about President Kennedy's plans to invade the Cuban Bay of Pigs, given to him by an old World World II associate, was handled far more cautiously than was the McCarthy issue. "Murrow and Fred Friendly discussed it as a possible 'CBS Reports' subject." It seemed too much to handle at the time, and shortly thereafter, Murrow was offered the directorship of the United States Information Agency (USIA). He readily accepted, thus giving up the liberal journalistic role of "people's watchdog" in favor of a more powerful position within the government itself. He was apparently so eager to have that job that he tried to suppress a BBC airing of "Harvest of Shame" during the time his appointment was being considered. He later "regretted and deplored this action" and the BBC didn't honor it.[13]

Murrow's career took an odd turn. He began in the 1950s by attacking McCarthyism and the dangers of military and legislative abuses of power, but by the 1960s was withholding evidence of just such abuses of power and affronts to democratic process. His about-face is no contradiction in the looking glass world. McCarthy was a rightwing extremist. Kennedy, on the other hand, was a liberal facing the threat of Communism in the form of a small island near Florida. These are the boundaries of television's ideological roadmap. McCarthy must not be allowed to destroy our rights, but Kennedy should be aided in destroying the one enemy television will never fail to help combat: Communism. Democratic principles governing both journalism and the presidency are set aside in the name of the "national interest." The guidelines which dictated Reagan's behavior at the time of the Grenada invasion, and the media response to it, were drawn up early in television history.

Murrow's move to a political career is particularly instructive because it is a common event. Because of their "competence," outstanding TV journalists are often given jobs in government. While their skills may merit this, it is a political tactic of great importance. The very independence of the media is blatantly destroyed when such alliances exist and are regularly sanctioned.

The state of documentary television since Murrow has been spotty. In the 1960s and early 1970s, when protest against the Vietnam War was heated and news of extreme government dishonesty was revealed through the publication of the *Pentagon Papers* and the broadcast of the Watergate Hearings, the media became more critical of the status quo and more openly liberal. In 1965, for example, ABC produced and aired a special report called "The Agony of Vietnam" which stated, "We cannot afford to see Vietnam only through American eyes," and surveyed the largely negative views of the war prevalent in other countries. In 1966, CBS produced a half hour program in which Senator J. William Fulbright, a strong foe of national policy in Vietnam, was allowed to express his criticism of the Gulf of Tonkin resolution, which had brought the U.S. officially into the war. CBS head Stanton was not pleased. "What a dirty trick that was to play on the President of the United States," he is quoted as saying. But there was no official censure.

More recently, as fears of military involvement in Central America increased, the networks produced several very fine reports on the region, pointing out the fascist, dictatorial nature of the governments we were defending in the name of "democracy." The liberal stripe of many national news reporters is apparent in these instances. The lessons of Vietnam, learned largely from the effective work of the antiwar movement, have not been forgotten by the Rathers and Brokaws.

Issues of war and peace bring out the polarities within our ruling bodies most clearly. Just as Fulbright fought involvement in Vietnam, Senator Thomas Dodd and others have been outspoken against presidential policy in Central America. The media, with its many levels of participation, reflects these differences and splits. Even here, however, TV is more cautious than the print media. Judging by his reaction to the Bay of Pigs, it is unlikely that even Murrow would have presented the *Pentagon Papers*, leaked to the *New York Times* through Daniel Ellsberg, on television.

The difference between print and video is subtle. Papers like the *New York Times* are no longer part of "mass culture." They are known and read by a select group of educated people who participate, directly and in various indirect, "opinion making" ways, in policy making. Only a few TV shows—"Nightline," David Brinkley's Sunday interviews with newsmakers, and the "MacNeil-Lehrer Report"—share that kind of small, select audience. In the chain of information, from the circles of power to the private living room, network nonfiction follows the prestige press with few exceptions. Av Westin's list of publications read by ABC news staffs each morning, quoted earlier, verifies this.

After studying these "opinion makers," the networks ultimately decide what to do on the basis of public and official response to events and views presented there. Progressive political movements, and the more progressive people within the networks themselves, form an important element in the range of opinion examined by the networks before taking positions. The antiwar and antiapartheid movements have impact for that reason. But even when the networks grant the seriousness of their efforts and allow them into the charmed circle of social happenings that matter, they are presented in very limited ways. Todd Gitlin's study of media treatment of the radical student movement of the time, *The Whole World is Watching*, gives a thorough account of how subtle the media was in preserving the dominant belief systems even as it seemed to be publicizing the movement's actions.[14]

Within this cautious framework, contradictory if real progress does at times occur. Central America and South Africa would not have been covered as liberally if not for the lessons of Vietnam. Activists cannot afford to stay out of the public eye for fear of being left out of the process of creating televised history, and national response to it. In fact, the ability of progressive newspeople to push through ideas for left-leaning reports depends upon their ability to point to supportive mass sentiment, as expressed in activism and coverage in print, as well as to the "newsworthiness" of such material in terms of the other economic, social and technical criteria used by the networks.

Documentaries Updated

Documentaries in the 1980s, except in times of national crisis, are produced under conditions and in ways which differ radically from those of Murrow and Friendly. First, the deciding factor in documentary production today is money. There are several other forms—magazines, talk shows and TV movies—which serve the public interest function better than straight documentaries because they are more popular with viewers while still handling major social issues. Reuven Frank, longtime head of CBS, has been quoted as saying that "the primetime documentary was invented so that we could stay on the air at the least possible cost when we had only a very small share of the audience."[15] This is because documentaries—many of which use file tapes and a simple studio set for a commentator and guest—are relatively cheap to produce.

Documentaries are not done more often because local affiliates don't like them. Often, affiliates refuse to carry network specials and choose to broadcast more lucrative reruns of popular shows instead. The only thing that stops local affiliates from entirely eliminating documentaries is the FCC public service requirement, lurking in the background.

The documentaries that are produced are different in content, style and tone from those made in Murrow's day. The air of caution that followed the "See It Now" McCarthy series spawned a complicated system of checks and balances which ensures that controversy will be minimized and entertainment value maximized. The interactions of those involved in planning and producing the show illustrates one aspect of this process.

Once a report is planned, the problem of sponsorship arises. The process by which a network seeks to get a particular sponsor to buy a report is complex. "About one hundred twenty subject ideas are thrown into the pot," from which the news staff chooses thirty. These are personally offered to a target company. The company then "chooses those titles among the thirty in which it is interested. Production then proceeds."[16] From this description, it is easy to see how cautious the networks must be. On rare occasions—the recent airing of the ABC movie "The Day After," about nuclear war, is one—a network's commitment to an idea, for its own reasons, forces it to run the show without sponsorship. In that particular case the network was right in its judgment. "The Day After" was a huge hit with viewers and will doubtless have many reruns with sponsors to spare.

What moves a sponsor to take on a heavy topic is primarily prestige. Large multinational corporations, whose image depends on prestige rather than commodity sales, generally sponsor special reports.[17] As we have seen, Alcoa was willing to sponsor "See It Now" only until it moved into commodity sales. Since the networks usually assume that sponsors favor "soft subjects," they think "soft" from the start, in a way that Murrow, at least early on, did not. The process as a whole has become infinitely more efficient. Each participant tries to second guess the others as a way of avoiding needless, usually expensive, delays and changes in plans. As an NBC "White Paper" producer has put it, "This does not mean that the networks won't do programs that can't be sold on subjects that are not popular. It means the network won't do many such programs."[18] Even here there are striking examples of courageous reports, such as those done recently on Central America.

Technology: Comedy or Tragedy?

What does this mean for the viewer seeking an understanding of her or his world? It means that lightness of topic, combined with a variety of ideologically tricky devices for framing and limiting that topic, will be the most predictable kind of documentary. A perfect example of the typical network report on a current, socially pressing issue was the June, 1985 ABC special, "The Future Is Now." This show attempted to explain, reassuringly, what the explosion of high tech, computer-assisted activity in every aspect of our national and personal lives would mean. Its premise was that "the computer is changing our lives," and that "We all must learn to relate to it." We have a "choice" of course, but the emphasis was on urging the frightened folks out there to dip into the high tech waters.

This message fits almost too obviously into the category of "socializing agent," which is a primary role of TV today. Far from having a "choice," the show indicated that we do not in fact have any choice at all. The computer is here and the only "choice" is whether or not to be ignorant and powerless. Already the ideological problems are clear. We are not being asked to consider and make a decision about technology. We are told after the fact—and in ways meant to be cutely seductive—that our kids are already way ahead of us and we had better catch up. According to the report, the role of parents these days is not to teach skills and values to children, but to keep up with the parenting provided by the scientific/industrial sector.

The style and specific content of the show is worth examining.

The emphasis on sports and show business razzmatazz was an especially slick example of the "ideology as candy" approach so popular with the networks. Computer technology is not really a joke, a sport or an entertainment. But in TV Land, as in Disney World, that is not at all clear.

The host of this "lighthearted look at computers," as *TV Guide* described it, was ABC's "Good Morning America" host, David Hartman. His job was not to explain things, but to experience them and learn about them along with us. Already, the mystique of scientific expertise was established. This topic was apparently beyond the understanding of our newsman/host. Hartman's role was to be taken from place to place and given games to play, gadgets to operate, minicars to drive, and so forth. Hartman was presented as a kind of primetime Captain Kangaroo. He was puzzled and amazed at each new gimmick. "Wow! Isn't this something, kids!" was the tone of his commentary. Like the members of local news teams, Hartman had been demoted from patriarch to "one of the kids."

The scenario also allowed for endless location jumping, so the background settings were in fact very much like a tour through Disneyland. From the rodeo to Paris; from an Indian reservation to a professional football game; from a space flight to a little church in rural Holland. It was pretty; it was colorful; it was a vacationer's dream, especially if economic problems made a real vacation impossible for viewers this year. It was all so light and clever. What could possibly be questionable about it?

The program was divided into four segments. The first covered the use of computers in sports related activities. By no means, of course, could an argument be made that sports related technology was either a major national concern or a major use of technology. But the fact that sports is a "national pastime" made it easy to relate to. Again, as with the Olympics and Super Bowl, sports are used in questionable ways to sell questionable national values.

The athletes featured were as atypical as the subject itself. How sports medicine handles injuries of rodeo clowns was thoroughly analyzed and explained. Problems of fitness fanatics also got time. The segment on pro football was of more obvious appeal. But the question "Why sports?" was still glaring, and never answered or even asked. Instead, the thrust of the piece was science as magic. "It's amazing what they do today!" was a common Hartman line. And the curing of athletic pain was treated as if it were the answer to global hunger. "We're not dealing with mystery," you see, "we know where the source of the pain is and we use state of the art technology to heal it!" What more could a taxpayer want?

After showing the use of computers in a variety of other, less than earth-shaking realms—church bell ringing, cartoon drawing, movie score composing—the program took up the "problems of technology." These were downright silly too. The "problems" were for the most part personal anecdotes of computer errors on credit card accounts and children's computers games. The benefits that balanced these problems were equally trivial. Just as the space flights have given us Tang and Teflon, computer technology, used in space flights, has given us life rafts—the kind used for space are now marketed commercially and have already saved at least one life.

The final segment showed children learning to use computers, while their parents were forced to tag along. It was all very personal, homey, and clearly developed with our daily lives in mind. What was left out was the historical, economic and social context in which computer technology was developed and will be used. The main use of computers, after all, is not life rafts or church bell ringing. They are primarily developed and used for military and industrial purposes. That there may be wonderful personal side effects to the development of new technologies is not the point. (I am personally dependent upon the computer I am using to write this book and would not dream of going back to the typewriter. Nonetheless, the personal comfort and efficiency of socially critical writers was not a factor in the decision to develop computers.)

"The Future Is Now" selected esoteric examples of the high tech revolution. What about weapons technology? What about the loss of jobs and the shift in economic spheres and activities that has already had such deep impact on workers? What about the larger philosophical questions of morality, psychology, and so on posed by using these technologies to educate children and do so many other things in which machine-human interaction is a major factor? It is not that every answer would be negative; it is that we are never asked to consider these issues.

Most telling, perhaps, was the list of sponsors that paid for this show and the particular commercials they chose to run. Most sponsors were themselves manufacturers of high tech equipment. Those that weren't tied their product sales pitch—for this show at least—to the mystique of technology. IBM ran three commercials for high tech leisure products. AT&T was very visible. The ads for Dodge cars were a parody of "Knightrider," a TV show about a high tech auto of the future. Sears focused on VCRs and TVs. Even Crystal Lite soda featured a very streamlined, mechanically loaded workout gym in which slimness itself was associated with technology—all geared, of course, to personal leisure time.

It was impossible to watch this show thoughtfully without noticing the subtle but all encompassing message it presented: life today is totally personal and pleasure oriented. Sports, games, performances and other goodtime activities are what technology will bring us. Don't bother your silly little heads about other matters; have a good time.

While computer games may seem a far cry from the McCarthy hearings, many of the formal aspects of today's documentary reports were established in Murrow's day. The isolated instances and cases are classic. The lack of social and historic context is too. Even the fascination with gadgetry, while warranted and perhaps even justified in itself, was a part of Murrow's success.

Television and the many other technological developments of our century are indeed amazing and awesome. No one would dispute this, and it is interesting to see technology demonstrated. Such programs effectively display the power of the human imagination and its ability to realize its dreams. Like sports on television, the pleasure in watching is real. In the grand scheme of things, such programs do have a place. It is only proper to sit back and congratulate ourselves on our achievements and to ensure that science is used in the interest of fun as well as serious matters. In the best of all worlds, I would hope these things would exist and be enjoyed.

In our own world, however, this kind of program plays a different role. Given the real scientific priorities of this country, and the lack of serious discussion in any medium of technological decision making, an hour spent watching this kind of thing feels insulting. Whatever pleasure we may derive from these inventions, we did not choose them nor do we have any idea what they are costing us, financially and in trade-offs for other social expenditures. In light of that reality, "The Future Is Now" was an exercise in bread and circuses.

When Crises Really Occur

While we are on the subject of technology and its mind boggling effects on our daily lives, it will be interesting to move from the ridiculous to what was presented, again by ABC, as almost sublime—nuclear technology. Summer is the season for news documentaries on TV because it is a slow time. Reruns prevail and no one cares much what's on TV because the weather is nice and it's vacation time. It is a perfect time to sneak in some low budget, low rating, "public service broadcasting."

The summer of 1985 was chock full of these specials. ABC in particular aired a new variation on the form which it hoped would become a regular thing. For three full primetime hours, it presented an "in depth" study of the implications of nuclear power—both for weapons and energy use. Following the broadcast, ABC's "Nightline" continued the discussion, calling upon such figures as Henry Kissinger to comment. This format was developed when the network began doing controversial TV movies about similar subjects.

This very lofty and serious program, "The Fire Unleashed," presented the ideological flip side of technology as fun and games. This time we got the bad news, the dangers and horrors which technology had introduced into our lives. Where the first show urged, "Come on, get your feet wet, you're gonna love it," this one said, "We have a very serious matter to discuss with you, one from which you may never recover." In fact, these two messages are the classic comic/tragic masks of American political mythology. On the one hand, this is supposed to be the very best possible system in the world. Thomas Jefferson promised us that. We are capable of anything we strive for. We are free to enjoy every blessing nature and mankind can provide. But when the system does not deliver, or when its irrationalities, injustices, tragedies and sufferings come into focus, then the message shifts. Suddenly it is not American democracy that is responsible for our fates but that old devil, human nature. "What could we do about it?" ask the powers that be. "You can't change human nature." Suddenly the Dr. Feelgood that created electronic music and sports medicine is really Dr. Faustus, making his evil pact with the devil.

Such classic narrative structures are imposed upon issues like technology in particular because they hit so close to TV's home. TV itself is a technology developed and shaped in ways unclear to most of us. The links between foreign policy and technological decisions of all kinds are necessarily obscured, ostensibly for "security" reasons, but in large part because they are hard to justify in democratic terms. In government rhetoric, fear and wonder lead us along as we passively accept the arms race and space program without much rational thought. Nuclear weapons have always come to us through a haze of terror and awe. It is numbing to consider the implications.

Nonfiction television has not been eager to tackle this subject until recently, when the antinuclear movement put it on the national agenda. Again, social action pushes the media to challenge itself with controversy. "The Day After," ABC's fictional drama, was an odd movie because it was impossible to show, through TV technology, anything vaguely approximating a real nuclear attack. Realism is not up to the job, especially within the limits of TV drama. But as nonfiction producers have developed expertise in state of the art visual technologies, they have learned to couch their messages in images and other visual effects that serve effectively not only to enhance but at times to alter their meanings. The documentary approach, rather than the dramatic, provided a way to present the nuclear issue in a style commensurate with its implications. That style, however, served to subvert the information it contained.

"The Fire Unleashed" was a visual *tour de force*. Where the network had used sophisticated equipment to shoot and relay "The

Future Is Now" from a variety of distant and awkward settings, this time a new tack was taken. Although the actual information presented and the "experts" chosen to explain and debate it were typical enough, the tone of the show was vastly different from most newscasts. Using poetry, quotations, and artwork culled from the best of the entire tradition of western culture and civilization, the producers managed to communicate a sense of higher wisdom which was almost biblical. Our imminent doom looked beautiful.

The program was divided into three segments, one on nuclear proliferation, one on energy and one on the arms race. The information provided was carefully "balanced"; different positions were presented on various policy issues and scenarios for the future. The segment on the history and behavior of the Nuclear Regulatory Commission (NRC), for example, was full of pro and con. Commissioners defended their policies while adversaries—the closest the show got to letting regular people participate—voiced loud objections. But this, like the rest of the overwhelmingly abundant facts, figures and opinions offered, led to no conclusion. In fact whether the segment aired was presenting arguable controversies or scientific and geographic data, the result was the same. There were too many opposing opinions to evaluate, too much intimidating and terrifying information to grapple with. The viewer was left with a sinking feeling that most of what was presented was beyond her or his comprehension, and those things that were clearly wrong and irrational were far too deeply established and inevitable in their forward thrust to do anything about.

The segment on proliferation, for example, was at once enlightening and paralyzing. Information was presented that Brazil, Argentina, Israel, Libya, India, and countless other nations and groups already had or were about to develop the capacity for nuclear weaponry. Israel's nuclear plant was even built with plutonium stolen from the U.S. In fact, espionage and "terrorism" were so often exposed and dramatized during this hour that if not for the lofty tone, one might have been watching a James Bond movie. According to the show, every crackpot and every suicide-bent Third World "terrorist" was busy building bombs to hurl at us in our sleep. There was image upon image of Third World military forces marching through streets, accompanied by tanks and drum rolls.

The segment on the arms race, however, did not emphasize force so much as reason and science. Rather than show American military forces and equipment, ABC allowed our leaders—interspersed with quotes from the likes of Einstein and Gandhi—to tell us what was what. President Reagan, former Secretary of Defense McNamara, the Joint Chiefs of Staff, Edward Teller and others were paraded before our eyes, flanked by lab equipment and book shelves, to give us the bad news. But in fact the most repeated visuals in this segment were patriotic symbols like the flag, the White House, the Capitol, the space flight launchings—and then, the bomb. This was one way in which images served to distort language. The Third World was full of "terrorists" while America was building bombs in the name of freedom, progress, justice and democracy. With less sophisticated visual technology, these symbols would have seemed merely hokey. But so slick were the images that they could be repeated—Big Brother style—over and over again without appearing as blatant indoctrination.

The quality and tone of this program deserves some analysis, simply because it was so successful an effort to subvert the emotion which the material itself might be expected to naturally elicit. Using the device of style itself, not entirely different from the emotionally and visually moving art forms used by the Nazis, is terribly subtle. The evening began with a series of images, culled from ancient wall paintings and other museum artifacts, depicting the beginnings of civilization—exactly in the images and tones we are used to equating with this theme through years of educational television, Art History 101 courses, high brow magazines and coffee table art books. The narrator, journalist Marshall Frady, intoned the following kinds of phrases—also familiar from such kitschy encounters: "Man...hunting, scavengering...mostly indistinguishable from other beasts around him... What lifted us from this primeval night...the urge to under- stand...to make beauty..." and so on. As the mellifluous words fell softly upon our ears, our eyes were treated to the rest of the Metropolitan Museum tour. Michelangelo, Van Gogh...and on and on to the present day's greatest (or most reproduced) artists. Finally, the atomic age and the famous words of nuclear physicist Robert Oppenheimer, upon developing the nuclear bomb, "Now I am become death." Cut back to narrator seen full form, hair blowing in the breeze, alone against a vast plain and a cloud filled sky.

The meaning of this kind of thing—whether we realize it or not— is programmed into our brains. The primitive beginnings, the rise of civilization with its promise of beauty, truth, wisdom, and then the tragic misuse of our powers to create death machines which we are destined to use, irrationally, to destroy ourselves. This is the classic structure of tragedy. We are the heroes. We are greater than any other creatures, in potential and even achievement. But like Oedipus, like Macbeth, we blow it. We fall prey to our character flaws. We allow pride and arrogance to tempt and trap us. We are become death.

This is in fact the justification—in Western literature and art—for the tragedy of "bad things happening to good people." In personal terms, it generally makes sense. Even historically, it is not always nonsense. But it is not a true picture of the tragedy of nuclear power. Dramatic tragedy, after all, treats things that have already happened.

Nuclear power and our national policies about it are very much in the making at the moment. That, ostensibly, is why a three hour documentary was appropriate—to help us, as citizens, decide what to do. There is no reason in the world—as the majority of Americans who support the antinuclear movement know—why it cannot be stopped. No reason, that is, that doesn't challenge the existing power structure and the thinking that keeps it in place. This is not a Greek tragedy. It is a political issue to be debated—mostly on network TV. In treating it as a drama, the message was that it was in fact over, inevitable, hopeless and beyond the control of such flawed and weak mortals as ourselves.

The show told us that our opinions were useless, and our options nil. It did this in large part by ignoring any historic context, any sense of how we got here. The arms race did not simply emerge full blown. As even the show itself made clear, the Soviets have only forty-six nuclear plants to our eighty-five. We started it and we are pushing it on. Historic context is often ignored in TV documentaries, but this one was different in an important way. It acknowledged the enormity of the problem and the intensity of our national terror and concern. And then, to find a way to seem to deal with those things without repudiating the policies that are its cause, it hit on a particularly odious and dishonest style. It used the tradition of Western culture—the world of high art.

Art images, as John Berger points out, are often used in advertising. They "lend allure or authority" and suggest "a form of dignity, even of wisdom, which is superior to any vulgar material interest... [because] they belong to the cultural heritage."[19] What this documentary was selling was not commercial merchandise, but it was similarly self-interested. It intended to sell us a policy which was not, in terms of hegemonic boundaries, up for debate. Its message was that all human wisdom and greatness had been applied to the problem; that we were in the best hands possible; and that there was nothing more we could do. Here again we hit the volatile area where "Communism," the ultimate threat to American democracy, looms large. To be "against nuclear war" is one thing. To oppose the existing policy which dictates our behavior toward the "Communists" is quite another.

There are many contradictions dramatized in this presentation. The program itself was conceived in response to political agitation on a global scale against our nuclear policies. In that sense, it was a victory for progressives. It would be unfair to write it off as having no positive value. The information presented in three long hours of videotape was substantial and useful. Those already attuned to TV esthetics and politics, or already convinced of the antinuclear position, could benefit greatly from the facts and figures released, many of them damaging to the United States. The NRC came in for some good muckraking. The balance of power between the superpowers was shown to favor us more than the administration likes to admit. The sheer volume of footage, there to be saved on videocassette, was invaluable to activists and documentary filmmakers.

Still, the show was unlikely to persuade the unconvinced that nuclear weapons should be banned. Its primary effect, because of style and tone, was to reinforce the helplessness already felt by most of us, and further entrench the legitimacy of existing agencies and decision making processes.

Having noted the similarities between the program's style and that of classy advertising, it is doubly ironic to look at the actual commercial messages which sponsored this show. Almost all of them were visual and verbal paeans to technology and progress. Image after image of office machinery, automobiles, even exercise equipment was offered us in the name of improved lifestyle, improved productivity, improved and more perfect human activity. Had these ads been analyzed—as they needed to be—as carefully as reviewers analyzed the program, a contradictory message would have emerged. The program said: technology is a sign of human nature's tragic flaw; it will destroy us with its awesome power. The commercials said: technology is our greatest, most beautiful achievement; it will provide perfect abundance and happiness.

The contrast between the 1950's documentary approach of "See It Now" and that of contemporary reports is telling. As video technology grew more sophisticated, the triumph of style over content was heightened. This allowed the networks to apply a variety of esthetically moving and impressive techniques to serious topics. On the other hand, the range of views examined, and the depth of the examinations have not changed as much as sometimes seems the case. Muckraking and the defense of individual rights and liberties is more often done on magazine shows, as we will see in the next chapter. Documentaries now serve the somewhat different purpose of expounding on, and so justifying, policies already in place. They rarely challenge hegemony; they explain it.

7

Magazines, Talk Shows and Soft News: Reality as Small Talk

The nonfiction form which has replaced documentaries as the primary vehicle through which national issues are presented and analyzed is the magazine/talk show. This kind of programming is actually a constant feature of network TV, day and night. These shows—"60 Minutes," "Donahue," "Dr. Ruth," "Lifestyles of the Rich and Famous"—are so diverse that superficially they appear to have little in common. It isn't likely that many people watch more than a few such shows on a regular basis. The early morning "Good Morning America" fan may not be up for "Late Night with David Letterman"; and the loyal viewer of "20/20" may never see Gary Collins' afternoon "Hour Magazine."

Nonetheless, these shows have more in common than the casual viewer may realize. They are all organized to be primarily entertaining and lighter in touch than Murrow's documentaries, to say the least. They all take the key social issues "in the air" as their subject matter—whether the form is panel discussion, report, interview or comic monologue. They all use brief, segmented formats to allow for less depth and a shorter audience attention span than Murrow assumed. They all tend to personalize issues and opinions by dramatizing the roles of individual thinkers and actors, as well as those of the hosts. And they all, in one way or another, lay out for us the permissible range of viewpoints on these topics.

In surveying so vast and varied an amount of video material, it is important to note that there are obvious and enormous differences among formats, and important contradictory elements within each form. Some of the stories presented on "60 Minutes" and "20/20" are the best and most serious social commentary on television. Some of the advice and discussion on daytime talk shows reflects socially advanced positions and plays a progressive role. As a whole and at times individually, these shows have great social influence. They set the agenda for what Americans will be discussing in subsequent days and weeks because they are so dramatic and so widely seen. They act as a sort of study guide for casual discussion, since the issues raised, and the drama with which certain features are presented, focus attention and help to determine perspective for viewers.

This form is also the most dynamic and elastic of all nonfiction on TV, the most likely to push the limits of hegemonic thinking in all directions. This makes it even more difficult to see the unifying ideological features of all the shows, and even of various segments of a single show. The sentimentality of daytime magazines, the humor of late night, and the sensationalism of some talk shows seem to have little in common with the social analysis of shows like "60 Minutes." Add to that the unusual variety of perspectives sometimes presented, the fact that individual segments may be more progressive or reactionary than is usual elsewhere, and the difficulty of mapping out the political universe of the genre increases.

The best way to survey this smorgasbord of formats and topics is probably by breaking them up into three categories: nighttime, morning, and afternoon series. In this way we can see the way different audience segments are informed by TV. In particular, the morning and afternoon shows are geared to women, while evening programming is meant primarily for working males. (Obviously there is a great—and increasing—overlap here. But the difference between male and female concerns is still dramatic enough, on average, to warrant very different shows. And since daytime programming is still the most blatant sexual ghetto on TV, it is worth looking at from that perspective as a way of understanding the changing, but still very sexist and contradictory, way in which women are thought of and expected to behave in this country.)

The roots of these forms go back to the very beginnings of television. The personal interview with a famous person, now a mainstay of all these shows, was developed by Edward R. Murrow not long after he began his "See It Now" series. "Person to Person," launched in October 1953 as the first celebrity-in-the-home interview series, was a spin-off of "See It Now." When asked by John Cassavetes why he did "this kind of show," Murrow said "To do the show I want to do ("See It Now"), I have to do the show that I don't want to do."[1] The show he did not want to do, ironically, has been far more influential than the more controversial show about which he cared so much.

In the case of the "Today" and "Tonight" shows, prototypes of our current morning and evening varieties, the development of an audience was gradual. The morning series, featuring Dave Garroway, premiered in the early 1950s to mixed reviews. Part news, part variety, critics and viewers alike had difficulty discerning the point. Introducing a chimpanzee, J. Fred Muggs, finally made the show a hit. According to producer Gerald Green, Muggs was an instant star: "Women proposed to him; advertisers fought for the right to use his photos...; actresses proposed to him,"[2] and so on.

The "Tonight Show" began with much the same format it now uses. Its first host was Steve Allen, but it was Jack Paar, a temperamental personality given to emotional and opinionated outbursts, who made the show a national institution. Looking at these three cases, it is easy to see how TV's current way of doing nonfiction evolved. Inside views of celebrities' lives, gimmicks and strong personalities were what caught on—far more than straightforward information or conversation. Audiences responded to TV figures they could relate to emotionally and to cuteness and humor that could be shared nationally. They still do. What passes for information and analysis on TV is almost invariably couched in, or interlaced with, these very elements.

Primetime News Magazines

"60 Minutes" is a television phenomenon. It is the only nonfiction series dealing with serious issues that has consistently remained at the top of the charts. "The highest rated public affairs program in television history,"[3] it began as a weekly series in 1975 and rose into the top twenty shows in the Neilsen ratings the next year. In 1977 it climbed to number four, and in the last few years it has held its own as the first or second most popular show in the country.[4]

At first glance, "60 Minutes" would seem to defy the generalizations just made about nonfiction TV, especially serious nonfiction. Unlike its popular imitator, "20/20," which allots a heavy proportion of its time to feature segments on cultural and human interest topics, "60 Minutes" has always concentrated on serious muckraking of the Murrow variety. Most of the time it presents stories based on the investigative reporting of its own stars, whose purpose, *a la* Murrow, is to expose injustice and set things right. Week after week, these stars report on political and commercial ripoffs and scams. They challenge the most highly placed public officials and take them to task for failing to live up to their public responsibility to serve the people. The expose of General Westmoreland's falsification of data about the military situation during the Vietnam war is only the most well known of a long line of muckraking, political exposes.

When "60 Minutes" isn't dealing with matters of state, more often than not it takes on similar evils in public institutions and businesses. If a mental hospital is abusing patients, if the criminal justice system is punishing an innocent person, if a major corporation is polluting the environment, you can count on "60 Minutes" to find out about it. Week after week, audiences sit fascinated by the sad stories of how the little guy is being taken by big business and big government. Follow-up reports often reveal that an evil has been redressed and a victim recompensed, released, or vindicated.

The popularity of "60 Minutes" attests to the widespread desire to see injustice righted, and the genuine sympathy Americans have for the little guy, as well as the general mistrust and resentment we all feel toward those in powerful places. Like the "Action Line" segments on local news, "60 Minutes" satisfies the general need to feel that problems are being solved and that those in power are being made accountable to us. Its emotional appeal is understandable.

On a case by case basis, there is often a lot that is commendable in "60 Minutes." Its populist approach to social and political life is itself refreshing. However, there are also a lot of problems with the show, both in its methods and its ultimate effects. In particular, its way of framing and structuring individual segments, and its editing techniques—which have recently come under public scrutiny—tend to create a certain perspective on the workings of society as a whole that is at best misleading. In typical TV style, "60 Minutes" reduces every injustice to a single case, an isolated personal experience. Because it takes the stuff of the evening news and places it in a more intimate context, it subtly transforms a political or social phenomenon into a personal narrative in which the dramatic and emotional features dominate, while the general political or social message is negated. As in the "Action Line" segments of local newscasts, the "60 Minutes" commentators become real, sympathetic actors in the story. And the visual settings—living rooms, offices, moving cars—add to the sense of personal narrative drama.

Structurally, the audience shares an emotionally or morally moving situation, and then sees it all come right in the end. The journalist has solved the problem, exposed the villain, comforted and assisted the victim. But what is never hinted at is the political context in which these little melodramas take place. Because each story is isolated from the others, the cause of the problem is always a single "evil" person or group, never an entire system in which such injustices and atrocities happen again and again. It is always the little guy who gets hurt, after all. It is always a business or government institution that does the hurting. The viewer is kept from seeing the connections, however, and encouraged to believe that each case is a fluke, and that the media, in its role of watchdog, can right the wrong.

Even when the show is watched week after week, year after year, with the same patterns coming up again and again, there is no sense that structural changes are in order. On the contrary, real comfort is transmitted by "60 Minutes" because it has a consistent message and world view, one which fits nicely with the view our government generally advocates. All evil stems from human nature. People are no damn good and must be watched like hawks, or they will steal your underwear. This conclusion may not seem particularly uplifting, but it is, in its own cynical way, reassuring. At least we know what we're up against—and what we're up against is not a changeable system that often gives rise to behaviors we deplore, that we might be challenged to confront, but rather certain immutable facts of human nature, the results of which can sometimes, in isolated instances, be reversed or momentarily quelled.

Recently, the technical tricks of "60 Minutes" crews have gotten a lot of attention because of legal suits brought against the show by people who claim to have been presented unfairly due to editing, out of context quotes, or outright duplicity on the part of the journalists themselves. If Dan Rather misrepresents himself to someone—promising to use an interview in one way and then using it in another—the Murrowesque virtue of the show is called into question. If lengthy testimony is cut and edited so that explanatory or qualifying material is eliminated, leaving a false impression of a speaker's experiences or views, the show is clearly presenting false information—every bit as false as what gets printed in the *National Enquirer*.

Despite legal hassles, the show's image has not really been tarnished. Why? Because we have become a nation accustomed to duplicity and manipulation, no longer expecting or demanding "the truth." More than any simple political shift, this subtle assumption of and tolerance for duplicity is the most dramatic legacy of the post-Murrow days. Murrow, for all his political limits, was usually an honest journalist. When the "$64,000 Question" replaced "See It Now," it put an end not to serious nonfiction reporting, but to the shared trust in media honesty. Having lost its virginity, network TV was never again quite so trustworthy, and rightly so. As technical sophistication grew, the temptation to edit verbal and visual material, and to dramatize its presentation, proved irresistible. The effects of exercising the simple "tools of the trade" have at times been politically outrageous.[5]

While "60 Minutes" does feature other kinds of reporting, it is primarily a "serious problem" show. It will occasionally profile a cultural figure or treat a light topic, but for the most part its lighter side is compartmentalized into the brief Andy Rooney monologue at the end of each show. Its popularity has spawned any number of similar magazine series which—rather than compete with the "60 Minutes" formula—have branched out into other areas. "20/20," the ABC entry, is the best example of this kind of diversification. Its range of topics and segment formats has been much more influential, and typical of what nonfiction programming is really about. "60 Minutes" covers the spectrum of social evils—in government, business, the arts, science, sports, etc.—generally using the expose approach. "20/20," on the other hand, treats the same areas but uses different approaches for each. This diversity has allowed "20/20" to present the broadest range of political views of any nonfiction show, and in many cases, remarkably hardhitting political segments. This is particularly intriguing because the very same show may present another segment, immediately following, which is as patriotically mushy and chauvinistic as the previous one had been militantly critical. The contradictions within network television are fascinating to chart in this program. A dominant attitude is nonetheless discernible in examining its various elements.

"20/20" usually has at least one "60 Minutes"-style expose, but it also does a lot of celebrity profiles and trend analysis. It may treat a scientific figure as a celebrity and interview her in the gossipy "Person to Person" mode, rather than investigating her actual scientific contribution and the controversies surrounding it. It is more like the early morning magazines in that sense—a hodge podge of news, glitter, expert advice and fun. Where "60 Minutes" uses the hardnosed, foot in the door, flash bulb in the eye approach to social issues, "20/20"—and most of the other magazines—prefers a more even-handed, "this is the whole picture" presentation of issues. They are not so much out to catch crooks as to explain to us what the issues are and—ever so subtly—lead us to certain conclusions. "20/20" does not have the same kind of coherent, oft-repeated message as "60 Minutes." Nonetheless, the hegemonic limits of network ideology are not violated because the formal constraints of the show's format do not allow for enough variety, enough depth or breadth of analysis, to suggest truly divergent world views strongly enough to challenge hegemony itself.

As in "60 Minutes," social issues are chosen for their timeliness and dramatized in a way that makes the reporter a persona in the proceedings. This is probably the most distinctive feature of this kind of journalism, as opposed to standard nightly news. It personalizes everything about the investigative process. Instead of fancily framed stills and graphs, it offers news figures as personalities, viewed and interviewed within the framework of their daily lives. Victims and other "subjects" are typically seen at home, on the street, at work. "Experts," on the other hand, are always seen in official settings: booklined offices, labs, and so on. Instead of copy read from a script, it offers real interaction between interviewer and subject in the form of easy conversation. It will frequently include cute shots of the reporter entering the story itself—trying out a computer or riding in a racing car. All of this adds casualness, personal warmth and drama.

"20/20" recently treated a social problem—school truancy—using all these dramatic features to reach a particularly reactionary conclusion. The reporter was Geraldo Rivera, a hip, liberal Latino supposedly at ease with the kids and neighborhoods he spoke of and with. The segment began with a few startling statistics. Truancy, we learned, is as high as 30 percent. In Boston, one-third of all high school kids are failing.

When the glib and dramatic interviews began, there was a clear difference between the tone, diction and content of the questions asked different figures. The audience of course, used to such race and class bias, was not expected to pick this up on a conscious level. Rivera asked the kids the most simple minded, condescending questions. "Didn't you worry you'd get caught?" he asked some kids in a video arcade. "Yeah," came the obvious answer. When experts, such as the high school principal, were questioned, things were very different. "Why do kids play hooky?" he asked the public school hack sitting with dignity behind a desk. The answer, filled with sociological gobbledygook, was received with respect. Yet this man was less likely to understand the real causes of truancy than the kids Rivera had so haughtily brushed off.

Without indicating that ABC had an answer of its own, the segment managed to end with clear implications. There were a series of shots and interviews about various legal and law enforcement strategies. One showed a court in which parents—in this case a Salvadoran refugee couple unfamiliar with U.S. culture and language—were lectured by a judge. Another showed a group of kids, some as young as seven, being rounded up in paddy wagons. "Eighty-five percent of parents make excuses," said one expert to Rivera with contempt. The final words, spoken by Hugh Downs, were clear and pointed: "It looks like parents are playing hooky from their jobs," he said with a sad nod of the head, as Rivera, now seated next to him, sorrowfully agreed. These two men had looked at the issue and drawn a conclusion for us.

No alternative questions or answers were suggested. Why not look at the school system itself, or the social and economic context in which these kids come to understand and judge the value of their education? Instead we, as parents, were made to feel guilty for not taking on more personal responsibility. But how? Most parents, in the communities shown, have no time, no child care, no social services to help them raise their kids. The next logical thought had to be: we had better put it in the hands of the authorities. And so they shall.

This clearly conservative viewpoint is not necessarily typical of "20/20." Rather, the show represents the full range of views in the spectrum of established belief. At times, it uses the form's conventions to push beyond these views a bit. Av Westin, whose policies on enforcing the Fairness Doctrine were quoted earlier, has been executive producer of this show, and it reflects the same perspective he subsequently brought to ABC News. Most reporters and segment producers probably do subscribe to the "liberal social activist" positions found in the prestige press from which they get their material. Because these positions are well represented on the show, corrective segments like the one described above are presented in equal number. Because the majority of segments are not hard issue, but "soft" cultural and human interest features, it would be impossible to characterize the show's politics in traditional terms. Its overall political perspective, within which sharp contradictions war, develops out of its stylistic and formal conventions and its emphasis, as we shall see, on the idea of "celebrity."

One of the cleverest features of "20/20," related to its preoccupation with celebrity, is its ability to integrate cultural and social material, thus using the blurriness of nonfiction content to present serious material in the most appealing way. A recent segment dealing with grassroots responses to plant closings, for example, used the popularity of Bruce Springsteen as a jumping off point. Springsteen allowed a tape of his acoustic performance of Woody Guthrie's "This Land is Your Land," the phenomenal closing number on his record-breaking 1985 tour, to be aired. This song, sung by Springsteen as Guthrie intended it—an anti-big business anthem affirming the rights of working people—is quite radical. It is also universally known and loved, as is Springsteen himself.

The piece used Springsteen's personal involvement in efforts to stop a plant closing in his home state to explore the national movement, largely invisible to TV watchers, to stop plant closings everywhere. In a rare departure, viewers heard workers and political organizers in many cities speak of their determination to fight back. The sense of collective action so broad as to constitute a national movement, and the sympathetic treatment of working people organizing against the power of the corporations, was unusual.

Danny Schecter, the producer of the Springsteen piece, also produced a segment about Native Americans facing removal from their homes, which began with a look at the efforts of rock star Little Steven Van Zandt on their behalf. Schecter is among the most creative and progressive producers of nonfiction television. His commitment to social justice is aided by his ability to use hot cultural issues and figures to explore controversial topics, thus staying within the confines of the celebrity-centered feature, but pushing its limits significantly. Springsteen and Little Steven are the very epitome of individualistic glamour and stardom, the cornerstone of "20/20"'s approach to life. But because they are social activists as well, they provide a legitimate way to say more radical things than usual. Here is a fine example of someone within the network consciously pushing the ideological limits as far as possible and succeeding because of an understanding of the system itself, combined with a knowledge of social activism and social issues not usually seen on TV.

The effect of such efforts is hard to judge. On one level, they reflect a minority perspective which is overwhelmed by the bulk of material around it. On another level however, like the moment of social criticism during Liberty Weekend, or the words and deeds of Jesse Jackson during the 1984 presidential campaign, they exist as powerful expressions of alternative versions of the looking glass reality. Those who saw the plant closing segment know that its effect was strong. Activists were bolstered by having their efforts dramatized and valued. Regular viewers of the show, and one time viewers who had tuned in especially to see the rock stars, saw and heard a new perspective given legitimacy. Those already set in their anti-worker, anti-minority opinions were not likely to change their minds. Those wandering around or reading while the segment aired were only marginally affected if at all. Nonetheless, many viewers surely were moved and made to think by these reports.

Having scanned the ideological poles of "20/20"'s perspective, we can wade into the mushier middle of things—the celebrity interviews and cultural features. The overriding tendency of these segments is to personalize and glamourize everything, to create a universe peopled by "media personalities" concerning themselves with media issues and concepts. The most popular new media forms of all kinds, for instance, *People* magazine and *USA Today*, are representative of this trend. The emerging contradictions are subtle and interesting in the media-zation of American life which TV has been instrumental in creating.

On the one hand, this excessive concern with celebrity and media visibility as a sign of significance is realistic. "Fame," as the media alone can bestow it, has become as sought after an American goal as financial success or happiness, according to recent surveys. People long to inhabit that looking glass empire, and we spend time, money and energy trying. It is indeed the big time, the promised land. The values inherent in that world are every bit as important as their coverage implies. Bruce Springsteen's relationship to the plant closing issue does deserve credit. As a celebrity, he has power to sway minds and hearts as a struggling political organizer in New Jersey does not.

But media self-concern is also self-congratulatory and narcissistic. Standard celebrity coverage would not draw connections between the lyrics of Springsteen's songs and the social reality they reflect, thus putting the stardom of the singer in perspective. Instead, it further mystifies and misleads us, inculcating the distorted views and standards of the powerful. In examining these shows, we need to acknowledge their moments of real insight. But we need also to realize that most of what is produced serves primarily to confound and hide reality.

Interviews with show business figures and other celebrities are most common. While they can be instructive, they most often are not. Again the networks serve as socializing agents by taking ideas and trends from more elite publications—newspapers, serious magazines and journals—and molding them to the dimensions of the twenty minute personal interview. Some key figure who fits the criteria for celebrity, in achievement as well as personal image, is selected to talk about a hot issue. Sometimes experts—movie critics and scientists— are brought on to discuss some trend or news event. Carl Sagan may discuss the concept of nuclear winter. Roger Ebert and Gene Siskel may discuss the *Star Wars* movies. These people are themselves media figures. They know the ropes and fit the image. Usually a celebrity discusses his or her own life and work.

The settings for these interviews are personalized too. Celebrities are taped in their homes or offices, their personalities embellished by the decor. Experts may sit in plush studios, but the settings are always comfortable and tasteful. It is when the questions are asked that the limits of the form come up. Once more, matters of social context and historic background are ignored.

One of the more interesting social issues raised by the trend toward special effects movies like *Star Wars*, for example, is their links to military research and their reflection of military values. Scientists from the Air Force-funded RAND Corporation often meet and work with people from Lucasfilm on a common problem: simulated war games. An interview with filmmaker George Lucas will almost certainly not touch on this issue. Nor will the financing and distribution of the films come up. What does it mean for example that several of the top ten film rental hits *globally* are recent Lucas and Spielberg epics like *Jaws*, *Stars Wars* and *Raiders of the Lost Ark*? It means quite a lot—especially to the Third World nations included in the figures.

Twenty minutes is simply too brief an interval to explore such broad implications of an artist's work, however. Most of the time must be spent presenting information about the person's rise to celebrity, and that is the major function of these interviews. An interview will typically give a tour of the subject's home or office, pausing to comment on significant objects that pertain to career highlights. It will reiterate the key ideas about her or his work, as established in the elite press. It will perhaps raise an issue which the press is currently debating. New territory is rarely staked out. Old ground is introduced and reiterated until the audience gets the point.

When social issues do come up, they are typically framed and limited by preordained strictures. The issue of sex and violence onscreen, for example, has not been resolved. Brian De Palma's films have outraged some feminists and those concerned with children's responses to violence. They have also been championed by defenders of "art." De Palma's own answer, on TV, is that "the camera loves sex and violence," and that his portrayal of those themes is true to the realities of capitalism which, he is sad to say, cannot be changed. References to unchanging human nature and built-in political biases in technology fall within hegemonic lines. The "other side," the side that fears for the children, also gets its several minutes to reply. The reason for the emptiness of the discussion is the lack of social context. Is all violence "bad" for children? Does this society in fact inculcate a love and respect for violence—state sanctioned violence—in kids, while disapproving of violence in less abstract forms?[6] The subject has endless possibilities, almost none of which will be treated.

The format is flexible enough to allow for some successful tampering, given a skillful, determined producer. *The Terminator*, a B-movie that became an unexpected hit, warranted treatment on "20/20" because it had been so widely reviewed in print. Rather than interviewing the film's director, the producer (Schecter again) chose to invite critic Peter Biskind, author of a book on the way in which Hollywood movies subtly express political positions, to discuss the futuristic film. Biskind, a sophisticated social and political analyst, called attention to the larger political implications of the movie's success. The producer's choice of experts, along with knowledge of the formulae, makes the difference.

Having surveyed the range of discord the form permits, we can turn to the formal techniques which create the dominant world view of these shows. That there are now so many magazine/talk shows, all variations on a set of simple themes, is itself important. Again and again, as the days and weeks go on, we will see—as we glimpse the screen and stop for a minute or two to pay attention—the same images and ideas repeated. We may see George Lucas on "20/20" discussing, and being discussed in terms of, what TV has defined as "the important cultural issues." On the ABC morning show, "Good Morning America," we may then see pieces of this interview, edited and selected to fill a much briefer, lighter segment. Even shorter bits and pieces may appear on any number of other network programs: CBS' "Hour Magazine," NBC's "Lifestyles of the Rich and the Famous," etc. Depending on the format and focus of each such show, certain increasingly glitzy and superficial items will be repeated.[7]

The effect of all this repetition is to establish certain faces, items and values as measures of success, happiness and meaningful activity.

The ultimate effect of this process of endless repetition of increasingly few and simple factors is a reductionism that fixes in the public mind certain largely meaningless ideas about these values. "20/20"'s version of art and culture is, as we have seen, already limited in texture and complexity. By the time we get to "Lifestyles of the Rich and Famous," whatever was actually meaningful—distorted and limited as it was—has been entirely eliminated.

In a typical recent case, publicist Henry Rogers, author of a book of "rules" for success, was featured on the talk/magazine circuit. Institutional analysis of his phenomenal financial success, in a business which is a parasite on the entertainment industry, was ignored. Instead, the parade of famous faces who had been hurled into prominence by this clever fellow was shown *ad nauseum*. Gossip and anecdotes about some of the best known stars were featured. Joan Crawford, whose public image had been thoroughly decimated a few years earlier by her daughter's book and its subsequent movie version, *Mommy Dearest*, was reborn through Rogers' anecdotes. This time she was a sweet, almost compulsively thoughtful and kind friend. This bit of gossip, from a morning show, was then reduced, on the more "how to" oriented "Hour Magazine," to one of several "rules for success" listed in Rogers' book. "Thoughtfulness," you see, was one of the principles of success recommended by the powerful Mr. Rogers. Finally, on "Lifestyles of the Rich and Famous," only the homes, art collections, entertainment patterns and other leisure activities remained of this man's life.

All of this points to a way of defining "success" for Americans. Not only are economic and political considerations lost, even work itself goes unmentioned. We are supposed to believe that becoming wealthy and powerful is a matter of following a few rules and then living out your days in luxury and decadence. This is patent nonsense of course. However, it is an important part of the myth of success in America. As the inequities of class widen, and the real mechanisms and behaviors that enable the few to "make it" become increasingly undemocratic and unfit to exemplify the media's supposed values, this kind of mystification and fantasy grows more important.

Once we have people believing, or at least lusting after these images and myths, we have a perfect setting for the real business of TV: selling endlessly expanding consumer products, lifestyles and values. The meaning of art is made simple and easy to grasp, yet still—for those interested—intellectually chewy and rich enough to satisfy. But what really occurs in the process of image reproduction is far more important to consumerism than intellectual or political debate. For one thing, we will see even more of those blockbuster movies selected for discussion. As if Lucas and Spielberg didn't already monopolize the global market and imagination beyond any historic precedent,[8] the networks—owned by the same conglomerates that own the film industry—help to further increase this lopsidedness and drive alternative films further out of the competition.

Once this is accomplished, the tie-ins—direct and indirect—are pushed—directly and indirectly. The aggrandizement of Lucasfilm, for example, adds weight to the heavy market for tie-in products connected to Lucas' films. Toys, clothing, games and so on are indirectly sold in the movies, and directly sold when advertised on TV. But in a more subtle way, all the accoutrements of Lucas' work and lifestyle are also pushed. Few watching can buy the mansions, cars, women and friends this man is seen to have, but a desire for cheap reproductions and lesser items is planted and watered through the endless repetition. In the public mind, it is the things seen on "Lifestyles" that are lusted after and saved for.

When a news figure is featured, the process is similar. When Claus von Bulow, twice tried for attempted murder of his permanently comatose socialite wife, was finally acquitted—after a trial filled with soap operaish scandal and emotion—Barbara Walters was there, on "20/20," with the first interview. This man, a cold-mannered aristocrat whose media image had been on a par with Dracula, was suddenly transformed to TV celebrity of the more glamorous kind. Ironically, Von Bulow fit the stereotype of fictional TV figures like Blake Carrington. It took a mere twelve person jury to kick him up from the status of evil villain to enviable gentleman. Like the polls during an election season, public opinion on the man had already been tested. Many people—fans of "Dynasty" and "Dallas"—already loved the guy, and who cares if he did or didn't murder his wife. Morality, after all, is a slippery thing in a capitalist value system. Acquittal was all that was required to allow him to be knighted by Walters. In his elegant home, he sat explaining it all to us ever so reasonably. His affairs and his financial status were made to seem the height of chic. And after all, aren't they? Once again, the primetime magazine acts as social and moral spokesperson for consensus. It's okay to admit that you love the guy, said Barbara.

It is through Walters herself that this message is conveyed. She is the national woman in the know, a socially important figure. Her tastes are ours. Her treatment of cultural and political figures alike is the essence of image creation. She has the ability to draw people out, but her bias is sharp. With established popular heroes, she is mawkish and fawning while she intrusively digs for the dirt, but with leaders of "unfriendly nations," her motherly disapproval is harsh. "No, no," she chides Fidel Castro, "You shouldn't have done that." She generally allows some level of personal charm to show through in her villains;

but that subtly serves to "explain" to the audience the appeal and power of someone so obviously evil.

The real difference between Fidel Castro and Claus Von Bulow, in Walters' eyes, is obviously not "evil"; it is a political judgment. As men, it is hard to imagine anyone making a case that Claus Von Bulow's life is somehow more noble or meaningful than the Cuban hero's. Fidel Castro, whatever one thinks of his politics, has led a life filled with commitment and action, values normally admired, even in villains, in historic context; Von Bulow is, by his own admission, a parasite. But one represents the values of capitalism and especially consumerism, as glamourized on TV as a whole, and the other represents a political system that opposes such lavish rewards for a useless life. The anticommunism of network TV, honored here so typically, is bonded to the consumerism upon which commercial television depends for its survival.

Morning, Noon and Afternoon

There is a continuum of merging forms in this area of TV. Magazines for primetime deal in some length with big newsmakers and issues which are seen as "reports" on the standard news. Morning magazines compress these interviews into much briefer segments and add elements of the talk show. They bring folks on to chat, on couches, against drapes and ferns, about whatever makes them newsworthy. There are breaks for local and national news and weather, and lots of local news style chatting among anchors. Daytime talk and magazine shows exclusively for women do the same with emphasis on home, parenting and other "women's issues." And late at night, punchy from work, kids and a few beers, we are allowed to be silly with Johnny Carson and David Letterman, who bring the same people on and make them—and us—silly for a while. Whatever the style or tone, the major ideological elements never vary.

Just as the segments of our real day tend to demand different elements of our personalities to emerge, so do the talk and information shows that follow us through our schedules. Television is in that sense a real mirror—translated into media symbols and images—of our daily lives. It makes us at home no matter what we are doing by doing the same things in the same manner. It is a neighbor, a friend, a "national comforter" in Tom Shales' words.

Early morning magazines fit this role perfectly. Everyone may be at home—Mom, Dad, kids. There is lot of psychological shifting needed to get up and go. We need coffee, small talk and comfort. We also need to get ready for the problems of the day, whatever they are. There is hard news and analysis—but not too much. There is discussion of women's concerns, like parenting and fashion. There is talk of weather, movies and major problems and trends. Mostly, there is a lot of celebrity. The emphasis on show business is interesting. Why would Farrah Fawcett loom larger in this time slot than the latest highjacking? Because popular culture is our favorite form of comfort and escape. No matter how bad things get, we can always turn to the beautiful people and focus on more pleasant things. They are our national fairy tales, our national royalty, our national gossip.

There is usually quite a bit of overlap in the three network morning shows. Each has a similar format and a similar, cozily furnished set. Usually the news and show business features focus on current events, which means the same guest may zip from one network to the next, touting a book or film, or explaining an event in which he or she participated. The Von Bulow interview done for "20/20," for example, was excerpted and previewed on ABC's "Good Morning America." Audiences, after tasting the delicacy, were sure to want more that night.

The brevity of each segment is understandable. At 8 or 9 P.M., a family may sit for twenty minutes or so at a stretch, but in the morning, such attentiveness is impossible. Breakfast must be made, kids attended to and so on. The format of these shows is geared to this routine. It doesn't ask much of us. We can move around the house and glance up from time to time to get the gist of any story. Any given moment's attention will probably be rewarded with a coherent, discrete thought. A simple question can be asked and answered while we clear the table. An interview with a famous surgeon, responsible for an organ transplant breakthrough, for example, will generally include two or three informational questions. A similar interview on prime-time will go into greater detail.

Another odd feature of these shows is their conglomeration of topics. After a light conversation with the reknowned acquitted murder defendant, a chat with a blonde starlet or model, some jokes among the hosts and a quick review of a hit movie, we may suddenly find ourselves confronted with a battered wife, an Auschwitz survivor or some other truly serious and grim subject. The uniformity of length and the framing of lightness and mirth tends to render these serious segments innocuous. They take up far less time on the whole than the light stuff and they are handled by our hosts with a psychological flexibility that is a model for all of us of what is required during a typical American day. They take it all in stride, just as, in reality, we must take in stride a host of similarly unpleasant, even traumatic facts and experiences during a day, and get on with our lives. We may be sexually harrassed, witness an act of cruelty, be exploited or robbed. Modern life demands that we not get too flustered or grim about any of this. Lighten up, have a Coke—just as the morning magazines do. If we must fall apart, file charges, or get a divorce, the morning shows help us to do these things too. Experts tell you how to make any crisis as smooth and painless as possible. Recovering from traumas as diverse as a child's bedwetting or nervous breakdown are handled in two or three minute segments in which the experts give us five simple rules or steps. "How to" is a kind of American religion whose links to the Protestant ethic of hard work and reward are evident.[9]

Woman's Work Is Never Done

Advice makes up most of the daytime programming between 10 A.M. and 5 P.M.—after the men and kids leave. No matter who happens to be home at the time, these shows assume that women will be the major viewers. And women, they know, whether they have outside jobs or not, have a day's work cut out for them. So much of the socializing and education of daytime TV is for women because it is women who cope with almost every emotional, social and physical crisis of modern life. To view these shows is to be astonished at what women are expected to integrate and absorb. While men are to be informed and children handled, women must do, do, do.

Women must not only follow rules, they must walk a fine and confusing line between liberation and reaction—a contradiction not yet officially solved by the media. Daytime's view of sexual issues—and other matters raised in the aftermath of feminism—is an ideological jumble of contradiction. There are the talk shows—"Donahue" and "Sally Jesse Raphael"—which tend to feature racy, controversial subjects and allow the audience—led by the enlightened host—to speak out freely. There are the more traditional magazines like "Hour Magazine" in which celebrities and experts help women do more traditional things like put on makeup, cook a flan and make a flower arrangement. And there are the new therapy-style shows in which a real doctor actually practices onscreen, either over the phone or right there in front of you, using actors to portray real clients and real problems. Most shows actually use a combination of traditional and hip approaches.

Although I have thus far avoided treating shows shown on cable, it is daytime TV that has been most affected by cable so far. Already the trendier topics and approaches on the various cable "lifestyle" channels and shows have started showing up on the networks. While the biggest winners in cable's nighttime programming are continuous news, music and feature films, daytime is flooded with new women's shows. There is so much to discuss and adjust to in the way of lifestyle issues that originality is still possible here. While most of the innovation is clearly liberal in approach, it is balanced by the smaller, but more ideologically dogmatic, Christian programming also geared to women. To see what is new and what is old in daily life, we can do some quick channel zapping.

CBS' "Hour Magazine" is the most traditional show. It uses the same content seen in the morning, except its only concern is household and social life. In a recent thirty minute period, there were five topics. First came film star Victoria Principal talking about her personal life and touting her beauty book—which listed eight "principles." Next came a couple who had delivered their daughter's baby on the freeway—just in case you should need to know how. Ryan O'Neal promoted a movie and discussed his personal life. Henry Rogers, the public relations honcho already seen several times that week, plugged his book on success—again with cliched rules for "how to" become one. A Hollywood gossip writer did and did not tell all. Her main point was outrage at the press for exploiting the drug and alcohol problems of stars and so making light of real problems. The irony here, as in the beauty and success segments, was its contradiction. "Wasn't it a shame about Mary Tyler Moore?" sighed the host, as photos and details of the star's problems were aired.

At their worst, these shows promise you things you cannot possibly have, and do and say things they pretend to abhor. They play on the desire in all of us for perfection and reinforce traditional meanings of the word. If we cannot be Victoria Principal, we can, as later segments reveal, take tips from other real housewives on those things we can reasonably expect to attain in the way of elegance and glamour: fancy table arrangements, high fashion for tots, French cooking.

At the liberal end of the network daytime magazine spectrum, far from the domestic, consumerist concerns of the traditional woman, are the shows in which actual women—and their families—participate. Whether it is "Donahue" or "Sally Jesse Raphael," these shows push the limits of what is acceptable, in topic and approach, including ideas and ways of living introduced by feminism and the lifestyle movements. The structures of these shows are looser, the content less predictable. Shock is one of the things that audiences hope for when they tune in. The introduction of new ideas and the inclusion of regular people in the formats are the two important features. They are participatory where "Hour Magazine" is dogmatic and static. Women are allowed to hear about somewhat racy things in these shows, and to mull them over and repeat them to husbands and kids if they choose. These programs, with many progressive and useful elements, are a sort of testing ground for changing social mores. The networks allow more play in these time slots because the audiences are relatively small and largely female. Like women's print magazines, they are bibles for the harried homemaker in a world of overwhelming change and responsibility. They may be the only places to turn when traumatic problems come up which are difficult to talk about. They are less superficial than the "how to" lists of celebrity salespeople. They are generally more respectful and sympathetic as well.

Phil Donahue has been doing this kind of thing for years. His technique is more sensational and more like the traditional shows than newer versions. He puts controversial or racy views or lifestyles onstage and lets the audience—really incites the audience—to go at them like bloodhounds. Sexual issues are popular. A program may feature women married to gay men or people who have overcome cocaine addictions. Usually these folks have a book, method or institution to push, and their own sets of rules to follow. Questions vary from the insulting to the intrusive. "Do you and your husband use the vibrator together?" may be asked. Donahue is also a stanch liberal in areas nonsexual, and is likely to bring on political dissidents as well as personally unusual guests. The result is to stretch the boundaries of traditional thought in these areas, to raise possibilities not before thought of. This is healthy.

Donahue's style, unfortunately, is often quite offensive in its sensationalizing of guests and their problems or ideas. His show began very early, as a local Chicago venture, and took off from there. Its popularity was certainly based to some extent on his own flamboyance. His effect, too often, was to give the show a freak show quality, stigmatizing the unusual guests in the process.

The new therapeutic and problem oriented cable talk shows are more dignified. Because the times have changed enough—and people's personal agonies and confusions have multiplied enough—we all see the need to take sexual and lifestyle issues seriously. Again, women and daytime are the proper times and audiences to discuss this situation because women must deal with it. Sexual variation and lifestyle differences have become recognized, within the framework of ideological debate and contradiction, as valid social issues.

The liberal therapeutic programs combine the raciness of Donahue's topics with the seriousness of the establishment advice shows. But the raciness is made to seem far less bizarre. What seems titillating on the networks seems quite sensible and ordinary when discussed by the hosts and therapists on daytime cable. To the extent that sexual repression has made women extremely eager to hear about, and hide their interest in, sex, the shows draw audiences. There is a real if limited kind of mass therapy involved. Once digested and absorbed, lifestyles and attitudes may change somewhat and the titillation may become normal concern. Network shows have already been influenced by this development.

It is cable that has brought about this trend, largely through the Lifetime channel. Lifetime started out as an all women's channel, a tribute to feminism's success. Economic problems, however, forced a merger with the Health channel. The result is a blend of health and women's concerns which implies that they are the same.[10] Thus feminism survives in pieces, but has been absorbed into the realm of consumerism. Women remain in their daytime ghetto. They maintain material and emotional life; they buy things. But these activities look, and are, in some important ways, different because of feminist values and perspectives. The victory is partial, but it is real.

Many of these shows come and go, changing and merging with enormous speed. Some are group talk shows on which real people come together to discuss and share a common problem and help viewers solve the problem in their own lives. These shows may offer advice and information on where to find help through social service agencies and support networks. This is a step forward. One typical "Woman to Woman" segment featured victims of date rape, an all too common event. Stories were told and responded to with appropriate sympathy and concern. Help and support were offered to women who had experienced or would experience rape in the future. A bit of the women's movement—limited as it was—was brought to viewers.

On some shows, actual psychotherapy occurs. The voyeuristic aspect of this kind of thing is obvious. Thankfully, actors usually play the parts of real people, or unidentified callers are quoted. Because of the commercial nature of TV, the exploitation of real people is always a huge danger. There is something painfully sad about having to turn to TV for help. As with game shows, this is not the fault of the participants, but of the way in which this society privatizes trouble, defines "shame" and provides nurture and support—or doesn't. The class bias against "airing one's dirty laundry in public" is based on the confidence of the wealthy in their ability to find and pay for more private forms of help. It is not a particularly healthy bias, even for those privileged enough to preserve it. In social terms, it is even less commendable. Social networks for expressing anxiety and obtaining support are essential to psychological well being. Politically, the open acknowledgement that problems are shared, that one's suffering is neither freakishly unique or entirely one's own fault, is liberating. As in women's consciousness raising groups, upon which these shows admirably model themselves, the realization that "the personal is political" brings both relief and power, at least potentially. In small measure these shows may broaden the reach of that message.[11]

The rightwing counterparts of these shows, as seen on Christian cable, are more varied, more slick and more popular than most people realize. While their primary subject is religion, an area rarely covered on daytime or primetime network TV, they manage to provide information and advice on just about everything the networks do, and in at least as sophisticated a manner. There are game shows, soap operas, rightwing rituals over which the Falwells and Bakkers preside, and musical variety shows. In each case, the range of topic and approach is circumscribed by a fundamentalist Christian perspective.

Talk and advice shows are the mainstay of Christian TV. Just as people watching "Donahue" and "Good Morning America" hear about how to do better as parents, spouses, and so on, so do the audiences of Pat Robertson's "700 Club." The cures offered—for sexual dysfunction, parenting woes, marital strife, illness, and everything else—are always based on a Christian, male-dominated nuclear family structure in which each member gives up her or his life to God—a God who speaks especially clearly to the father and husband.

Anyone who has watched these shows is aware of their power. There is no contradiction or disagreement. Labor problems, global political crises and lust for thy neighbor's wife are all cured by the same method. So are emotional illness, physical debility and homosexuality. There is the same reassurance, the same personality types chatting and sharing, the same swift pace and range of subject found on non-Christian TV. There is even, surprisingly, the same awareness and concern about the changing lives of women. "Women's Liberation" is no stranger to CBN. Christian wives and mothers have a lot to say about the importance of "doing your own thing," being a "partner" to your mate, and so on. The definitions of these things are odd, however. They manage never to challenge any rightwing idea about the family, chastity, and so on.

In the end, what we see on women's shows is the profound and often progressive influence of feminism, tempered by the power of television to redefine the concept in its own terms, to muddy its political ideas by blending contradictions and shifting the focus from social change to accommodation. Sexuality and femininity are great battlegrounds today. Right and Left are at war over them. When the dust settles, the networks and primetime will have somehow integrated the most important aspects of both. In the case of feminism and Christian fundamentalism, the results will surely reflect the struggle of political activists, progressive and reactionary, in the larger social world. The issues of pornography, abortion and gay rights are in heated contention at the moment. To the extent that the actors manage to influence the media and participate in it, they will affect both society and its TV mirror image. While the end result will undoubtedly be clouded by George Gerbner's concept of mainstreaming, progress may still occur. It will ultimately depend on the participation of various groups in a complex battle.

Nighttime Talk and Soft News

The original nighttime talk show was the late night "Tonight" show, back in the early 1950s. It established the major topics and limits that have prevailed since. It also established the concept of "fame as a value more precious than money, power, virtue, and kindness" by confusing "notoriety with persuasive power and visibility with impact."[12] It introduced the idea that celebrity alone was reason to listen to what someone had to say about any number of issues. Because it is a late night show, sexual innuendo is its mainstay. Rarely is anyone allowed to give a serious view on a serious subject. Everything is a joke to Johnny Carson and Joan Rivers.

While it is not widely known, there is a method of deliberate political censorship. Not only do guests go through rigorous preinterviews in which specific topics and approaches are mutually agreed upon, but there is also a great effort made to ensure that no one will in any way raise a political issue.[13] Anyone chosen to be a guest, especially if she or he is not appearing expressly to plug something, is checked carefully for what will be said. Only the most clever and bold celebrity will overturn the applecart by surprising the host with a controversial topic or view. Susan Sarandon once did that. An activist in MADRE, a woman's group opposed to U.S. intervention in Central America, she refused to follow Carson's lead and insistently repeated and expanded upon her views of American foreign policy. She has not been on since. Under these circumstances, personality and celebrity are all that the show can possibly "sell."

More recent nighttime shows have used different forms and approaches to continue and expand the national obsession with show business and celebrity. Soft news shows are the most visible examples of this. There are a variety of these shows that come and go, but there are two established formulas. We have already looked at "Lifestyles of the Rich and Famous." Another show which is usually dumped in the same superficial category is "Entertainment Tonight." The syndicated news show about the entertainment industry deserves some attention, however, because it is very different in important ways. It really is a news show, and it really does provide information found nowhere else on television. While its overall format, and many of its segments, appeal to the trivia-lover, it treats the entertainment industry as hard news. It gives economic and political news about the industry, much as the new cable "money" shows give such information about the financial world. It is specialized data of a kind anyone concerned about media will find useful.

"ET," as it is called, is a model of contradiction. It inflates and furthers Hollywood hype even as it debunks it. It alone consistently acknowledges that Hollywood *is* an economic and political world. The first few entries on the show are generally given over to serious things. When, in June of 1985, terrorists hijacked a plane and held Americans hostage, "ET" alone ran a serious survey of the way in which the networks handled the event, complete with media analysts' commentary. The head of CBS news, for example, made some general remarks about the role of television in this kind of political crisis—as close as we are likely to get to hearing network executives say anything about their theories and strategies. Media critics from national papers offered insightful comments on the visual effects created by the particular way in which the incident was handled. Others discussed the problems of media access or lack of it.

This way of calling attention to how the media "creates" news through its technical strengths and weaknesses is unheard of and important. It takes seriously the very issues raised in this book. Other items reported that night were the painting of a swastika on Screen Actors Guild president Ed Asner's door, and the buyout of *Us* magazine by *Rolling Stone*. This report included information on how a promotional strategy is developed in the magazine world, as well as segments on various cultural events, projections for the next season by ABC heads, and other industry transactions of the day.

Sometimes the show features political actions engaged in by entertainment people. In fact, almost any such event will be covered on "ET" and nowhere else. Protests aimed at the industry by groups concerned with racism, sexism, anticommunism or any other reactionary bias show up here alone. So do industry labor problems. It may well be the only place where progressive people within the industry are visible as social activists.

Even the star interviews are fuller and more informative than most, because they provide a sense of what it is really like to be a media worker with a seriousness that no other celebrity feature approaches. The daily features, the top five of every media form, box office grosses, openings, and so on, are interesting from a variety of perspectives.

"ET"'s ultimate message is that show business is the big time, for reasons that are anything but useful or progressive. In one sense this show does exactly what its detractors claim: it makes of glamour, celebrity and hype a bigger deal than it already is. But the fact is that it already is a very big deal, in ways most other shows deliberately mystify and deny. Such are the ironies and contradictions of television.

8

Made-for-TV Movies and Miniseries: Reality as Melodrama

When "The Burning Bed"—a made-for-TV movie about Francine Hughes, the battered wife acquitted of setting her husband's bed on fire—aired on NBC last fall it drew seventy-five million viewers and was the fourth highest rated TV movie ever. Its downbeat theme and grim "video *verite*" style made the movie an unlikely candidate for mass appeal, yet it drew the rapt attention of much of mainstream America and was rerun on primetime only six months later. "The Burning Bed" points to major changes in the role and nature of TV movies.

Made-for-TV movies and miniseries hold a unique position in primetime network broadcasting. They are the special events around which regularly scheduled series revolve. They are the "pills and modules the networks drop into their schedules for relief from the series habit." In an average season the three networks combined schedule about one hundred movies that have been developed and financed explicitly for television. Together, "they underwrite more original movies than all the studios combined." By 1980, TV movies were filling about 20 percent of primetime. By now the figure is even higher.[1]

The reasons for this development have to do with the changing roles of home TV and theatrical movies over the years. In the 1950s, when the major studios finally accepted the arrival of TV as permanent and significant to the future of American leisure patterns, they agreed to rent films to networks. Movies proved from the start to be high rating draws. However, Hollywood's rates were high, and grew higher still when the studios saw the profits networks were accumulating. By the mid 1960s, network executives reasoned they could cash in more substantially on the advertising revenues movies brought in by producing their own movies. They were right. By the mid 1970s sensational made-for-TV movies like "Little Ladies of the Night" and "Cry Rape" were outdrawing even current Hollywood rentals in

141

ratings.[2] When you consider that in the mid-1980s a TV movie costs about $2 million to produce, as compared to $9.4 million for a feature film and $14.3 million for a season series, the payoff is obvious.[3] Moreover, TV movies may often be rerun, and some are theatrically released in Europe.

It is not only money that has hurled the TV movie into such a position of prominence in TV programming. Given the ideological nature and social role of home TV, any genre that is singled out for such special audience attention will not for long be left as pure fluff or sensationalism. From the start, executives were willing to gamble on an occasional serious topic because of the need to be socially relevant on occasion. In 1977, one such venture, the miniseries "Roots," based on Alex Haley's best seller about the history of Blacks in America, astounded everyone with its blockbuster ratings. From then on, the potential for cashing in on serious, relevant themes was tapped more and more frequently. The combination of big bucks and artistic prestige—something TV had long despaired of achieving—was too good to believe.

By the 1980s, serious TV movies like "The Burning Bed," "The Blue and the Gray" (about the Civil War), and "Something About Amelia" (about incest), had become national events, with news shows presenting special segments to accompany them and publishers preparing study guides to send to high school and college teachers around the country. So universal was the the interest in "The Day After," the 1984 movie about the aftermath of nuclear war, that antinuclear activists were able to organize extensively around the event, calling public meetings and discussions which often developed into ongoing groups.

The form that TV movies now take, and the role they play as major social events around which national public debate on social issues takes places, grows out of this twenty year history. Again, the combination of functions on TV has shaped the made-for-TV movie. It is a unique form which differs in important ways from both theatrical films and weekly dramatic series.

Of all the TV genres we are examining, made-for-TV movies are the most philosophically interesting and categorically problematic. Some are pure fiction, some essentially "based on fact," some a mixture of both. It is the "based on fact" movies that I consider here as nonfiction. These are movies—usually called "docudramas"—which tell, in classic TV movie form, the story of an actual life or event. Still, the form demands at least some marginal tinkering with truth. It is never true "documentary." That is, it does not use actual footage of historic events and interviews with real people to tell its story. It uses actors, staged settings and dramatically written scripts in which dialogue is invented and events are themselves at times omitted, embellished, conflated and so on; hence the term "docudrama." Some TV movies and mini-series are properly called historic dramas rather than "based on fact" movies because, while they use historic background and details and even incorporate actual characters from life, their principals and plots are wholly invented.

The term "based on fact" does not imply the same kind of "real people and events" actuality as the other nonfiction forms. To complicate things further, it is even difficult to make clear distinctions between these movies and certain fictional ones which treat similar subjects and are almost identical in narrative and thematic strategy. I am including the genre in this study somewhat arbitrarily; it is a borderline case, to be sure. The analysis presented here will perhaps confusingly bounce from one variety of social issue TV movie to the next quite freely because the boundaries are so vague and the dramatic similarities so obvious.

"Based on fact" movies and their fictional siblings which treat important social issues mark the cutting edge in that blurry continuum of fiction and nonfiction TV forms. They provide a way of demonstrating how and why network TV came to so conflate truth and fantasy in all its forms. For this reason, they throw more light on certain key aspects of the concept of "nonfiction television," as it is used here, than more typical forms. It seems particularly important to discuss this form.

From its inception, the decisions about a social issue movie reflect, in exaggerated form, the ways in which other nonfiction forms—even nightly newscasts—are produced: with an eye toward visual and dramatic concerns at least as much as absolute truthfulness. In initial concept meetings, it is theme and form, not fact or fiction, that are discussed. All nonfiction TV takes the shape it does because it is conceived and executed largely on the basis of formal, esthetic considerations.

When a TV movie about a social issue is planned, chances are, whether it begins with fact or not, the producers will freely use fictional material to make the topic "work as a movie." Robert Greenwald, who works primarily with social issues by choice, prefers "true stories" because "they usually have more drama." However, once underway, he may "move away from fact" whenever necessary. A movie about the juvenile justice system, for instance, which began as fact, ultimately moved away from it when Greenwald found "I didn't have enough to make a whole movie." He then "combined two themes I was interested in, plant closings and juvenile detention" to "make the story work."[4] As we can see, creative considerations take precedence over historic, although not thematic ones. That is also true, however, to a greater extent than is usually realized in nightly news reports. Concern for dramatic footage and narrative structure is always a factor. Ideology is also a factor, although that word is not used in story meetings. To serve the public interest—the rationale that permits serious social drama—while not offending the corporate sponsor or Standards and Practices, means producers must stay within a certain range of topics and approaches.

Sources for social issue movies may be almost anything. The concern for reestablishing family closeness played up on the AT&T "Reach Out and Touch" commercials may have originated with the same source material as the human interest magazine show feature on the "fate of the family." Creators of both see the same market research studies and news reports. "I look at TV commercials to look for a trend," says producer Deanne Barkly, who actually used the telephone commercials as the basis for a movie story idea.[5] That the material which ultimately becomes a serious social issue movie can as easily come from a real event, a social trend or a TV commercial, with no noticeable difference in end result, may seem bizarre. Bizarre or not, it is true, and it says something about the peculiar dramatic style that characterizes all TV programming.

Social issue movies, both "true" and invented, follow the same strict formulas. There is a single heroine or hero to whom things "happen." The protagonist's individual efforts are seen to effectively solve personal and social problems. Plots are simple and spare so that no one will fail to understand them. Little room is left for the development of atmosphere, nuance or ambiguity of character. Issues are seen as isolated rather than endemic to society, and therefore they are resolved through a single heroic action. Historical perspective is almost nonexistent, even, surprisingly, in historic drama. The events simply begin and end in temporal isolation; there is usually no past or future. There is almost always a happy ending, an answer to problems, a new horizon to walk off into. Finally, characters and settings generally reflect the values and lifestyle presented in commercials.

Even a movie like "The Day After" was presented not as political drama but as domestic crisis. Its settings were the usual mainstream American living rooms. Its characters were straight out of "Father Knows Best" and "The Waltons." When the bomb dropped, it disrupted a myriad of personal crises. And when the ads came on, they too were family oriented. "Are you worried that your kids won't make it to college next year?" asked the man from IBM ironically. "Well, get them a home computer." This lack of political or historical perspective fit well with the movie itself. Like most TV movies, "The Day After" allowed for no past, no public world, no class or race differences, at least not as significant social factors. Everyone was a member of a nuclear family, but no other group designation seemed to exist. The hero, a doctor, was a professional male, a father of course. Every household contained furnishings and appliances, every character wore clothing and used grooming aids, mirroring their counterparts in the ads. The plot allowed for no dalliances that didn't obviously and immediately build the main action. In made-for-TV movies, as critic Stephen Farber has said, "the purely transitional scenes that create mood and atmosphere...are inevitably rushed or abbreviated while the evocation of character through purely visual storytelling is less highly refined"[6] than in film.

The intrusion of the political world, through the device of the home TV set around which each family's life revolved, served to make nuclear war an essentially private domestic problem in the fictional "Day After." In exactly the same way, the intrusion of personal life and its problems, the fictional Mitchum character and his family, made the supposedly "nonfictional," historical "Winds of War" primarily a domestic drama too. That is what TV always does to historic and social issues. It domesticates them, personalizes them, makes a purely private and individual matter of every problem which in reality we face collectively. These issues seem totally beyond change, except insofar as our limited personal powers allow.

This is not to say that TV movies are generally stupid. On the contrary, they are often quite serious, stylistically and emotionally realistic and even helpful to those suffering from the problems treated. In the better offerings there is often intelligence, insight and even depth. Since these movies are one shot deals, dependent on huge promotional campaigns with inviting come-ons for ratings, they can risk unpleasant or complex subjects now and then. "TV isn't afraid of downbeat stories," says Lawrence Schiller, producer of the TV version of Norman Mailer's *Executioner's Song* about convicted murderer Gary Gilmore, "because it doesn't depend on word of mouth."[6] "Executioner's Song" was seen theatrically all over Europe, but only on TV here. Bad box office for grim films like *Raging Bull* had made U.S. distributors wary.

Even topics which seem primarily titillating can at times be treated with sophistication and seriousness in TV movies. "You need an idea that will grab an audience in one sentence," says Greenwald. And while this can be pure exploitation and junk, it can also be a topic like incest, which is too serious and demanding to make a big box office theatrical hit. TV is contradictory. It can—must—do several things at once. So it is not surprising that in spite of the common disdain in which TV is held, more and more people have come to agree with TV producer David Wolper that "cinema today is popcorn fare, while TV has taken over the role of serious drama."[8] Overstated as this is, it bears a grain of truth.

Sex and the Modern Female TV Viewer

Historical epics like "Winds of War," about World War II, are among the most common forms of TV movies, especially miniseries. They serve an obvious educational function. They teach the major beliefs and values of our culture to a society largely disaffected, badly educated and consumed with the pleasures and traumas of personal life. Before looking at them, however, I would like to look at the other most common type of TV movie, the one which treats personal and domestic crises, most typically of the kind experienced by and of concern to women.

In fact, the area in which TV movies have most successfully usurped the role of cinema is that of "women's films." In the 1930s and 1940s, movies like *Stella Dallas* and *Mildred Pierce* dramatized the conflicts and contradictions of female experience in a sexist, material- istic world. Now TV does this. This is understandable and in keeping with TV norms. TV, after all, is a domestic medium meant for family consumption. It has always favored domestic drama—whether in soaps, sitcoms or movies—because of its audience, and because of its social and commercial functions. Women, as discussed in the previous chapter, buy most of the consumer goods sold on TV. Women handle much of the emotional and social negotiation and nurturing that comes with social and moral upheaval. And TV movies—like the products they sell—are often about this kind of thing.

The range of issues and qualities in these women's films varies quite a bit. Most common, and generally most popular, are the movies about sexual issues, the titillating, often downright trashy entities like "Dallas Cowboy Cheerleaders" and "Hollywood Wives." But even "trash" says something real, something socially relevant to women. It is no longer accurate or useful to dismiss sexual themes as mere sensationalism or escapism. Sexuality for women in the post-feminist 1970s and 1980s is very much a social issue, as we saw in the discussion of daytime magazines. Sexual repression and stereotyping have plagued and inhibited women throughout the modern era. Women— particularly "nice respectable" wives and mothers—have been largely deprived of a public arena, language and imagery with which to discuss and analyze their sexuality. TV's producers and sponsors have responded to this.

Whether or not TV executives care about feminism, they do care about women viewers. They know that women are intrigued by sexual themes that explore areas considered "taboo." Of the top twenty all-time rating champs of made-for-TV movies, seven have been sexually titillating treatments of themes of concern to women. Most seem to be about adult or teenage "runaways" from middle class respectability. The theme of illicit sex, especially when it involves women from middle class families becoming somehow involved with prostitution, has proved a near certain audience draw.

Most of these movies are presented from the woman's or girl's point of view. "Dawn: Portrait of a Teenage Runaway" and "The Minnesota Strip," for example, are composite docudramas—the term used for "based on fact" movies—based on real cases in which teenage girls run away from unhappy homes and end up as hookers. In this formula, the girl's family is seen first. They are portrayed as insensitive to her needs and feelings, perhaps because of preoccupations with other things. Sometimes they are emotionally abusive and puritanically repressive about her social life. Dawn's mother actually drove her away out of jealousy at her husband's greater affection for his daughter. When the girl leaves, she discovers a street world which seems to offer freedom, but which in reality offers danger, degradation and exploitation. A social service agency intervenes. Usually, she reconciles with her family through therapy. In Dawn's case, she finds a substitute family, better than her own, to adopt her.

On the one hand, we have a dramatization of certain common fantasies of sexual rebellion and escape from middle class repression. On the other hand, we have a neatly affected resolution to these problems and a vision of the traditional family structure as flexible and capable of responding to a young woman's needs. Not least, of course, we have a cautionary vision of the dangers that await the woman who tries to escape the protection of the middle class family. It's a vicious world out there and it makes more sense to stay within the family unit than to venture out into the dark world of sexual freedom.

A more interesting TV movie, "A Touch of Scandal," aired in 1984. It starred Angie Dickinson as a very liberal public official (she supports the farm workers, gay rights, etc.) running for office. Her husband/manager, played by Don Murray, has severe sexual hang-ups. He hasn't slept with her in years because, "It's not one of my priorities." Just once, Dickinson uses the services of a young male hustler, an ex-client of hers. The Byzantine plot involves blackmail, car chases and other paraphernalia of the cops and robbers genre. What is interesting is the wholly supportive attitude the movie takes toward Dickinson's need for, and right to, sexual pleasure. The movie ends with the scandal averted, the office won, and the husband agreeing to see a therapist. Neat and clean again. Still, for women in the audience, the message was clear: women are sexual beings who, when respectable marriage fails them, are justified in seeking satisfaction outside the bonds of matrimony—even as far outside as paid prostitution. Again, of course, the solution is found in patching up the bad marriage through counseling and therapy.

Not all TV movies about sexual themes are this sympathetic to women. Some reflect an obvious male backlash against what seems an aggressive encroachment by women onto traditional male turf. Movies about incest and other forms of sexual abuse of children, for example, are generally presented from a male—even a patriarchal—perspective. The role of the male as owner/protector of society's children is often featured when TV treats this volatile theme. A 1984 TV movie called "Kids Don't Tell" was typical. It was about a male documentary filmmaker doing a film on sexual abuse of children. As he became more emotionally involved with his subject, his wife's behavior grew more and more bizarre. Portrayed as a bit of an airhead anyway, she became increasingly demanding and frivolous, trying desperately to draw him away from his "unpleasant" work. Her resistance to discussing what was to him a matter of critical importance—both socially and emotionally—intensified, pulling them further apart. The outrageous resolution to this fantasy of patriarchal power and authority was predictable: the wife had been an incest victim herself. The husband, with his boundless compassion and insight into the problem, was able not only to produce a social document which would help all society's abused children, but was also, on the domestic front, able to comfort and "cure" his pathetic, childlike wife of her personal trauma.

The image of sex offenders in this movie was as reactionary as its personal politics. They were nothing less than evil demons, determined to continue their nasty practices and incapable of guilt, remorse or compassion. The political solution was inevitable: since rehabilitation was seen as an impossible liberal myth, incarceration, implicitly for life, was the only logical answer.

This movie was admittedly dumber than most. Even a better, more sophisticated and liberal treatment of the topic of incest—the much acclaimed "Something About Amelia"—presented an essentially male perspective on a topic which should have focused on the suffering and exploitation of the female victim. This movie, about a respectable middle class family, probed more deeply into the psychology of the perpetrator and the family dynamics which too often make male abuse of female children a fact of family life. First, the marriage of the parents was presented as lacking in sexual intimacy and emotional communication. The father, a nice guy played by Ted Danson of the popular situation comedy "Cheers," turned to his daughter for the things his marriage lacked. When the daughter, in desperation, told a teacher about her unbearable situation, her mother was unwilling to believe the story.

In the end, through the efficacious use of various social agencies—the law, the school, therapy—the father was able to admit and apologize for his behavior and, gradually, to change. The family was preserved and the daughter and mother could once again love and welcome back the sinner. While there were many positive aspects to this well made movie, from a feminist point of view there were also problems. For one thing, the father was the central character. Only he was shown feeling regret, remorse and excruciating emotional pain. Only he was seen to change and grow. The women were largely props in this essentially male saga of guilt and redemption. Never was the issue of institutional sexism mentioned, despite its role in encouraging, even permitting, the males in a family to use their female dependents sexually. Yet, a full 98% of incest victims are females abused by male parents or other family members, a fact brought out in the discussion which followed on "Nightline."

The movie did many important things. It informed its huge audience of the dimensions of this very real, generally hidden, problem. It proposed therapy—with its implicit assumption of human decency and ability to change—as a solution, rather than the "lock 'em up and throw away the key" law and order tack of "Kids Don't Tell." It did not address the social roots of the problem; and it did not sufficiently acknowledge the torment of the female victims. Amelia was never even seen expressing rage or hatred for her father. He was, after all, her father. From the movie's point of view, the need to keep the family together by patching up Daddy was far more important than dealing with real female grievances.

An interesting contrast to "Something About Amelia" was the 1985 treatment of a family coming to terms with a homosexual son, "Consenting Adult," based on Laura Z. Hobson's novel (itself based on an "actual case"). The issue of male homosexuality, unlike incest, strikes at the very core of society's patriarchal assumptions about masculinity and its social functions. "Consenting Adult" did a fine job—within the limits of TV's ideological imperatives—of exploring and critiquing those assumptions. Like "Amelia," "Consenting Adult" put the "crisis issue" in a broader context, making the connections between the individual family members' attitudes toward the key issue and their own personal hangups about emotional relations, sexuality and parental control.

The father, a high-powered businessman played by Martin Sheen, was recovering from a stroke. The sexual problems within his own marriage, however, predated his illness. The mother, a suburban housewife, was clearly—and typically—the moral and organizational force within the family. Used to controlling her children, even getting her primary sense of worth and achievement from this job, she was a domineering, at times overbearing, figure. The movie dramatized the classic stages of each parent's coming to terms with the son's announcement—as a virginal college freshman—that his sexual interests were exclusively toward men. An older, hipper married sister was the voice of reason. She lectured her mother on the need to let go, to let her children make their own decisions and do their own thing. Her need to dress and do her hair as she saw fit was compared to her brother's need to make his own choices about sexual partners. The mother, at first shocked, then guilty and ashamed, finally came to accept and even embrace her son and his new lover.

This is what TV movies do best. They show us how to handle current, emotionally difficult problems in a healthy, relatively enlightened and progressive way. Out-of-the-closet gays are here to stay, and the movie tells all us parents out there we had better adjust to it. Gay sex is okay, normal, not an "illness" as the amazingly stable and self assured young hero explains to everyone in earshot—from his shrink to his roommate to his Dad. If you learn to see that, you won't lose your loved ones, won't destroy your family, and your own emotional and sexual life may well improve as a result of your loosening up a bit about things like this.

This movie was quite moving because of its emotional intelligence and sophistication. Its only weakness was that, like most such movies, it assumed that "the family" was an upper middle class suburban one existing in a social and political vacuum. There was no gay liberation movement anywhere. There was no sense of social background or context, beyond a brief mention of AIDS and a surly, "These kids and their 'lifestyles'!" In fact, there was no world at all outside the Beverly Hills landscape against which all the action took place. Issues of class and race did not come up. The young man was a swim team champ and pre-med student; he was blond, gorgeous and impeccable. So was his live-in lover, another pre-med student. In the end, when Mom could finally bring herself to invite this boy to Christmas dinner, it was as though she were dragged kicking and screaming into something most mothers would drool over: not one but two handsome, blond, "my son the doctors."

Working class families in TV movies are treated very differently from the classy folk in "Something About Amelia" and "Consenting Adult," who are more or less the descendants of Ozzie and Harriet and Ward and June. When movies based on actual events do treat working class and Black families, the solutions offered are not different, however. The genre seems to work to bring all of us into the white, middle American fold, at least in our beliefs, values, and lifestyles.

Among the best of the TV movies of family crisis was "The Burning Bed." It managed to present domestic violence seriously and compassionately. The violence itself, while useful in drawing audiences, was not sensationalized. The perspective was in keeping with feminist analysis. Still, it managed, through tampering with facts, characterizations, and—not least—the ironic subtext created by the commercials, to limit its feminist message.

"The Burning Bed" is told in flashback, as Francine Hughes (Farrah Fawcett), having turned herself in for killing her husband, tells her story to her court-appointed lawyer (Paul Masur). The structure is spare and economical. Each segment relates a significant turning point in Fran's journey to desperation. We first see her as a teenager in the early 1960s smitten by the worldly Mickey (Paul LeMat) with his Elvis Presley pompadour and air of worldliness. No one has ever seemed to need her so much; his every cliche brings stars to her eyes.

Immediately after the wedding and move to his parent's home, the violence begins. The scene in which he first hits her is loaded with sociological and psychological information. She has bought a new blouse to please him and he reacts with jealousy. Moments before we learned that Mickey had no intention of finding work and was prone to booze. Fran is already pregnant, feeling trapped and terrified.

The scene is incredibly powerful. The setting, a shabby house filled with too many people with too many problems, reverberates with tension, fear and hostility. Having established Fran's shock and fear, Mickey's irrational rage and the parents' refusal to acknowledge any problem, director Greenwald allows the inevitable blows to erupt wildly and end as abruptly. The emotional and atmospheric resonance of the scene, done with a rawness unusual for TV, is nonetheless constrained—almost squashed and flattened—by the structural and ideological requirements of the form. There is simply no time or space in this form to elaborate on emotional nuance and implication. There is information here, a lesson about male violence and family and state complicity. When the emotional impact threatens to stretch the boundaries of that ideological framework, it is the emotional impact that is cut off.

The movie continues relentlessly to portray the escalation of Mickey's destructiveness and Fran's desperation. The story is classic. Fran loves her children, even believes she loves Mickey. How else could she have married him? Every agency and family member corroborates this simple message: you are "a family," you must take the bitter with the sweet. In the end, Fran's desperate act to save herself and her children seems too inevitable to question. Throughout, there is the marvelous, lowkeyed sense of the ordinariness, the dreariness, really, of this kind of life.

The violence and its larger implications about human nature, sexual relationships, and the repressive role of the traditional family, is always muted and contained because the movie has a simple, one-case-at-a-time approach. Fran's solution is a plea of temporary insanity devised by her white, middle class lawyer, who wears his three piece suit like a uniform from another civilization. This plea was in fact used by the real Francine Hughes. It was developed with the help of feminists, however, who organized a defense fund and publicized the trial as a political trial. That the movie leaves feminism and the women's movement out; that it credits an individual—a traditional TV hero at that—is typical of these movies.

The reason for the muted quality of the film's subject—violence—is that violence is not entirely what it is about. It is about solving the "problem" of violence with methods which reflect the values TV always champions: the law, middle class respectability, individual action. The Hughes story differs from most TV movies in focusing on a working class family, but what a family it is! It is nothing like the "real" American families that smile out at us, again and again, in the soap and furniture polish ads that sponsor this "women's" movie. These ads reflect the world of Francine Hughes' lawyer (and of the families in the movies discussed earlier). It is a world of order, reason, cleanliness and the kind of joy that comes from having your husband notice that you used Downy—especially if he's the kind of husband who does important work and cares about women. This irony is implicit of course. It is no part of the director's intent. The production of the movie proceeds without giving thought to the ideological subtext created by commercials. Nonetheless, the experience of watching a network movie is one in which this subtext figures. It is important to point out, too, that while "The Burning Bed" was "based on fact," it differed in no significant way from the fictional movies examined above.

Occasionally, there are TV movies about women who actually confront social issues arising from the community or workplace, rather than the family. These tend to be among the best of the genre. But they too end with simple, contradictory messages about women and society, social activism, and the possibilities of making effective, broad changes in the structure of American institutions.

"Lois Gibbs and the Love Canal," also produced by Greenwald and "based on fact," told the story of a working class housewife's struggle to organize her neighbors to fight the corporation responsible for polluting the water their children drink. Like "The Burning Bed," the "Lois Gibbs" heroine changed from a passive, obedient wife and mother to a fighter out to save her own and her children's lives. While the movie was stylistically less impressive than "The Burning Bed," it made up for that with an almost unheard of dramatization of real political organizing among working class women. Its subtle portrayal of the way Gibbs and her friends develop an understanding of what they are up against, and a determination, rooted in anger, to win, is memorable.

Gibbs is portrayed as a woman bent on justice at all costs—even her husband's job and the family's livelihood. When her husband understandably balks at his wife's mission, she allows the relationship to end and goes on alone. Again, however, there is no hint that Love Canal is anything but an isolated case, no attempt to broaden the message to a general indictment of corporate greed and lack of social responsibility. The villains, whether corporate or governmental, are merely mean, hardhearted men. They represent no one but themselves and their sins are never broadly social or political.

Gibbs wins her case but her future is unclear. Like Fran Hughes, she is seen as acting primarily as a wife and mother. There is a subtle subliminal message too: if you get too serious about politics you will lose your man. Most importantly, the movie shows that social problems, women's problems, no matter how deadly, can be solved on a case by case basis.

Taken as a whole, movies about women and social issues are among the best things on TV, artisticly and socially. The blending of fact and fiction, didacticism and art, which the TV movie form requires, works very well at engaging women viewers and speaking seriously to their problems. Whether the issues are sexual or social, they portray women as active and effective, as the centers of human activity. Women are seen as sexual beings, and as subjects, rather than objects. They may take on the male power structure and educate men about human and emotional relations. Often, they are friends and co-workers. Most importantly, they are seen as powerful in any number of ways.

These movies tend to distort the role of social and political institutions quite a bit. The extent to which we are influenced, and stifled, in our efforts to achieve our dreams of personal happiness and social justice by powerful, all pervasive institutions is played down, while the role of individual action and character is exaggerated. This is a necessity given the need to create personal, human interest stories dictated by the form itself. As heroic tales they are effective for those very reasons. When, as in the Francine Hughes and Lois Gibbs stories, social institutions are incorporated to a greater extent than usual, the heroism is even more impressive and believable. This is not achieved as often as we might wish, but it happens quite a lot.

History as Melodrama

While the movies we have been looking at have not all been based on "real life," they have all attempted to approximate social reality and incorporate elements of fact and verisimilitude. In that sense, they are the same as the movies we are about to examine: the officially proclaimed sagas of real historic events. We have already sketched out the formal and stylistic characteristics of made-for-TV movies and miniseries: their emphasis on simple, clear plot development and elimination of ambiguous, complex psychological and atmospheric factors; their tendency to present all issues as principally personal and domestic, moral rather than political; their upbeat messages about social solutions to these problems within the framework of existing values and structures.

Looking more closely at two representative historical miniseries, we can see how these very features—rationalized by network producers in terms of technical necessity and the need to draw mass audiences—are quite political in nature and implication. The way history has been treated on TV is fully in keeping with the personal, domestic values of the family, consumerism and individualistic solutions to all human problems, even political ones. That is the politics of TV.

The series I have chosen to examine both treat major issues of historic import, but from radically different perspectives. "Roots," the 1977 miniseries based on Alex Haley's book about the experience of Blacks in America from slavery to the present, was ground-breaking in content and record-breaking in ratings. The 1985 series "Robert F. Kennedy: The Man and His Times," also focused on the question of race relations, among several other political and social themes. But it did so from the perspective of the Kennedys, a ruling class family whose power and influence, not to mention charismatic attractiveness, comes as close as this country has ever allowed to royalty, a dynasty of the kind now regularly celebrated on primetime soap operas. Yet, the effect of both series was to reinforce the same view of family life, human nature, the American Dream and even American imperialism. Moreover, just as the TV movies about women's sexual and domestic problems tend to reinforce existing values and institutions while often espousing notably progressive attitudes, so do these seemingly different miniseries.

The thing that made the popularity of "Roots" such a surprise was its focus—from a Black perspective—on the reality of racism, often in its most brutal forms. Night after night, audiences sat in rapt attention as scenes of rape, disfigurement, beatings and other forms of inhuman cruelty—all done by whites to Blacks—assaulted their senses and sensibilities. For "eight consecutive nights, January 23rd to 30th, 1977, a record 130 million Americans—representing 85 percent of all TV-equipped homes—watched at least part of the series." The final episode attracted a staggering eighty million viewers, surpassing *Gone With the Wind* and the eleven Super Bowls as the highest rated TV show of all time. All eight episodes ranked among the top thirteen programs of all time. More than 230 colleges and universities decided to offer courses based on the series.[9] Such critical and popular success was previously unheard of.

What did it mean? Why the fascination with such a bleak view of white history? Why so little backlash? An enormous element of the show's appeal must be credited to the Civil Rights Movement and its long range effects. Having been educated by Blacks a decade earlier about the evils of racism, past and present, America had digested the bitterest pill of that message: the responsibility of whites for racist injustice and atrocity. The Haley book came on the scene as a perfect vehicle with which to translate that message to the small screen, in the public interest, certainly, and in a form that would at once entertain and educate.

The significance of this TV event, and the audience response to it, must not be underestimated. "Roots" stands as a major event in American social life: a shared national encounter with the realities of racism, especially the sexual, economic and violent aspects of it. For the first time, a cast of Black actors and actresses took center stage in a major media event in which their stories were central rather than peripheral. Just as "The Day After" and "The Burning Bed" made nuclear war and domestic violence national issues of debate and discussion, so did "Roots" take center stage in national consciousness. It was truly a phenomenon.

Its success rested to a great extent, however, on the way its subject matter could be fit into the pattern already established for social issue movies. Like women's movies, this series laid out the dimensions of a tragic social problem, only to show the problem being gradually resolved within the strictures of American democratic process. Particularly, the series tended to portray the triumph of the American Dream, its ability to expand its bounty to satisfy even the demands of a Black minority brought here as slaves, through the virtues of the family unit and the drive for monetary success.

Even the popular press felt compelled to comment on the series' generous use of sex and violence in rather sensational ways. As *Newsweek* pointed out, "ABC could not resist applying the now standard, novels for television formula: lots of softcore sex, blood, sadism, greed, big-star cameos and end-of-episode teasers."[10]

Beyond these obvious dramatic ploys, the real appeal of the saga was in its portrayal of the central importance of the family in American life, and its almost lightheadedly optimistic view of what Blacks could, and indeed had, accomplished in their quest for the American Dream. Coming on the heels of movies like *The Godfather*, "Roots" played on the growing interest in family and ethnicity in America, with all its implicitly clannish and reactionary undertones. It also rationalized and revised much of the history it presented by using a standard dramatic form: the rags to riches success story of the family who came, literally, from nothing, and pulled itself up—without the advantage of boot straps—to a position of respect and prestige in American society. Alex Haley's book—upon which the series was based—was subtitled "The Saga of an American Family." One critic described the series as "a dramatic allegory comparable to a medieval morality play, being neither fact or fiction, but a didactic popular entertainment."[11] Haley himself thought that the appeal of his work derived from the average American's yearning for a sense of heritage and from the "equalizing effect" of thinking about family, lineage and ancestry, which are concerns shared by "every person on earth."[12]

The many historical inaccuracies of "Roots" have been extensively documented by historians. Haley himself has admitted to several. His depiction of Kunta Kinte's tribal origins in Africa, for example, are full of distortions which Haley justifies in the following way: "Blacks long have needed a hypothetical Eden like whites have."[13] The African scenes, as shown in the televised version, were largely truncated anyway. ABC was eager to get the action out of Africa and into white America. According to producer David Wolper,

> The TV audience is mostly white, middle class whites. That's why we got out of Africa as fast as we could. I kept yelling at everyone, get him to Annapolis, I don't care how. Tell the boats to go faster. Put on more sails. I knew that as soon as we got Kunta Kinte to America, we'd be okay."[14]

Almost every segment of "Roots," moreover, ended on an upbeat note of success, achievement, hope. The heroes, through the generations, are the male heirs of Kunta Kinte who struggle valiantly and successfully not for themselves but for their families. Chicken George, for example, returns from his triumphs as a cockfighter in Britain not to fight for freedom, but to serve his immediate family.

The individualistic, family-oriented approach is typical of all TV movies. Its political implications—its sins of omission—are in this case particularly serious. As historian Eric Foner has noted, "the narrow focus on the family inevitably precludes any attempt to portray the outside world and its institutions." To do this, he continues, "would undermine the central theme of 'Roots'—the ability of a family, through unity, self-reliance and moral fortitude, to face and overcome adversity."[15] Political values—freedom, social consciousness—have no place in this saga. It is a family success story, pure and simple, and its implications for Black viewers are clear, and ultimately reactionary: do not look to political movements for Black liberation; look instead to the family and the quest for personal, material success.

Ironically, seen from this perspective, "Roots" has more in common with the saga of "Robert F. Kennedy and His Times" than one would ever have imagined possible. Here too we have a male hero, a loyal member of a tight knit, ethnic family for whom political struggles are perceived in terms of individual and family goals almost exclusively.

Like "Roots," "RFK" takes great liberties with history. John Siegenthaler, a journalist who worked with Robert Kennedy in the Justice Department in the 1960s, when Kennedy was Attorney General, points out many of them. "In order to serve the peculiar demands of docudrama, situations were created that never occurred, lines are delivered that never were spoken, developments that spanned months or years were telescoped into minutes and even seconds."[16]

What Siegenthaler calls the "demands of docudrama" are more ideologically significant than he imagines, or at least admits. He is actually quite content, for example, with the portrayal of Bobby Kennedy himself. "His love of family, his unswerving loyalty and his passion for social justice come across accurately," says this former friend and colleague. Only the portrayal of John F. Kennedy "as one whose big role was to help his younger brother run the federal government" and the "counterfeit caricature of James P. Kennedy, Sr.," seem to bother him.[17] But here we are quibbling about individual personalities, not political or historical matters. The fact is that "Robert F. Kennedy and His Times" was—as its very title asserts— about the younger brother. Its political and personal messages were bound to be presented in terms of its central character's role, and not his brother's.

The interesting question about this series is why Bobby Kennedy, and why in 1985? The answer lies in the tensions that exist between the often liberal, idealistic values of media producers, and the politically conservative needs of their corporate and governmental superiors. It is a tough tightrope to walk and TV movies dramatically reveal how cleverly it is done.

As the media had it—including such Left liberals as the *Village Voice*'s Jack Newfield (who appears as a character in the series)—Bobby was the most liberal Kennedy, the most principled Kennedy, the most socially conscious and concerned Kennedy. It is that media image that the series resurrects and embellishes, using its standard techniques of historical and personal omission and distortion.

In the age of Reaganism, Robert F. Kennedy quite understandably would appeal to the producers of TV movies. Unlike brother Jack, whose moral lapses and imperialist policies have by now been widely exposed, Bobby was a pure family man and, apparently, a principled liberal. It is that image of the public servant from a wealthy, ruling class family that the series pushed.

As an historical figure, our hero was presented, in classic TV style, moving from one national and international conflict and crisis to the next, upholding the principles of justice and honesty against all opponents and singlehandedly winning each battle. His battles with Jimmy Hoffa, Lyndon Johnson and J. Edgar Hoover were presented as so one-sidedly black and white as to defy belief. All three opponents were neurotic, immoral and scheming caricatures. All the better and more satisfying to see them slain by the moral virtue and purity of our hero.

Embarrassing or difficult historic moments—the Gulf of Tonkin is the most glaring—are simply eliminated. Again and again, Bobby is the voice of progressive reason. He argues for and personally involves himself in the fight for Black civil rights, for economic and political rather than military policies in Southeast Asia, Latin America, and so on. Moreover, his one publicly exploited character flaw—ruthlessness—is proven beyond doubt to be false. He has a "personality" problem, not a social or political flaw, as his wife Ethel understands and repeats throughout the series. The flaw is that he lacks the easy charm and charisma of brother Jack. But since Jack is portrayed as a preppie fraternity boy anyway, the "flaw" is made to work in his favor. Unlike Jack, he is not shallow or glib, but has the kind of depth that excuses, even requires, a flaw or two, especially if it implies sincerity. And no matter what his personality flaws, he does manage to do whatever is needed and ends up being right anyway.

It would be wholly misleading, however, to focus only on the series' presentation of history as a battle of one pure soul against the mass of idiots and crooks in high places. "Robert F. Kennedy and His Times," no less than any other TV miniseries, takes place in the context of—and primarily in the physical surroundings of—the personal family realm. Ethel and Bobby's marriage is idyllic and perfect. Every key decision Bobby makes involves a long process of personal discussion and debate with the ever-available, ever-sympathetic, ever-wise Ethel. Bobby is continually shown snuggling kids, knee deep in diapers and bottles. There is no question that Bobby's public role is subordinate to—or at least indistinguishable from—his family role, both as a member of a Catholic ruling class dynasty and as a husband and father.

The structure of the series is, again, a lot like *The Godfather*. The scene continually shifts up and back between the Kennedy home and the wider world he personally, and single-handedly, alters and improves. But unlike the Hollywood movie, there is no irony here, no sense of contradiction between the demands of the secluded, loving, emotionally involving family, and those of the nasty political world of ruthlessness and deceit. Where Coppola showed how concern for family could—and did—lead to the most heinous, bloody and immoral of public acts, the chronicle of Bobby Kennedy's life does exactly the opposite. There is no such contradiction as long as our hero can be shown acting consistently and effectively in the public realm on the basis of the same values that inform his private life. A neat trick, but one which TV has developed, literally, to an art.

This brings us back to the amazing similarity between the Kennedys and the descendants of Kunta Kinte, as portrayed in TV miniseries. As long as you do not deal with capitalism as a system with moral implications; as long as you do not deal with racism as an institution deeply embedded in the successful workings of our society; as long as you don't ever present social and political movements as influential, even crucial, in achieving progressive social change; then you can actually present the descendants of ruling class families and Black slave families as being essentially identical.

The range of made-for-TV movies is great in both quality and political attitude. Like the magazine form, it allows for a wide range of perspective, although the contradictions which that fact raises are not obvious. TV movies are always isolated events. They do not reflect upon one another. Looked at as a whole, however, generalizations can be made. At their worst, they can be reactionary; at their best, very progressive and worthwhile, more so than the most popular theatrical films today. Still, they are forced to remain within a tight set of dramatic boundaries, the implications of which are more than esthetic in effect. It is to the credit of the most talented and serious producers and directors in the field that so many controversial and provocative examples exist to chip away at the face of hegemony.

9

Commercials: Television's Ultimate Art Form

> As a teenager, reading both Karl Marx and *Honey* magazine, I couldn't reconcile what I knew with what I felt. This is the root of ideology, I believe. I knew that I was being "exploited," but it was a fact that I was attracted.
>
> —Judith Williamson

It would be inconsistent to end this book without looking at the commercials which have been mentioned so often throughout. If we understand nonfiction television to be made up of forms which partake of elements of entertainment, information and sales, commercials certainly fill the bill. They may be the most perfect form for achieving this neat mixture. Certainly they are emotionally powerful, often fun to watch and filled with information and propaganda urging us to buy the commodities described.

It is hard to categorize the commercial as "art" or "information"; it uses elements of both. I have already treated forms which do this to a greater or lesser extent, although with less ambiguity. One withdraws from the label "art" in spite of the esthetic and fictional elements of commercials. They are not entirely informative either, however, since they do invent fictional narratives which serve as homilies, pointing up the commercial message.

As with made-for-TV movies, I chose to include commercials because of what they illustrate about TV's method of blurring categories rather than any pure definition of commercials as "nonfiction." They are so much like so many other forms, and in so many ways, that they are an important element in the overview of network TV's evolution in an institutional context. They serve, as no other form does, to illustrate the direct role of the corporate sponsor in influencing TV's esthetic and ideology. Sponsors no longer directly control program content, but do control the very similar content of commercials. To see the parallels between the style and message of the ads and those of programs is enlightening. It helps to make real the indirect role of sponsors in all TV production.

Perhaps because of the uneasiness described by Judith Williamson, so many of us, when confronted by the power, range and appeal of commercial advertising, refuse to acknowledge its significance. We know we are "being exploited," but "it is a fact that [we are] attracted," as Williamson says. "Publicity is the culture of consumer society." But "because we are...so accustomed to being addressed by these images, we scarcely notice their total impact."[1] And if we do notice, we feel better couching our perceptions in analytical rather than emotional or esthetic terms.

It is far more common to hear admissions of, and arguments for, admiration and even love of such TV series as "Hill Street Blues" and "Cheers" than for the commercials which frame and punctuate them. Yet, in technical skill, creative energy and production costs, most TV commercials are far more elaborate, slick and amusing than the shows they sponsor. Even a decade ago, a thirty second Campbell Soup spot in which Ann Miller danced Busby Berkeley style on the top of a soup can, cost $250,000. At that rate, a ninety minute drama would have cost $45 million—half again what Warren Beatty's film extravaganza, *Reds*, cost years later.[2] As Erik Barnouw has noted, "the commercial is a central element of TV entertainment, outshining most other elements."[3] Media critic Jonathan Price agrees. In his provocatively titled *Commercials: The Best Things on TV*, he lists the many ways "commercials outpace programs" and concludes: "if commercials are artful, the art is objective, not subjective; capitalist, not rebellious; part of a social activity, not a personal means of expression."[4] Whether "art" or not, it is a fact that 74 percent of viewers admitted, in a recent survey, to finding commercials "fun to watch."[5]

It is the power of commercials to entertain and persuade—their artfulness—that makes them a cornerstone of the corporate structure. Multinational corporate conglomerates buy 81 percent of all TV advertising time.[6] Commercials and programs do not conflict with, so much as complement, each other. In technical and stylistic matters, commercials have always set the standards which other programming forms have followed. The use of special effects, fast cutting and montage have been longtime commercial staples which news and dramatic forms have only recently begun to imitate. Even the character types, plots and themes of most fictional programming are determined, far more than most people realize, by the conventions of the commercial message, rather than vice versa.

History: There Really Was a Time When We Had No TV, Dear

When, as babies, we are first introduced to the TV screen, it is a permanent, central fixture in our homes, a totem around which the family gathers to "watch the news" or share a favorite drama or comedy. The first words a child utters, the first words she spells, the first songs he sings are, often as not, from TV commercials (as the producers of "Sesame Street" understood) rather than the nursery rhymes of earlier generations.

Those of us who remember the post-World War II advent of home TV are now in midlife. Soon there will be no one alive for whom TV's rise to cultural supremacy is lived memory, rather than an eternal fact of life. It makes sense, then, to trace the development of this institution in terms of the informing role played by commercial advertising in shaping it. For the rise of advertising and home TV are intimately linked.

In 1952, the sale of radio time accounted for more than 60 percent of every broadcast advertising dollar.[7] By 1954, TV boasted $500 million in advertising sales, while radio brought in only $44 million.[8] Vance Packard's classic study of the roots of TV advertising, *The Hidden Persuaders*, gives extensive evidence of the ideological aspects of that dramatic development. For a consumer society, real "need" was no longer the impetus for buying. The fact that "most Americans already possessed perfectly usable stoves, cars, TV sets, clothes, etc." made necessary a corps of new "scientists of desire" or "merchants of discontent" whose job it was to "stimulate" consumption artificially among those who "do not yet know what they need." The problems of this new, powerful profession were more esthetic than informational. The industry was eager to hire "gifted artists" whose job it was to "cope with the problem of rapidly diminishing product differences."[9] This they did, using a combination of "fact" and "fiction," imaginative and informational materials which have come to characterize the blurry world of TV in general.

By the 1960s, TV advertising had become so expensive that commercials had shifted almost entirely away from one or two minute spots to thirty second spots.[10] This put even greater demands on creative, graphic artists to use highly condensed montages of visual imagery accompanied by the briefest, often-repeated verbal messages. The move from factual information to visual and emotional appeal, based on symbol and image, was complete.

The formal and symbolic sophistication of contemporary television commercials, combined with their unabashed mixing of fact and fiction, hype and information, have had profound effects on our national political consciousness. For one thing, TV commercials tend to encourage people to see their identities in terms of what they consume, rather than what they produce. A worker with two cars and a color TV, for example, will gradually begin to see himself or herself as a member of the "middle class" rather than the "working class."[11]

According to Erik Barnouw, even the decline of American socialism is in part a result of the success of advertising. As words like "freedom," "love," "success," "fun," even "revolution" became attached to consumer goods rather than social structures, the appeal of socialism, or any radical reform, lost its urgency and meaning. In 1932, notes Barnouw, "the Socialist Party drew 884,781 votes." Such a figure has not been approached since. Of course other factors—particularly McCarthyism—have played major roles in this decline, but the power of television cannot be overlooked in analysing this political trend.

> [If] socialism had promised workers a share in the better things in life...television proclaimed it a birthright. The picture window of television showed that everyone could live there... Its images were a lesson in living. Soon it was spreading its message in a hundred lands, proclaiming the good life, the age of the consumer.[12]

In looking at the role of the commercial on network television, three things must be considered. First, the esthetics and techniques of TV ads have had enormous impact on the way in which programs themselves—both fictional and nonfictional—are visually conceived and executed. Next, the major dramatic and thematic conventions of commercials have had a seminal influence on the very content of both drama and informational programming. And finally, how viewers experience the flow of TV—from news to drama to ads—influences the meaning of every program we watch. This again is primarily attributable to the role of the ads. They can either reinforce or counteract the apparent "message" of any given program.

Marketing as Art

The esthetic power of advertising is a crucial component of its political role, because what advertising is meant to do demands the ability to transform mere commodities—through the use of images— into quite other things: objects of human desire, to be exact, which embody qualities impossible for material objects to really possess.

Raymond Williams has written about "the system of organized magic which is modern advertising." Far from being a sign of our society's overly materialist bent, says Williams, advertising "is quite evidently not materialist enough." It does not so much sell us material goods to fill material needs as it delivers myths and fantasies. Advertising "is the consequence of a social failure to find means of public information and decision over a wide range of everyday economic life. This failure is the result of allowing control of the means of production to remain in minority hands."[13]

In other words, the qualities and values promised us by the rhetoric of democracy are not being delivered. And so we have a huge industry—the advertising industry—whose function it is to fix in our minds the idea that these values can be realized through consumption, that using certain products will bring the fulfillment we all need and seek. Love is sold in ready-to-bake biscuit and cookie mixes. Success comes with a new car. Excitement and adventure, especially of a romantic and sexual nature, is contained in elaborately packaged perfumes and bath products. Progress and human betterment arrive through technology and science. Democracy itself has come to be defined almost entirely in terms of the vast range of product "choices" available to us.

Because of the enormous ideological burden placed on advertising in a world where things are generally getting worse and worse for more and more of us, it is reasonable to consider ads as paradigms of the worst TV messages about politics, human relationships and the good life. This is where esthetics plays its most subtle and powerful role. The impact of the visual image, especially when it is juxtaposed in rapid succession with many other images, is both compelling and emotionally affecting.

One of the most powerful and misunderstood features of TV commercials—and programs—is the way in which form itself, rather than mere content, communicates meaning. Most analysts of advertising are content to point out the absurdities of the overt messages. Of course the use of a new toothpaste or shampoo is not going to lead directly to true love. Of course the purchase of the proper breakfast cereal or fabric softener will not make husbands and children suddenly appreciate and express adoration for their wives and mothers. But advertisements are not linear or rational in method. They create meaning through juxtaposition of like and unlike, real and fictional elements. They take "certain elements, things or people from the ordinary world" and rearrange and alter them "in terms of a product's myth to create a new world, the world of the advertisement."[14] They function much as dreams and poetry do. They combine elements of reality with wish fulfillment fantasies in a way which touches us where our desires are deepest, and most unfulfilled. If, as Althusser says, "Ideology represents the imaginary relationship of individuals to their real conditions of existence,"[15] then TV commercials are ideology of the first order.

Examples of typical TV commercials bear this out. Everyone has a favorite example of a "really good" commercial. Usually it is visually startling. The series of Chanel perfume ads, run regularly during the Christmas season, are as good as any. There's the sexually suggestive one in which a physically beautiful man dives into a luxurious pool and comes up between the legs of a physically beautiful woman. The images of luxury and sensual perfection combine with pure eroticism to connect the product with an ideal of sensual pleasure and luxury unavailable to all but a few jetsetters. There's the more romantic ad in which a montage of sophisticated urban images—ultramodern glass highrises, soaring airplanes, and such—are intercut with brief scenes between a man and woman, dressed in sophisticated elegance, mouthing the "John," "Mary," romantic cliches of 1930s Hollywood. In the background, the Ink Spots sing "I Don't Want to Set the World on Fire," from the same romantic era. In all, it makes no linear sense. But the feeling and the promise are crystal clear. Older viewers, most likely to be buying Chanel for Christmas, will be reminded of the romance and glamour of their youths, as interpreted and remembered by Hollywood.

For younger viewers, the most effective ads are equally suggestive, but in a different way. The 501 Levi commercials are as artistically impressive as anything they sponsor, including most of the music videos they so strongly resemble. Street scenes of hip kids—having fun, being cool, hanging out—are shot in a funky "video *verite*" style that contrasts with the sophistication of the Chanel ads. The text reinforces the visual message: if you buy 501 jeans, you'll be as cool and laid back as most teenagers dream of being. "And now my hard to please woman's havin' a hard time pleasin' me," sings the proud but ever so casual owner of the 501s.

It is amazing that most of these ads last a mere thirty seconds. They manage to put together a range of images and emotions with a minimum of verbal explanation. Slogans are simple and often repeated and spelled out graphically. All the advertiser wants you to remember is the feeling you got from the ad, and the name and look of the product. They literally "promise you anything but give you Arpege." Advertising "is never a celebration of a pleasure-in-itself. [It] is always about the future buyer. It offers him an image of himself made glamorous by the product it is trying to sell. It makes him envious of himself as he might be."[16] But that "might be" is a fantasy, since the goods offered, in and of themselves, never embody the values that commercial art attaches to them.

From another angle, advertising is "an elaborate social and cultural form" which responds to "the gap between expectation and control"—in an economic system in which there is "a controlling minority and a widely expectant majority"—by creating a "kind of organized fantasy" which

> ...operates to project the production decisions of the major corporations as "your choice," the consumers' selection of priorities...[and] pretends to a linkage of values between quite mundane products and the now generally unattached values of love, respect, significance or fulfillment.[17]

It does this primarily with visual arts.

Marketing as Melodrama

Most commercials include elaborate dramatic situations and characters. They are miniature melodramas where narrative and imagery combine to promise fulfillment—whether emotional, social or economic. The typical forms taken by ads, the people shown, their problems and the solutions offered are all in keeping with the larger messages of TV programming. Just as perfume ads promise us a life of luxury, a la "Lifestyles of the Rich and Famous" or "Dynasty," and car ads promise the excitement of the Indianapolis 500, "Knight Rider" or "That's Incredible," most narrative ads promise us things we desire, things we have every right to enjoy, but which most of us will never experience.

Among the most common kinds of ads are those for over-the-counter medications, household and business supplies, appliances, and processed or prepared foods. Ron Rosenbaum reports that in the first week of September, 1977, "close to 50 percent of the spots on the CBS and NBC nightly news shows, and nearly a third on ABC" were for medications.[18] He lists nearly forty different product ads—from Dentucreme to Ex-Lax to Geritol to Pepto-Bismol—all of which were meant to inform us that the many ominous signs of the inevitable "debilitation of the body" could be quickly and easily eradicated with a pill, a cream, a suppository. We all know the way these ads go. First someone agonizingly tries to hide from loved ones the physical condition that is robbing her of her ability to have fun with them. Sometimes it's a middle-aged woman whose arthritis or constipation interferes with her plans to enjoy her husband or grandchildren. Sometimes the same woman agonizes over her husband's ailments. Lately, there has even been an ad in which a young wife's "headache" interferes with her sexual pleasure. In each case, someone suggests a cure. In each case, the results are miraculous. No more pain or "irregularity" to interfere with the joys of family life. No more ailing husband or child to worry over. No more headache to impede the sexual revolution. And it is all done through the marvels of chemistry and modern medical science.

The most elaborate versions of this theme are probably the ads for coffee and telephone services. Again and again, we are shown little dramas in which breakdowns in relationships are healed through brewing a cup of coffee or dialing a long distance phone number. The drama is symbolic of course. Coffee, after all, in our culture, suggests human beings cozily getting together in intimate situations. The husband who blows up and apologizes is forgiven and the damage healed with a cup of coffee. Sisters bridge the gaps that separate siblings in nuclear families by sharing coffee. So do employees and bosses. And every possible emotional trauma that comes with the endless mobility, the breakdown of family and community ties that characterize modern life, is healed through the simple slogan, "Reach out and Touch Someone" via AT&T.

What makes the best of these ads—the "Reach Out and Touch" campaign, the Brim and Taster's Choice series—so memorable is characterization and situation. It is hard to miss the fact that every situation assumes a prototypical formula for happiness which is based on the nuclear family, and each ad addresses familiar issues facing that institution today. Like soap opera, these ads dramatize the current circumstances we have been in and felt awful about. Then they suggest a fool proof answer. Even the ads for Visa credit cards exploit interpersonal problems common in a world of changing sex roles, in which "true love" followed by babies is still the ideal. For career women who "travel a lot," Visa can be the ticket to meeting a new man. "I just got my new card in the mail," says the female executive to her male counterpart, in the mailroom of their urban apartment building. "Want to try it out?"

All these "plots" and "characters" are unmistakably identical to the "plots" and "characters" that make up most of network TV programming, whether nonfiction or drama. On TV, all problems are presented as unique and individual, with no relation to history or other social forces. They are solved through the intercession of expert "heroes," often scientists, law enforcement officials, or representatives of other commercial or government institutions. Cures are rapid and complete. Health problems, for example, whether on the nightly news, "St. Elsewhere," or "The Guiding Light" are personal tragedies which only the most eminent doctor, using the most up-to-date equipment and drugs, can solve. There is never a question of using less expensive techniques and so, perhaps, solving the real health problems of this nation—the lack of affordable care for most people. The very idea that there are alternative ways of viewing these problems, much less that we as citizens might participate in debates and decisions about them, is denied.

It is no accident that TV celebrities are often chosen to promote these products. "I'm not a doctor, but I play one on TV," says a spokesman for some instant cure. Again we are faced with the blurring of fact and fantasy, the confusion about who and what are "real" on TV. It is quite common to see a soap opera star advertise a household cleaning product on the very show in which she portrays a housewife. This does not confuse or irritate viewers. On the contrary, it adds to the sense of television as all of a piece. The associations viewers have with these media personae are what make them effective spokespersons for products guaranteed to solve our life problems. Again, commercials are the prototypes for "real" programs, plots and characters.

Most commercials take place in the kinds of homes, recreational facilities or workplaces that are models of everything commercial TV presents as the good life. These settings are the most blatant and powerful forms of propaganda for the consumerist lifestyle. Every beleaguered housewife fighting ring around the collar or waxy, yellow buildup lives in a sparkling clean, brand new, fashionably appointed home. The envy and guilt felt by many women watching these ads is a spur to consumerism that goes beyond the mere buying of the advertised product. You may in fact try Oxydol. But whether you do or not, the vision of a spotless, beautiful home will stick with you. It will subtly lead you to buy a variety of products not even mentioned: furniture polish, floor wax, new appliances and furniture, kitchen canisters and draperies.

Multinational corporate sponsors are often the most concerned about pushing capitalist values as equivalent to the good life. Since many do not sell individual consumer goods, they see advertising as a way of bolstering the corporate image in a general way, in an effort to counteract bad publicity about corporate responsibility for widespread social evils. These advertisers sponsor "prestige" programming—TV movies and specials. "People who watch television that they think is exceptional in quality tend to remember advertisers," notes David

Poltrack, CBS vice president for research.[19] These ads typically show industry itself as the source of human progress. They often feature workers testifying to the joys of sharing in this good work.

The Flow Is the Message

The overall effect of this juxtaposition of ads and programs is interesting to analyze. In a typical hour of soap opera, for example, the problems of characters and commercials blend almost perfectly. Domestic crises such as adultery, rebellious teenagers, accidents and natural disasters, and weddings and funerals are standard fare on soaps. It takes the characters far too long—in most viewers minds—to straighten things out and get to the happy ending. The ads tell a different tale. Just as the viewer is feeling frustrated and distraught over a favorite character's blindness to some human truth, or refusal to seek help for some problem, the show will cut to a commercial where the very same actors, wearing the same kind of clothes and living in the same kind of houses, will give us the quick answer, the fool proof cure.

Children's shows are the most extreme examples of the merging of content and commercial. There are now entire half hour programs featuring as heroes the very toys that sponsor the shows. First we see the Smurfs as heroes; then we are told where we can buy our very own set. The adventure shows are punctuated with ads for games and gadgets which will bring the same kind of adventure into your child's life. The cereal and snack ads play on the child's need to fit in, be part of the crowd. Everyone is eating Sugar Snaps, kids are told.

There is no way to appreciate the impact of TV—fiction and nonfiction—without understanding the sheer ideological impact of hearing and seeing different versions of the same propagandistic messages over and over again. What seems like a lot of fast cutting from form to form is in fact a very clever format by which messages are reinforced through the rapidly shifting but constant replaying of key images and ideas. Cultural analysts Michelle and Armand Mattelart have referred to "the syndrome of repetition" as a major factor in the power of "the American image industry" and the global popularity of such American cultural products as "Dallas" and *Raiders of the Lost Ark*. The meaning of an image

> emerges from the relationship between this image and others that the audience has already seen. This process...constantly nourishes the memory of the American image industry.[20]

In the same way, the juxtaposition of various familiar images in the flow of TV programming tends to reinforce their ideological power.

The effect of the flow on viewers is even more subtle and powerful in those cases where shows and ads seem to be delivering very different messages. In fact, advertising is one of the most important ways in which network TV manages to present some alternative views and values without undermining its ultimate consumerist, jingoist thrust. When a downbeat theme is presented, dramatically or informatively, the ads will invariably undercut the negative implications and send the viewers off to bed feeling confident and safe. We saw this in our discussions of TV movies like the "The Day After" and "The Burning Bed." The intent of the producer or director to make a socially critical point will be independently undermined by the upbeat, consumerist message of the ads with which it is punctuated.

As cable television moves in on network turf, the problem of getting people to watch commercials, rather than zapping the keypad or leaving the room, has begun to worry ad agencies. But those concerned with this problem have a lot of things going for them. For one thing, like all popular TV products, ads are the stuff of our common social communication: the small talk of a society filled with strangers and loners; the jokes of a nation eager to forget the many aspects of their lives that are not at all funny, and over which they feel no control. How else explain the fact that Walter Mondale's only real media points during the 1984 presidential campaign came from his use of a Wendy's slogan: "Where's the Beef?" And who in this country doesn't know about the sexy Jordache ads, the hilarious Express Mail commercials, the arty series of Anacin ads featuring dramatic monologues by serious actors impersonating workers?

In a recent *TV Guide* article, a CBS executive worried that zapping was becoming a big problem for advertisers. "We all have this gut feeling that something dreadful is taking place," she said. But no sooner is the problem named then it is easily solved. "The answer is simple... We have to create a zap-proof commercial: a commercial so good that viewers won't want to change the channel."[21] Judging from past performances and from the enormous creative and financial resources available to ad agencies, that is certainly not the impossible dream.

10

Cable's Cornucopia and the Future of TV

So far I have discussed network broadcasting and how the three major networks produce nonfiction television. But it is clear that in the last few years the entire system of television and other electronic leisure equipment has been evolving in radically new directions. With the development of cable and satellite broadcasting, and the popularity of home video recording systems, the way in which people watch TV, and the form and content of what they watch, has already undergone significant change. "In May 1981, RCA, parent of the National Broadcasting Company, announced that it was going into the cable television business." According to media analyst Edwin Diamond, "this date marked the birth of a new era."[1]

The advent of cable, with the enormous range and beaming power it gets from satellites and its compatibility with telephone and computer technologies, has paved the way for a veritable communications revolution. Such hyperbole is used a lot in this country of sales pitches and instant obsolescence, but it happens—in this rare case—to be accurate. There is indeed a communications revolution afoot in the land. And it has the power to reshape many aspects of our daily lives as well as major aspects of our social and political environment.

The power of cable, and the nature of the changes it will bring to our lives, originates in its technological differences from broadcast television. Where traditional TV was based on a limited electromagnetic spectrum which produced a system based on scarcity of channels, cable offers almost limitless channel abundance. Not only is there potential for over one hundred channels of information, entertainment and various kinds of data; many other kinds of communication are also possible. With cable, large and small communities can provide local public access channels to citizens and groups. Cable can provide interactive services ranging from video games to educational courses for credit to public opinion polling to home shopping and security systems. It can provide information retrieval from data banks and the ability to send specialized material to special audiences, such as investment brokers and medical professionals. Cable can also serve as a communications network for a municipality, linking schools, libraries, hospitals, police and fire departments.

The reason for this qualitative difference is cable's use of a wire—a coaxial cable—which is strung along telephone poles and connected to households much as the telephone is. Unlike television, the cable is compatible with many other kinds of communication. It is conceivable that in the near future a single wire will carry all voice and video communications into the home.

Cable was not developed in a laboratory. It began as a grassroots phenomenon in the late 1940s to solve the problem of TV reception in difficult to reach rural areas. Via cable, TV was brought to areas that were previously geographically inaccessible.

Cable technology remained rural until the 1970s. In 1976, Home Box Office (HBO) leased a transponder on the Satcom I satellite as a way of broadening its market. It was an instant success. Satellite hook-up gave cable just what it needed to penetrate major cities. All of a sudden, cable had more than mere improved reception to offer. By transmitting movies into homes all over the country, uncensored, unedited and free of commercials, HBO had a service with a real demand behind it. By 1980, virtually every big city in the country was wired or in the process of negotiation for a franchise. Most demanded multi-channel systems with the ability to provide the most sophisticated services. Warner Amex, which offered an interactive system called Qube, won franchises in six major cities from 1977 to 1980.

In the years since then, cable has had its ups and downs, and its share of forecasters of doom. With the demise of any given cable network, or the increase of "churn" (the rate of disconnection by cable subscribers), news of cable's end is predicted in publications from *Variety* to the *Village Voice*. Only a month after the debut of MTV—the music video channel that has revolutionized the rock music business and shook the foundations of advertising, movies and TV itself—one critic decided the widely praised rock-video network was in trouble because it was losing money. But as Les Brown has said, "The problem with the view from the present is that it is shallow. The past has the depth of hindsight."[2] It is a universal truth that each new development in communications has been greeted with predictions of imminent doom. When television made its public debut at the New York World's Fair in 1939, the *New York Times* predicted it would never measure up to radio broadcasting. Expense, technical complexity, and shortage of channels were the reasons given.

This kind of shortsightedness is responsible for a myriad of dogmatic proclamations about the future of cable. In this world of fads and passing fancies it is understandable that people are quick to write off any radically new technological development. However, we need to step back and observe such phenomenon from a more complex and sophisticated perspective. In the same way that broadcast television was at first dismissed and downgraded in importance, only later to be ignored as too obvious to merit further comment, so has cable and its related features been treated. I am not suggesting that every fad and fetish to come down the pike should be assumed historically significant. Nor am I suggesting that it is always possible for informed observers to make accurate judgments about new technological developments. What I am suggesting is that the methods used to make such judgments in mainstream organs of opinion are misleading and mystifying, and purposefully so.

Cable television at this moment is among the technological developments about which there is much confusion and mystification. There is no doubt that television itself has changed our lives and our ways of understanding and relating to our society and one another. There is no doubt that the same will be true of cable. One reason for this is that the social role of communications as a whole is so much more politically, socially and economically crucial than in any previous age. In a world where transnational corporations undertake global financial negotiations via satellite communications systems, with no physical properties involved, not even the symbolic paper notes known as money, one can only imagine the kind of havoc that would ensue should the entire international communications workforce suddenly go on strike.

Looking specifically at the workings of communications in the "merely" cultural realm, we see much the same enormity of power and importance. In fact, to see culture as a "mere" marginal realm today is horrendously myopic. Broadcast television has gone far toward integrating information, art and consumption by its blending of advertising, news and entertainment. In time, cable will take this trend far beyond its current level. Consider the device known as interactive cable. It is a mechanism—developed and functioning with the development of cable itself—by which viewers in the home may respond to what they see and hear and in effect change it. Its liberating potential is vast. It creates the possibility of collective viewer participation, thus upsetting the unilateral system by which we sit passively and receive a foreordained set of images and messages. Viewers could communicate with one another and with the source of the program, democratically deciding how they would like even a dramatic program to turn out.[3]

In fact, the interactive capability of cable has been among the least successful features offered, although the most highly touted and hyped at first. Why? Not because its potential was overrated. Far from it. It was simply never used to provide the kind of democratic communication system for which it was conceived. Cable programmers, seeing no further than their broadcast experience taught and their superiors allowed, merely repeated the old patterns. In broadcast TV, audience participation was limited to, say, the letter writing habits of dyed-in-the-wool soap fans, demanding that this or that character or development be maintained or changed. In imitation of this limited use, Qube, Warner Amex's interactive system, ran an afternoon show in which viewers could ask an "expert" questions and vote for what star they would like to see and talk to as a guest. Similar to shows like "Star Search," which allows viewers or audiences to choose which contestant will be given a contract, Qube allowed viewers to vote on the spot by pushing a button on the channel selection keypad. No one in power has ever requested or rewarded an innovative idea for using interactive cable to broaden our cultural experiences.

But this is not to say that interactive cable is not going to be used. It is simply not going to be used to allow viewers more participation in entertainment programming. Where it is clearly destined for institutionalization is in the realm of consumption—always television's most vital communications function. In the business pages of the April 13, 1984 *New York Times*, a report entitled "Using Qube to Market Cosmetics" described a trial marketing technique by which Ralph Lauren Cosmetics ran demonstrations of consumer cosmetic makeover sessions, after which viewers could make appointments to receive such treatments by way of the Qube interactive keypad. Of 11,000 people who watched, 800 made appointments and 48 percent showed up. A Kraft sponsored program, potentially viewed by 50,000 Qube subscribers in Columbus, Ohio, received requests from 3,000 viewers for copies of Kraft recipes offered during commercials. No more "Take this address down," then address, stamp, and pay for items. Now you need only press a button and billing, mailing and order choices are instantaneously taken care of. This is what a commercial TV system is going to use its high powered technology for.[4]

Interactive cable will be put to other uses also. Community networking is a valuable feature already in use. So is global business conference networking, which allows companies to save travel time and money, not to mention wear and tear on employees, by holding meetings via satellite. There is no question here of who the technology will benefit, no matter its innate attractions for other users.

In the process of allowing us to communicate with police, fire and other agencies, and to retrieve information from libraries and other resource centers, many terrifying possibilities also emerge. What about the ability of computers to record and save minute details of our interactions with these agencies? Records of every police department interaction and every bit of information we request can be kept. So can records of any political opinion we might express in a TV public opinion poll. Here two-way becomes, again, one-way; interactive becomes reactive. *They* will know what we thought. We will have no control over what they do about it. The decisions about what agencies we will be able to contact and in what circumstances, what information we will be encouraged and enabled to retrieve and what will be unavailable, and so on, will be made, as usual, by those in power.

In the area of education—to take one example of how cable is already being used in ways which signal social changes—we can see some of the long term personal, domestic implications of the new technology. Nancy Morrison, a twenty-eight year old office worker, is typical of the growing number of people who are getting college degrees via their living room TV sets. "I'm a product of television," she says. "I have always found television to be helpful and informative." So far she has taken four courses for twelve college credits and expects to take many more. The reasons are convenience and time. For a mere four campus visits and eleven home sessions, she can get the equivalent of fifteen hours of college credit. Most TV classes have multiple airings so that students who miss one session can easily make it up at odd hours. And with the development of home video recording equipment, the process is even simpler. "If I knew I couldn't be home to watch a segment," says Morrison, "I simply set my Betamax and viewed it at my leisure."[5]

The courses offered on TV are technically more sophisticated than they used to be. To replace the early "talking heads" style university professor giving a lecture, there are highly produced documentaries like "Vietnam: A Television History," first aired on PBS in 1983. Students can take these courses for credit at area colleges simply by coming in for exams, which are created along with the "courses" by the national producers. The centralization and privatization of this system is significant. No more will individual professors with individual points of view, styles, reading lists, and exams be necessary. Students can sit alone in their living rooms and view generic lectures—done up in high video style—accompanied by nationally produced and distributed readings and study guides, all neatly finished off with an exam.

This is not an entirely bad thing. As Morrison attests, "I really like the quality of the work. I feel that you have to be a more aggressive type student, and I like that."[6] But you also have to be a much lonelier student, and a student with no classmates to work with, no professor to consult, no alternative views to consider. This is one of the more troublesome aspects of the new electronic technologies. There is a potential—a very attractive potential—for developing lifestyles which are totally isolated and technology-centered. One can easily imagine a home of the near future with an entire room filled with interactive electronic equipment, at which an isolated person sits before a viewing screen and control board with glazed eyes, mindlessly pushing buttons to make "decisions" about shopping, banking, political issues, career choices and just about everything else. When the day's work is done, it's time for relaxation with a good movie or rock video, all at the same lonely—but safe and convenient—screen and control board. No need to leave home, get a babysitter, risk the dangerous streets of this increasingly violent society.

But Will It Fly?

What does all this amount to if cable does not take off and saturate the country? To answer that question, we need to return to the realm of facts and figures before moving on to programming itself. Much of the confusion over the future of cable stems from the fact that what is publicized and offered to us as information is not necessarily a full reflection of reality. While the media rushes to inform us about the demise of a given cable network or the profits and losses for a given quarter, it does not—once again—provide us with the necessary structural context in which to interpret this information. On the contrary, it deliberately mystifies the matter by presenting material wholly outside of such a context. "Much of the general confusion about cable arises from its uneven penetration across the country. While some cities are still years away from being wired, others already have highly advanced systems."[7] Replacement of old equipment and acquisition of expensive new items will take time too. As Jack Schneider, president of Warner Amex, explains, the breakdown of habits developed "in at least thirty years of broadcast network training of consumers" will be replaced by "new consumption patterns," not to mention viewing and other leisure time patterns.[8]

In the meantime, there are many ongoing negotiations and developments that provide ample evidence of what the future of cable will be. For one thing, what seems like an anarchic display of free market economics, in which mavericks like Cable News Network's Ted Turner are jumping in and swimming to the head of the school, is nothing of the kind. Once more the glamourization of exceptional individuals is made to obscure political and economic realities. Turner is undoubtedly a clever and imaginative entrepreneur. But he is as much an exception to the norms of capitalist reality as are Blake Carrington and J.R. Ewing. In reality,

[While] hundreds of companies are actively involved with the new communications technologies, most of the prospecting on the electronic frontier is being done by a relative handful—the familiar media conglomerates in broadcasting, publishing and motion pictures. With their huge financial resources and mass media expertise, these companies range all over the field, many of them involved with the ownership of delivery systems as well as with programming.[9]

The handful of companies involved in cable includes, not surprisingly, the three major broadcast networks: ABC, CBS and RCA, parent company of NBC. These three giants not only own stockpiles of old broadcast programming (which will continue to be the basic fare of most cable systems until new programming can be produced), they also employ the personnel with knowledge and experience in producing such programs. More to the point, they have established relationships and influence with the FCC. Their ability to lobby successfully for whatever rulings will serve their interests, and against the interests of such upstarts as minority and citizen groups, makes them hard to beat. There are any number of examples of how the FCC has ruled in favor of existing economic interests and made it very difficult for smaller, poorer groups to have any input at all.[10]

As "natural selection" among the big fish works itself out, actual statistics reveal economic and cultural health in the cable industry. The cable growth rate "exceeds the forecasts of virtually all the experts." In 1980, there were 4,225 cable systems serving sixteen million homes. By mid-1983 there were 5,700 systems serving thirty-three million homes. While some systems have gone by the boards, certain key services—like the movie and sports channels and MTV—have experienced massive profits. Within two years, the Movie Channel's advertising proceeds jumped by 33 percent while Cinemax's jumped a huge 114 percent.[11] Ted Turner's Cable News Network, the twenty-four hour a day continuous news service, has already revealed its potential for shifting viewing patterns in nonfiction categories during times of political crisis. On June 30, 1985, the day a group of Americans taken hostage on a TWA jet in the Middle East were released, CNN had its highest ratings ever. It "had higher ratings than the ABC, CBS or NBC affiliates from 6 A.M. to 6 P.M., counting just homes that receive CNN."[12]

Zapping: A New American Pastime

In cultural terms, the process needs to be approached differently. There are certain features of cable which have already made such a dent in traditional patterns of leisure consumption and tastes that they alone have made cable a cultural phenomenon. Music video is the most obvious example. By its fourth anniversary, MTV had become a cultural phenomenon which few could avoid. Its imprint on movies, fashion, broadcast television programming and viewing norms is unmistakable. Kids watch MTV and demand that their parents subscribe. And who doesn't wonder, at least a bit, what all the fuss is about? Once one decides to check it out and subscribe, the die is cast.

While many people do give up cable service—often because their communities have weak and problematic systems—many more keep and begin to fool around with them. It takes a long time to acclimate oneself to cable and the content of its various options. While the programs and ideological messages communicated by the new systems are, for the most part, mere extensions of the old, the effect of using the new technology is not so obvious.

Cable's most significant programming feature has been "narrowcasting." Where broadcast TV, using three major networks, has always been characterized by the blurring of entertainment, advertising and information, cable offers a different pattern, one which intensifies and accelerates the blurring of distinctions. Narrowcasting is the term used to describe how cable provides whole channels that cater to a relatively small, select audience. CNN, for example, has two continuous channels transmitting two versions of the day's news—one providing continuous half hour summaries of the day's headlines, the other giving more detailed reports along with other news features.

With each cable channel providing its own singular or combined abundance of specific program types, and each using its own method of making money and financing itself, no single channel will ever be quite as influential or "popular" as the networks still are. (In 1985, with all of cable's gains, it is still the networks that are the staple viewing favorites for most Americans.)[13] Some channels are purely informational or educational. You can get financial news all day and night; Christian programming continuously; many specific lessons and courses at various times; news and rock videos constantly; movies with no commercial breaks on several twenty-four hour channels which are subscription financed; and a variety of other subjects—foreign language and culture shows, sports and health, lifestyle and exercise, congressional and local government coverage, children's shows, arts programs—all at any given time.

With this abundance, it is understandable that cable has been accompanied by a rise in sales of video cassette recorders which allow us to view our own or rented cassettes, as well as record programs we cannot watch for later, more convenient viewing. According to *Variety*, VCR "penetration in the U.S. in 1986 should reach 39% (15% sales increase) and in 1987 it should be 50% (10% increase)." Merrill Lynch, the company whose figures *Variety* quotes, expects that "VCR penetration will peak in the U.S. and Japan at 75%."[14]

Moreover, in a related development, mail order record companies have become big businesses as a result of narrowcasting. In the same issue of *Variety*—devoted to a survey of video—"the abundance of affordable ad time on new [cable] national networks with millions of viewers" is cited as the cause of this success. MTV is obviously the biggest vehicle for pushing record sales of all kinds—and the cause of much of the current boom in the music industry generally. But many other channels also sell records by mail successfully. Christian music gets touted on CBN, which reaches a whopping 22.2 million homes, exceeded only by ESPN's 27.5 million. Slim Whitman, a formerly unknown country and western singer, has sold an amazing two million albums via ads on Ted Turner's "superstation," WTBS.[15]

All of this alters the way in which TV is used and experienced. On the one hand, viewers may be far more selective in their choice of programs and viewing schedules. They may choose to watch an entire week of their favorite soap opera in a single evening. They may watch a rented movie on Saturday night, with friends, and then catch up on the news or sports events they missed on Sunday morning. In this sense, there is more "freedom" and "individual choice" as defined by the media conglomerates. But as we have seen again and again, this endless choice is quite restricted. It is a mere spate of variations and recombinations of similar and familiar ideas, forms and experiences.

When we do sit down to "watch television," we do it very differently with cable. TV viewing has been characterized by a reluctance to change channels, unless there is a very good reason. If you leaf through an issue of a broadcasting trade publication, you will see full-page ads for syndicated programs which tout their effectiveness as evening lead-ins to primetime. In other words, the airing of a popular syndicated show at 7:30 is a good way to ensure that viewers will continue to watch that network affiliate throughout the evening. If this is a comment on the relative low quality and similarity among network offerings, it is worth reflecting upon. One reason people watch TV as a flow rather than as a series of discreet programs is that there is generally very little to choose from and very little difference among channels or even forms.

With cable, the viewing experience, if not ultimate content, is radically different. The viewer sits or lies down with a palm size remote control channel selector keypad at her or his side. Where network viewing is characterized by a constant screen image full of shifting images and sounds, cable viewers quickly learn to "zap." Zapping is the rapid shifting of channels by pushing the buttons on the keypad. One way of doing this is to start from the top and quickly push the up or down button so that every channel can be quickly reviewed. Should something look interesting or unusual, the viewer stops and checks it out, staying tuned in for a longer time—perhaps until a commercial comes on—or deciding, on further examination, to move on. Another way to zap is to shift up and back between or among several channels which are simultaneously airing programs of interest. Most typically, zapping has come to be used as a way of avoiding commercials. A viewer might watch the news, and when an ad comes on, quickly zap to MTV to catch a quick video, the length of which is about the same as a commercial break.

Advertisers have responded to zapping in several ways. One is to use very short, high intensity clips which get their images and messages across in a flash. Another is to move to commercials which are themselves as entertaining, or more entertaining, than most programs. This is not actually so different from what commercials have always, implicitly, been. But now the intention is more explicit, more urgent. Commercial trends—continuing characters and situations, expensive and imaginative visuals and editing techniques, narrative and dramatic elements, subtle and sophisticated humor—are simply being extended and polished to an even more impressively creative sheen.

This development of the art of commercials goes hand in hand with one of the major developments of TV generally, as a response to cable. Where TV has always organized itself and shaped its programming to fit the rituals and requirements—ideological and aesthetic—of the sponsor's product, the commercial, cable has intensified that development. We have seen how the news and other nonfiction shows tend to use short, highly visual segments filled with simplistic, easily grasped messages. Now this has reached an unheard of level. On cable TV, things move so quickly that no zapper will have to wait long to get the point of any given program. You know immediately that you have hit CNN "Headline News," for example, or the Christian Broadcasting Network. And if you aren't sure, you won't have to wait more than a few instants for identification.

It is not surprising that CNN and MTV are among the most successful cable ventures. Both use rapid change and highly intense visual clips as a mainstay. Both blur commercials and content. It is often impossible to tell the difference between the two. "Headline News" is just that—a series of headlines accompanied by abbreviated announcements of the "just the facts ma'am" variety, and not too many of those. The ads are almost identical. How can you tell whether you are watching: a news report about new automated office equipment or an ad for IBM? A report on a new medical breakthrough or an ad for a new cold cure now "available over-the-counter for the first time?" A report on the latest hostage crisis or an ad for *Time* or an encyclopedia?

With MTV, the situation is even more confusing. It is not an exaggeration to say that the ads and channel identification graphics and clips are generally more interesting, exciting and amusing than the videos. MTV has the most imaginative graphics and funniest promotional clips on the air. The MTV logos, which shift and change before your eyes like a psychedelic school of chameleons, are a visual delight. And as quickly as a video may go from heavy rotation and Top Twenty status to oblivion, the old logos disappear and are replaced by a new set.

Since MTV has an unusual legal status, by virtue of the fact that its content—music videos—are considered promotional clips for record albums, the confusion is even greater. MTV pays nothing for the very same clips NBC will pay thousands of dollars for. Why? Because record companies consider them a form of free advertising. Videos have in fact been around for a long time and have traditionally been used for this very purpose: to get radio stations to play songs. When MTV came along, all interested parties got an offer they could not refuse. MTV has low overhead; the record companies get enormous exposure; the musicians need not run around from city to city, exhausting themselves by performing live for relatively small, already sold audiences.

If MTV is the most extreme example of the total commercialization of TV, it is only a dramatic sign of the times. Every broadcast and cable network, to maintain advertising revenues, must tailor content to ads and to the phenomenon of zapping. This means that the more a program's content approximates the look and feel of a commercial, the more likely it is to hold fickle viewers' attention. Thus the development of what Edwin Diamond has called "disco news"—quick, superficial, entertaining "news" items. The ever more sophisticated use of visual imagery, created with rapid editing techniques and rock music backgrounds, adds to the effect: the emphasis on images and sounds at the expense of verbal content. Thus, the mainstreaming described by Gerbner, the tendency of television to water down and muddy ideological concepts, is bound to grow more intense.

Hegemony Reconsidered

On any given day, a cable TV subscriber will have access to some twenty to fifty different channels offering information, entertainment and commercials. For the present, the bulk of available programming is still produced by the three network owners, ABC, CBS and RCA, owner of NBC. Whether new sitcoms, dramas and movies—theatrical or made-for-TV—or reruns of older such offerings, the themes, settings and actors will be very similar. Several different versions of the news will also be offered, again presenting similar perspectives, visuals and ads.

The sheer quantity of Hollywood-produced media product experienced by Americans daily is staggering. The Waltons, just a few decades ago, led lives now inconceivable to most of us. In place of the extended family, held together by rituals of work, church and community socials, we have a new family unit headed by the TV set. Religion, culture, social values, lessons in work skills, history and health care, story-telling—all come to us from the small screen.

One of the most impressive features of this electronic media universe is its ability to bring together, through the homogenizing tendency of mass culture, so many different fragments of American life. The fragmentation of society is after all what TV was originally meant to correct. In the decades between the broadcast of the first sitcom and the start of the latest, family life has disintegrated even further, as has the pull of the church and the ability of schools and other social agencies to handle the increasing problems of youth, the aging, the ill and the culturally uprooted.

The image of family life presented on "Leave It To Beaver" is as foreign to most of us today as that of the Waltons. Through television, however, we receive a new, updated image of family life which accommodates itself to the most dramatic changes while maintaining a sense of family unity—a family pulling apart at the seams perhaps, yet still "a family." Single parents, working women and stay-at-home men, even interracial families now appear in sitcoms. And the reruns of the old 1950s classics become a kind of photo album of national family history for us all. To that extent, television, the destroyer of history, actually preserves some part it. The part it preserves, however, is the part invented by the media itself. "Our history" is now literally television history; our ancestors are as much the Cleavers and Nelsons as the fading figures in our real photo albums.

Television also bridges cultural gaps in national unity. While we may bemoan the loss of authentic peoples' culture—the demise of real country music, blues, gospel—the fact is that mass culture has taken elements of all these traditions and blended them together. The Nashville Channel has brought country to all of us. Authenticity is lost, to be sure. But in the name of hegemony, the music videos played on that channel are similar enough to those on MTV and other rock programs to draw crossover audiences. The "Rhinestone Cowboy" has an audience far larger than Hank Williams ever commanded.

We have also seen how even the fundamentalist religion preached on the Christian Broadcasting Network has incorporated elements of more progressive ideologies, most notably feminism. Christian programs like "The 700 Club" have long used Johnny Carson-style decor and format and almost all Christian talk shows now have rock music as a steady inspirational background. Rock, gospel, country, and rhythm and blues blend together into a common mass-produced popular style on TV today. Whether you watch a single, narrowcast channel or zap from cultural region to region, the effect over time is the same. "Liberty Weekend" epitomized this tendency toward homogenization of diverse cultures and styles into a newly remodeled melting pot.

Ideologically, the process has been similar. Nonfiction forms are the bulk of narrowcast programming. Nickelodeon fills the days of children with lessons in handling school and family crises, and information about agencies to which kids can turn when family members are unavailable or nonexistent. Even the dramatic features, as in network TV movies and mini-series, are as much lessons in handling currently common problems as entertainment. As kids drift further and further from the values and emotional safety of the family, nonfiction TV picks up the slack. Domestic violence and abuse are common themes of children's TV. Information about the world that awaits the runaway, the drug abuser, the kid who lashes out violently against the world that so disappoints her or him, even the immigrant from a Third World nation—all are presented to kids primarily through the TV channels they alone are meant to watch. Nonetheless, the major changes brought by narrowcasting are stylistic, not ideological. The world view presented to kids, the range of options and solutions offered for the intensifying social and emotional difficulties experienced by so many adolescents, is essentially in keeping with the beliefs and attitudes that have always characterized nonfiction television's treatment of social and personal problems.

Contradictions in the New TV: The Case of MTV

The changes in television delivered by new technologies are quite complicated. While dominant ideas and values are largely preserved, other important aspects of the TV experience change, sometimes for better, sometimes worse. The emphasis on visuals, music, and a fast pace certainly alter its content. As long as new technologies serve commercial interests, certain unsavory elements are inevitable. Instant gratification and sensation are irresistible hooks with which to catch fickle audiences. The new forms which these technical and commercial factors produce, however, also create opportunities for more positive developments.

MTV, the continuous music video channel, provides a good example. The mindlessness of the commentary that accompanies rock video programs, its emphasis on consumption and lifestyle aspects of the music rather than social content, and its tendency to destroy all sense of cultural history by playing only songs currently popular, are deplorable. Still, if MTV can be singled out as the vanguard of anti-intellectualism in television, it can also be viewed (although it rarely is) as the narrowcasting network most likely to present alternative social visions and progressive political material.

To see music videos in a more positive light, one must be aware of the contradictory nature of popular culture and how alternative social visions fit into the overall texture and flow of continuous music programming. A casual viewer, turning for the first time to MTV and watching for a brief time, may be stunned and appalled. To be sure, the "veejays" who announce the music videos do not say anything of substance. They are not allowed to. They exist solely to illustrate and sell products, records, lifestyles, youth culture. Music-video style, in itself, is apt to put off an adult viewer since it is so strange in both form and content. The bizarre clothing, the abstract, nonnarrative structure and design and the hard rock sound and pace may well astound devotees of Crosby, Stills and Nash, much less Lawrence Welk.

Still, MTV's ability to narrowcast to an exclusively young audience could, in the hands of socially progressive, sophisticated artists, allow the transmission of material rarely seen on other channels because of its implicit and at times explicit social and political attitude. To the extent that rock music has its roots in race and class feeling and experience, rock videos contain more footage of working class and Black culture, and more expressions of social rebellion than other channels, although one must watch regularly and at length to be convinced of that.

The acknowledgement of the importance of "material things" in the music of Madonna and Cyndi Lauper was mentioned in the earlier discussion of game shows. Their videos are but a few of the healthy depictions of working class, Black and female experience and attitude seen regularly on MTV. MTV has been rightly chastised for its blatant use of sexist imagery. In that regard it is really no different from other TV fare. What is more unusual is that MTV frequently airs videos, like Lauper's and Madonna's, that are boldly and independently sexual on their own terms, terms which often reflect working class attitudes toward middle class hypocrisy, not only in matters of money and female sexuality, but generally. Steady viewing will almost surely be rewarded with several videos which are artistically daring, socially rebellious or openly critical of those in power and supportive of those most dramatically misused by them.

Obviously, given what we know of hegemonic dynamics, even the socially challenging messages on MTV are limited and contradictory. Youthful rebellion is largely channeled into partying and consuming by the framing devices of veejay commentary and ads. It makes up a very small percentage of total airtime in any event, and it is often marred by sexist and racist innuendo.

Nonetheless, MTV has been effectively used by progressive musicians to bring political messages to teenage America. Most notably, MTV has taken up the network tradition of airing marathon events in support of various causes. As with the networks, these superstar concerts are presented primarily as charity fund raisers; but unlike the networks, MTV focuses on social and political victims and includes music which is itself socially conscious and often militant. A kind of hybrid of the 1960s political protest tradition and the more conservative telethon, these concerts are a fascinating jumble of contradictions. Nonetheless, they make possible the survival, in distorted forms, of some important political traditions.

The number of college kids involved in protest movements against oppression in South Africa, Central America and even the American working class is small compared to the number of kids who watch MTV from time to time. For that reason, the superstar concerts in support of Amnesty International and dispossessed farmers—watered down, politically contradictory and oriented toward band-aid charity solutions though they may be—are political experiences for MTV watchers. They feature some of the most progressive performers in this country saying more radical things than usual. Calls for public protest as the only effective way to right social injustice were heard again and again during the Farm Aid concert. Such encouragement to overt political agitation was culturally justified because it called upon the tradition of linking rock and protest that developed in the 1960s. Only on a rock channel, in the name of rock tradition, is the spirit of militant demonstrating likely to be so often and enthusiastically recalled, at least on commercial television.

The point is not that MTV is a political godsend. It is what it is: a commercial network within a hegemonically conservative but contradictory system. It does on occasion open a small door to alternative visions of society and human nature. These occasions are created by human beings working together in sophisticated and determined ways. The more aware we are of this process, the less likely we are to miss the rare moments when they succeed, hidden as they may be among the ads for blue jeans and acne cream. In that sense, viewer response itself is an acquired skill.

Problems and Solutions

Social critics are known for condemning television and even blaming it for the very social problems it seeks to ameliorate. Since Marshall McLuhan suggested to a fascinated world that "the medium was the massage"—that in and of itself it has the power to produce certain emotional and ideological effects in viewers—there has been a tendency among those concerned with social issues to fall into the trap of technological determinism. At its extreme end, this position holds that video technology itself leads to passivity, anti-intellectualism and antisocial behavior.[16] An economistic variation on this theme states that the power of the state and corporate owners and controllers of the media is so vast and the resistence of the viewer so weak that TV programming amounts to ideological brainwashing of the most simplistic, Orwellian variety.[17] Viewers are powerless to resist the pull of the manufactured message.

Obviously, there are valid insights in both positions. We have discussed the psychological, emotional and ideological power of nonfiction television throughout this book. There is no question that it serves the powerful well, and more cleverly than many critics realize. Nor is it false to say that the power of the medium is bound to increase and consolidate. The new technologies, and the amount of time spent using them, indicate just that.

Television did not, however, cause any of the social problems it addresses. It was sent into the game, so to speak, to try to salvage what was left of a disintegrating social fabric. As the disintegration has grown more severe, television's role has become more crucial. But even as television grows in importance, it also grows as a social institution plagued with all the contradictions and difficulties of every such arena in modern life. It depends upon viewers and workers for its survival and it is affected by the social atmosphere it helps to shape. The contradictions that these factors produce will not disappear. They may well intensify if those within and outside the industry focus energy and attention on making that happen.

One of the reasons there has been so little organized resistance to the hegemonic dominance of television is that it is unusual to think about television as a social institution. The structures and groups that uphold and maintain it are basically invisible behind the glaring facade of the small screen and its looking glass world. One of my motivations for writing this book was to try to counter that very tendency, to bring into the open the material bases and human dynamics which are in fact television.

One of the most interesting ways to experience television programming is to visit a set or location when a show is in production. Hours and days may be spent going over a single scene in which the two principals will repeat the same eight or ten lines again and again. As this is going on, and between takes, one will see vast amounts of sophisticated technology being moved and operated by scores of trained workers. Several directors, scores of make-up, costume, hair, prop and script workers, and a variety of other highly skilled men and women literally bring the program into existence.

Watching this physical activity, one is struck by the mystification of the star system. These two people do relatively little, after all. They are handled, coached and ordered about as they repeat a series of lines out of narrative context and in a physical setting which is almost entirely dominated by things having no relation to the emotional or physical life they are pretending to live. The role of "media workers" and the socialized workplace they inhabit is very much like the shop floor of any production plant. The conversation is similar—full of irreverence, grumblings and sophisticated understanding of the industry and its dynamics. As workers and as viewers, we participate in the media as social groups and can to some extent change the nature of what we see and even the structure of the process by which we see it.

Those who would see TV abolished tend to view it as a undifferentiated and unchangeable monolith. They seem unaware of the possibility of changing social structures to make them serve different interests and needs than they do now. Nor do they seem to recognize the truly marvelous aspects of video technology, perhaps because they have not noticed those moments and hours when it really does what it is capable of doing: broadening our vision and inspiring our souls. We would be greatly impoverished without the capacity to share, as a nation, in cultural and political life. No live theaters of performance or debate come close to creating a common life in the way that television does.

The problem is to make that system work for us and not against us. As things stand, we have a very limited power. But power in the media is no more out of reach for the powerless than in any other major institution. As the Jesse Jackson campaign illustrated, the problem of gaining electoral power is connected to the problem of gaining some control over television coverage. It is myopic to work for greater control over any political or economic institution without at the same time planning a media strategy. Television is by now an integral aspect of all political activity and cannot be ignored by those attempting to effect social change. Whether we are working for economic justice, an end to nuclear weapons or the right of women to have abortions, we cannot dream of winning over the majority of Americans, much less inspiring them to act, without using television as much and as effectively as possible. This holds true whether we are positioned within or outside the industry.

Seen in this light, as a new and crucial arena of political struggle, the world of television comes a little more into focus. The task of influencing, much less controlling, any level of the entertainment industry is overwhelming. On another level, however, to even contemplate such a task is healthy. It demystifies the "looking glass" image of television as a permanent, impenetrable kind of Emerald City of the imagination and forces us to focus on the material realities we have just been considering. It changes the terms of our relationship to television from passive to active. It shifts the emotional balance a bit as well, changing the question from "how can we dare to tackle such an immense structure" to "how can we afford not to?"

We are talking, after all, about the control of reality, of the meaning of concepts and language which, in the Age of Communication, is an enormously significant aspect of the struggle to gain and maintain real political power. Yet our relationship to media too often resembles Alice's relationship to Humpty Dumpty. "When I use a word," said Humpty Dumpty, "it means just what I choose it to mean, neither more nor less." Alice counters that "the question is whether you can use words to mean so many different things." Humpty Dumpty has the last word, however. "The question," he says firmly and correctly, "is which is to be master—that's all."

Alice is at a disadvantage in her looking glass world because she cannot figure out the rules. Nor can she see any signs of her companion's fragility, the weaknesses in his apparently substantial structure. We are more fortunate. We can figure out the rules by which to negotiate the world of television. We can even see the cracks marking those places where its current rulers are potentially weak, vulnerable to being shattered. With these analytical maps, we can gain significant ground in the terrain of hegemony. We have seen it done by others, as producers and activists in the political and creative realms, with no more powerful an arsenal of weapons than each of us has separately, and far less than we might have if all those with something to gain by challenging the media joined together.

Notes

Chapter 1

1. *Nielsen Report on Television, 1984* (New York, 1984), pp. 3, 6.

2. The new trend in universities to teach "Communications Studies," is, not surprisingly, geared to vocational training in a field now expanding. Communications majors, like business and education majors, do not study the media so much as learn how it works and how to work within it.

3. See George Gerbner, "Communication and Social Environment," *Scientific American* (September, 1972), pp.153-170; and Gerbner, "Television as a New Religion," *New Catholic World* (March-April, 1978).

4. The most recent and comprehensive study of monopoly control of the entertainment industry is Ben Bagdikian, *The Media Monopoly* (Boston, 1983).

5. See Elayne Rapping, "Cable Capable of Reshaping our World," *Guardian* (January 26, 1983), p. 21.

6. See Todd Gitlin, *The Whole World is Watching* (Berkeley, 1980); Gaye Tuchman, *Making News* (New York, 1978); Edwin Diamond, *The Tin Kazoo: Television, Politics and the News* (Cambridge, 1975); Edward Jay Epstein, *News from Nowhere* (New York, 1974); Herbert Gans, *Deciding What's News* (New York, 1980).

7. Gaye Tuchman, *The TV Establishment* (New York, 1974), p. 1.

8. For a useful discussion and bibliography of both these theories, see Michael Selig, "From Manipulation to Limitation: Leftist Views of Conflict and Contradiction in the Commercial Media," *Jump Cut* (Fall, 1985), pp. 18-20.

9. Janice Radway, "Identifying Ideological Seams: Mass Culture, Analytical Methods and Political Practice," *Communication* (April, 1986), pp. 93-121.

10. Douglas Kellner, "Network Television and American Capitalism," *Theory and Society,* (January, 1981).

11. The *Tabloid* Collective, "On/Against Mass Culture Theory," *Tabloid* (1980), p. 11.

12. Raymond Williams, "Base and Superstructure in Marxist Cultural Theory," *Problems in Materialism and Culture* (London, 1980), p. 38.

13. Antonio Gramsci, *Selections from the Prison Notebooks* , Q. Hoare and G. Nowell-Smith, eds. (New York, 1971), pp. 276-7.

14. Interview with Robert Greenwald, May 11, 1986, Culver City, California (forthcoming, *American Film*, December 1986).

15. *ibid.*, p. 8.

16. Todd Gitlin, *Inside Prime Time* (New York, 1983), p. 203.

17. Greenwald, *op. cit.*

18. Gitlin, p. 165.

19. George Gerbner, "The Mainstreaming of America," *TV Guide* (October 20, 1984), p. 21.

20. Greenwald, *op. cit.*

Chapter 2

1. *Nielsen Report on Television, 1984* (New York, 1984), pp. 3-6.

2. Raymond Williams, *The Sociology of Culture* (New York, 1981), pp. 110-11.

3. Raymond Williams, *Television: Technology and Cultural Form* (New York, 1974), pp. 26-7.

4. Stuart and Elizabeth Ewen, *Channels of Desire: Mass Images and the Shaping of American Consciousness* (New York, 1982), pp. 16, 57.

5. Vance Packard, *The Hidden Persuaders* (New York, 1957), p. 16.

6. Erik Barnouw, *The Sponsor: Notes on a Modern Potentate* (Oxford, 1978), pp. 82-3.

7. See Michael Grossman and Martha Kumar, *Portraying the President* (Baltimore, 1981) for a thorough documentation of the way in which the media and federal government work together in presenting news from the White House.

8. Todd Gitlin, *Inside Prime Time* (New York, 1983) p. 257.

9. Raymond Williams, *The Sociology of Culture* (New York, 1982), p. 54.

10. Raymond Williams, *Television: Technology and Cultural Form* (New York, 1974), p. 19.

11. See Richard Bunce, *Television and Corporate Interest* (New York, 1976).

12. Tuchman, *op. cit.*, p. 3.

13. See Tuchman, *op. cit.*; and Muriel Cantor, *Prime Time Television: Content and Control* (Beverly Hills, 1980) pp. 11-17.

14. Erik Barnouw, *Tube of Plenty* (New York, 1977), p. 41.

15. Tuchman, p. 7.

16. Douglas Kellner, "Network Television and American Capitalism," *Theory and Society* (January, 1981).

17. *ibid.*

18. *ibid.*

19. *ibid.*

20. Erik Barnouw, *Tube of Plenty* (New York, 1975), pp. 398-439.

21. For an interesting discussion, of this issue, in which both sides are articulated, see the interview with Archie Shepp in Douglas Kahn and Diane Neumaeir, eds., *Cultures in Contention* (Seattle, 1985). Shepp recalls arguments he had with his friend, Bill Cosby, when Cosby was doing "Sesame Street."

22. Muriel Cantor, *Prime Time Television: Content and Control* (Beverly Hills, 1980), pp. 11-17.

23. For a survey of Fowler's proposed changes see Les Brown, "The FCC Proudly Presents the Vast Wasteland," *Channels of Communication* (March/April, 1984), pp. 27-8.

24. *ibid.*

25. Alan Wells, *Mass Media and Society* #9 (Palo Alto, 1980), pp. 355-9.

26. Av Westin, *Newswatch* (New York, 1982), pp. 231-2.

27. James Traub,"Low-Power Television: Broadcasting in a Minor Key," *Channels of Communication* (November, 1985), p. 62.

28. *ibid.*; and Fred Glass, "Cracks in the Tube: How Socialists Can Break into TV," *Against the Current* (Winter, 1982), pp. 38-45.

29. Tuchman, p. 10.

30. Tuchman, pp. 13-4.

31. Edward Epstein, *News from Nowhere* (New York, 1973), p. 94.

32. Les Brown, *Television: The Business Behind the Box* (New York, 1971), p. 30.

33. Todd Gitlin, *Inside Prime Time* (New York, 1983), p. 56.

34. Erik Barnouw, *The Sponsor* (New York, 1978), p. 106.

35. Gitlin, p. 10.

36. Gitlin, p. 253.

37. Gitlin, p. 257.

38. Roger Noll, Merton Peck, John McGowan, *Economic Aspects of Television Regulation* (Washington, D.C., 1973), p. 100.

39. *ibid.,* p. 104.

40. *ibid.,* p. 110.

41. Tuchman, p. 30.

42. Tuchman, p. 5.

Chapter 3

1. Ron Powers, *The Newscasters* (New York, 1977), p. 53.
2. *ibid.*, p. 6.
3. *ibid.*, p. 29.
4. *ibid.*, p. 30.
5. *ibid.*, p. 6.
6. *ibid.*, p. 17.
7. Edwin Diamond, *The Tin Kazoo* (Cambridge, Mass., 1975), p. 76.
8. Herbert Schiller's *The Mind Managers* (Boston, 1973), deals with many of these features in detail, and discusses their ideological effects. His seminal work is done in the tradition of strict manipulation theory however.
9. Ann Salisbury, "News That Isn't Really," *TV Guide* (February 11, 1984), pp. 5-10.
10. Tim Patterson, "Eyewitless News: An Amusing Aid to Digestion," in *Alternative Papers: Selection from the Alternative Press* (Philadelphia, 1982), p. 458.
11. *"Cross Currents," Channels of Communication* (May-June, 1983), p. 11.
12. *ibid.*
13. Powers, p. 203-8.

Chapter 5

1. John J. O'Connor, ed., *American History/American Television* (New York, 1983), p. xviii.
2. John Berger, *Ways of Seeing* (London, 1972), p. 149.
3. Information for this section from Erik Barnouw, *The Image Empire: History of Broadcasting in the United States, Volume III—from 1953* (New York, 1970) pp. 85-239.
4. Erik Barnouw, *Tube of Plenty* (New York, 1977), pp. 271-2.
5. *ibid.*, p. 212.
6. *ibid.*, p. 309.
7. *ibid.*, p. 309.
8. *ibid.*, p. 337.
9. *ibid.*, p. 339.
10. *New York Times* (August 9, 1984), Section H, p. 23.
11. Gregory Bush, "Edward Kennedy and the Televised Personality in the 1980 Presidential Campaign," in O'Connor, *American History/American Television*, p. 329.
12. Leonard Goldenson, "Broadcasting and Politics: Meeting the Challange," *Variety* (January 16, 1985), p. 158.

13. A.W. Singham, "Foreign Policy Held Hostage: The Jackson Rescue Mission," *Freedomways* (First Quarter, 1984), pp. 20-21.

14. Todd Gitlin, *The Whole World Is Watching* (Berkeley, 1980), p. 288.

15. Charles Fant, "Televising Presidential Conventions, 1952-80," *Journal of Communications* (Autumn, 1980), pp. 130-139.

16. *New York Times* (June 3, 1984), Section A, p. 14.

17. David Hoffman, "President Says TV Becomes a Neighbor as Families Change," *Washington Post* (August 28, 1984), p. 23.

18. *New York Times, op. cit.*

19. Michael Grossman and Martha Kumar, *Portraying the President* (Baltimore, 1981), p. 14.

20. Mark Hertsgaard, "How Reagan Seduced Us," *Village Voice* (September 18, 1984), p. 10.

21. Grossman and Kumar, p. 248.

22. Hertsgaard, p. 12.

23. *ibid.*, p. 17.

24. *ibid.*, p. 20.

25. *ibid.*, p. 23.

Chapter 6

1. Erik Barnouw, *Tube of Plenty* (New York, 1977), p. 168.

2. Barnouw, p. 170.

3. Daniel Leab, "*See It Now* :A Legend Reassessed," in John O'Connor, ed. *American History/American Television* (New York, 1983), p. 1.

4. *ibid.*, p. 2.

5. *ibid.*, p. 15.

6. *ibid.*, p. 9.

7. *ibid.*, p. 18.

8. *ibid.*, p. 18.

9. *ibid.*, p. 19.

10. Barnouw, p. 181.

11. *ibid.*, p. 184.

12. See lisitngs in Alex McNeil, *Total Television* (New York, 1980).

13. Barnouw, pp. 278, 285.

14. Todd Gitlin, *The Whole World is Watching* (Berkeley, 1980).

15. Edward Epstein, in *News from Nowhere* (New York, 1973), p. 128.

16. *ibid.*, p. 129.

17. Erik Barnouw, *The Sponsor* (New York, 1978), pp. 86-88.

18. Epstein, p. 129.

19. John Berger, *Ways of Seeing* (London, 1973), p. 135.

Chapter 7

1. Erik Barnouw, *Tube of Plenty* (New York, 1977), p. 178.
2. *ibid.*, p. 488.
3. Alex McNeil, *Total Television* (New York, 1980) p. 641.
4. Craig and Peter Norback, eds. *TV Guide Almanac* (New York, 1980), pp. 562-570.
5. Douglas Kellner has analyzed the technique of "60 Minutes" in a particular episode in an unpublished manuscript, *60 Minutes vs. The Liberal Church: An Alternative View.*
6. For an interesting discussion of this issue see Raymond Williams, *Television: Technology and Cultural Form* (New York, 1974), pp. 119-134.
7. This is an example of what Armand and Michelle Mattelart describe as the effect of image repetition, or "the syndrome of repetition" in *International Image Markets* (London, 1984), p. 94.
8. See James Monaco, *Media Culture* (New York, 1977), p. 297, for listings of the top grossing international film rentals in recent years. For updates, see *Variety.*
9. For an insightful discussion of this point see Judith Williamson, *The Dynamics of Popular Culture* (New York, 1986), p. 103.
10. See Walter Karp, "What Do Women Want?" *Channels of Communication* (September-October, 1984), pp. 17-19.
11. Joel Kovel discusses this issue in *The Age of Desire* (New York, 1981).
12. William Henry III, "From the Dawn of Gab," *Channels of Communication* (May-June,1984), pp. 42-3.
13. See Gaye Tuchman, "Assembling a Network Talk Show," in Tuchman, ed. *The TV Establishment* (New York, 1974), pp. 119-136.

Chapter 8

1. Todd Gitlin, *Inside Prime Time* (New York, 1983), p. 157.
2. Douglas Gomery, "Television, Hollywood and Movies Made for Television," in John O'Connor, ed. *American History/American Television* (New York, 1983), pp. 208-230.
3. Gitlin, p. 164.
4. Interview with Robert Greenwald, *American Film*, forthcoming Dec. 1986.
5. Stephen Farber, "Making Book on TV," *Film Comment* (November, 1983), p. 46.
6. Farber, p. 46.
7. *ibid.*, p. 47.
8. *ibid.*, p. 45.

9. Leslie Fishbein, "Roots: Docudrama and the Interpretation of History," in O'Connor, pp. 280-82.

10. Harry F. Waters, "The Black Experience," *Newsweek* (January 24, 1977), p. 59.

11. Eric Foner, article in *Sevendays* (March, 1977) reprinted in David Wolper, *The Inside Story of TV's "Roots"* (New York, 1978), pp. 263-4.

12. Fishbein, p. 289.

13. *ibid.*, p. 289.

14. *ibid.*, p. 290.

15. Foner, *op. cit.*

16. John Siegenthaler, "Remembering the Kennedys," *USA Today* (January 28, 1985), p. 1D.

17. *ibid.*

Chapter 9

1. John Berger, *Ways of Seeing* (London, 1972), p. 139.

2. Erik Barnouw, *The Sponsor* (New York, 1978), p. 81.

3. *ibid.*, p. 79.

4. Jonathan Price, *Commercials: The Best Thing on TV* (New York, 1978), p. 270.

5. Barnouw, p. 82.

6. *ibid.*, p. 83.

7. *ibid.*, p. 34.

8. Edward Jay Whetmore, *Mediamerica* (Belmont, California, 1985), p. 270.

9. Vance Packard, *The Hidden Persuaders* (New York, 1957), pp. 14-17.

10. Maurice Mandell, *Advertising* (Englewood Hills, N.J., 1980), p. 107.

12. Barnouw, p. 116.

13. Raymond Williams, "Advertising: The Magic System," in *Problems in Materialism and Culture*, p. 186.

14. Judith Williamson, *Decoding Advertisements* (London, 1978), p. 23.

15. Louis Althusser,"Ideology and Ideological State Apparatusses," *Lenin and Philosophy and Other Essays* (London, 1971).

16. Berger, p. 131.

17. Williams, p. 192.

18. Ron Rosenbaum, "The Four Horsemen of the Nightly News," in James Wright, *The Commercial Connection: Advertising and the Mass Media* (New York, 1979), p. 201.

19. Peter Kerr, "Full-Time Sponsors are Shopping for Quality Shows," *New York Times* (July 7, 1985), Arts and Leisure, p. 19.

20. Armand and Michelle Mattelart, *International Image Markets* (London, 1984), p. 95.

21. Howard Polskin, "Every Time You Zap, Madison Avenue Shudders," *TV Guide* (October 13, 1984), pp. 21-2.

Chapter 10

1. Edwin Diamond, *Sign Off: The Last Days of Television* (Cambridge, Mass., 1982), pp. ix-x.

2. Les Brown, "Perspective: Beyond Boom and Bust," *Channels of Communication: 1985 Field Guide to the Electronic Media* (November, 1985), p. 5.

3. See Raymond Williams, *Television: Technology and Cultural Form* (New York, 1975), p. 139.

4. *New York Times* (April 13, 1984), Section Y, p. 43.

5. Barbara Gubanic , *Pittsburgh Post-Gazette* (August 9, 1985), p. 6.

6. *ibid.*.

7. Les Brown, "Cable TV: Wiring for Abundance," *Channels of Communication: 1985 Field Guide to the Electronic Media* (November, 1985), p. 25; *Channels of Communication: 1986 Field Guide to the Electronic Media* (November, 1986), p. 36.

8. Aljean Harmetz, "Cable TV, Buoyed by Popularity, Looks to Future," *New York Times* (May 4, 1982), p. 16.

9. "Players: Powers That Be," *Channels of Communication: 1985 Field Guide to the Electronic Media* (November, 1985), p. 64.

10. See Elayne Rapping, "Cable Capable of Reshaping Society," *Guardian* (January 26, 1983), p. 21.

11. Les Brown, "Cable TV: Wiring for Abundance," *Channels of Communication: 1985 Field Guide to the Electronic Media* (November,1985), p. 25.

12. "Cable TV Chalks Up Its Highest Ratings Ever," *Variety* (July 10, 1985), p. 51.

13. Les Brown, "Broadcast TV: Winner and Still Champion," *Channels of Communication: 1985 Guide to the Electronic Media* (November, 1985), p. 52.

14. James Melanson, "VCR Sales Biz Nears Maturity," *Variety* (July 10, 1985), p. 77.

15. "Direct Response Disk Companies Enjoying New Life on Cable TV," *Variety* (July 10, 1985), p. 79.

16. See Martin Esslin, *The Age of Television* (San Francisco, 1982); and Jerry Mander, *Four Arguments for the Elimination of Television* (New York, 1978).

17. The most cogent spokesman for this view currently is Herbert Schiller. See especially his *The Mind Managers* (Boston, 1973).

Index